PRAISE FOR THE AUDACITY TO BE YOU

"Like most people, I was taught the lie that I have to pretend to be someone I'm not to be accepted and loved. Dr. Reedy's work has helped me unpack that lie and to explore and hold space for what's underneath: the real stuff— the broken and the rotten stuff. I'm learning to be ok with feeling feelings, being imperfect, and with not always fitting in. I'm also learning that this is how I find my innate goodness and beauty. This is what it means to be whole. This is freedom. I'm deeply grateful for this work as I can't think of a greater gift to pass on to my children."

—Emily Baldoni, Actress, Entrepreneur, Wife, and Mother

"Dr. Reedy's work has granted us the liberation of better understanding what we can and cannot control, given us real perspective on how being the perfect parent is an impossibility, and helped us gain more confidence and peace within the daily challenges of raising our children."

—Tony, Emmy, and Grammy winner Audra McDonald and Tony nominee Will Swenson

"Abdu'l-Bahá once said, 'When one is released from the prison of self, that is indeed a release, for that is the greater prison.' On my personal journey I have often found myself locked in the prison of self with no clue how I got in or how to get out. It is a prison where shame, and unexpressed/unrealized pain festers...where I find myself overcome by shoulds and overwhelming feelings of not being enough. In *The Audacity to Be You*, Dr. Reedy shows us the link between our shame and our struggle to love each other by helping us make friends with our 'Dirty, horrible, rotten selves.' This book is an incredible tool that can help any of us shackled with judgments and shoulds find compassion for ourselves and hopefully a way out of that prison."

—Justin Baldoni, Actor, Director, Husband, and Father

"*The Audacity to Be You* is a deeply powerful book that lovingly invites you on a journey to explore what it means to be human. Five years ago, I found myself in Brad's client chair and for the first time, I knew what it was like to be okay in the world. I often want to be right; I feel shame, live in fear, and react with judgment. The difference now is that I know that it's okay to have a horrible, rotten self, and perhaps she isn't actually horrible or rotten after all. Every week I rediscover my work, my wounds, and my magnificence. While reading *The Audacity to Be You*, I again felt discovered both by Brad and by myself. Brad has a way of seeing me even through the pages of a book."

—Madeline Cardon, Client

"Most self-help books I want to throw across the room. This one I want to keep by my bedside forever. Its polite yet persuasive invitation to join its author, Dr. Reedy, on his quest for radical self-acceptance changed my life. It will change yours too."

—Christa D'Souza, author of "The Hot Topic"

"*The Audacity to Be You* widens our eyes to see that "using new lenses" can help us attain clarity, better perspective and goodness as humans. I first met Brad at one of his Evoke Wilderness Parent Sessions in NYC. Brad's words were raw, confusing, challenging, honest and weirdly addictive. Like many, I thought that the best way to help your struggling child was to work all the angles to "fix them;" not at all to courageously look in the mirror at your SELF. Brad's words were transforming, life altering, as they helped me to understand that the best and truly only way for parents/care givers to help their struggling child was to work on better understanding their own self. After six years and (over 150 meetings) of supporting parents through listening, empathy and validating, I find myself sharing Brad's words or talking about the power of his Wilderness Programs or recommending his first book at every meeting. Brad has transformed lives by sharing his own journey."

—Deann Snook, Co-Founder Warrior Families Support Group

"Brad Reedy has been an instrumental part of my life both personally and professionally. With his humor, kindness, relatability and absolute WISDOM, he has helped me to free myself of my stories of shame and become a far more compassionate and more available therapist and person. If you have the chance to learn from Brad, don't walk... run. You won't regret it."

—Molly Carmel, LCSW, author of "Breaking Up with Sugar: Divorce the Diets, Drop the Pounds, and Live Your Best Life"

"In Dr. Brad Reedy's newest book, *The Audacity to Be You,* he continues to offer a completely singular voice in the field of therapy and relationship development. Dr. Reedy brings a clarity and force to our collective work of being human. Whether you're a parent raising a struggling teenager, a practicing therapist or mentor, or in an intimate relationship with another, this book points us back to ourselves and our own source of compassionate wisdom. In this exceptional book Dr. Reedy challenges us to learn what it means to see and share your real and authentic self as your true gift. By sharing stories, case studies and personal reflections, he shows us a way."

—Sanford Shapiro, M.Ed., Learning and Education Specialist and author of "The Light Within," a children's book on working through anxiety

"Dr. Reedy has written a must-read book for those involved in the wilderness therapy field or anyone with the courage to grow as a human being. If you are willing to take the bold risk of looking at all parts of your *Self*, then read this book and learn from a seasoned expert."

—*Will White, DA, LCSW, LADC, Co-Founder, Owner Summit Achievement Academy, author of "Stories from the Field: A History of Wilderness Therapy," and host of the podcast, Stories from the Field: Demystifying Wilderness Therapy*

"A wonderful read... how to change your past... a compassionate, reassuring, immensely readable inspirational, relational recipe book on how to be oneself as a person and how to inspire change in others. Brad casts light on solutions that illuminate pathways and techniques that provide the "desired" outcomes related to the good intentions within ourselves and help mend our old past inspired habits that cause, pain, doubt and shame with techniques that bring joy, freedom and intimacy to ourselves and to those we love and care for. Professionally and personally, a must read."

—*Hamish White, CADC, Founder of Recovery Counselling Services in Toronto, Canada, a family centered outpatient addiction recovery agency*

"I am thrilled that Dr. Brad Reedy has provided another fantastic read furthering my own perspective on being a parent, being my authentic self, and finding me. As I face me and my stuff with increasing regularity, doing the self-care that Dr. Reedy shares about in *The Audacity to Be You*, I improve the ways I show up as a father, a husband, and a therapist. Thank you for teaching me it is ok to be me."

—*Matt Hoag, Ph.D., Co-Founder Evoke Therapy Programs and Clinical Director of Evoke at Entrada*

THE AUDACITY TO BE YOU

LEARNING TO LOVE YOUR HORRIBLE, ROTTEN SELF

Brad M. Reedy, PhD

Clinical Director and Cofounder
Evoke Therapy Programs and Host of
Finding You: An Evoke Therapy Podcast

For my therapist, Dr. Jami Gill, who showed me what it means to be a *Self* and love an *Other*.

"Why were we, each of us, taught the notions we had been taught about being 'correct,' when these exact notions ensured our failure in the world?"

from "The Letters of Juliet to the Knight in Rusty Armor"

The stories and ideas in this book are based on real events. The names, details, and identifying information have been changed to protect confidentiality.

CONTENTS

CONTENTS

CONTENTS

ACKNOWLEDGMENTS

From Joseph Campbell's, *The Power of Myth*:

… when you reach an advanced age and look back over your lifetime, it can seem to have had a consistent order and plan, as though composed by some novelist. Events that when they occurred had seemed accidental and of little moment turn out to have been indispensable factors in the composition of a consistent plot… And just as people whom you will have met apparently by mere chance became leading agents in the structuring of your life…The whole thing gears together like one big symphony… It is even as though there were a single intention behind it all…

Thank you to Joseph Campbell for identifying the signposts along the way that have given my life greater meaning.

Thank you to my therapist and my wife, the two people who, more than any others, have loved my horrible, rotten *Self*.

Thank you to the clients I have worked with who took the risk to show themselves to me. Thank you for modeling the courage and teaching me many of my greatest lessons. And I am sorry where I failed you.

Thank you to those who gave me feedback on versions of this book: Suzette Hearn, Linda Phillips, Beth Miller, Rick Heizer, Kaysha Sorensen, Pamela Hamilton, Meredith Bluestine, Peter Brown, and Patrick Logan. Thank you to Dawn Hansen for your editing and guidance.

Thank you to my Evoke Therapy Programs' Family.

Thank you to my brother, Rob, for loving me regardless of the mess or success in my life.

Thanks to my favorite editor and the coauthor of my life, My Favorite *Other*, my wife, Michelle.

Thank you to my four children, Jake, Emma, V, and Livi, for the gift of being your father.

FOREWORD

By J.D. (Jami) Gill

HUMAN BEINGS DEVELOP IN CONTEXTS. IN LARGE

measure we may be seen as the product of our background experiences. We therefore unwittingly expect the world to be like what we have known. The relationships we had with our parents form the basis for the relationships we have with each other as adults. What didn't work before, doesn't work now. The pattern is passed along. Also, in this way, we unwittingly shape our children to be like us. Everywhere we look it seems the same.

We have only our own histories to guide us—that, and the advice of friends and books about relationships and parenting. We are thrown into the middle of these interactions with some picture of how they will be, and this picture seems to us quite reasonable. As partners, we are drawn to the same kinds of people we have known, and we do the same things with them we have done before. As parents we are over-tired, new at everything, and guided by our backgrounds. We don't have a great platform, as a rule, on which to ground a whole new phase of life.

With our children and partners, we learn there are good times and bad times. Children and partners are not perfectly designed for us, and we are not perfectly designed for them. They have their own wishes and ways of being. We want to interact positively with them, but at times they drive us crazy. They do dumb stuff. Our children hate vegetables, bedtimes, and getting clean. They come to mock us. They are always wanting something, even when it seems they have everything—at least they have more than we had. Why are they so ungrateful? Sooner or later the day comes in our interactions with others when we lose it. We may scream or threaten, scaring the child to death. We have found our limit. The child has found our limit too. We don't know what to do.

In addition, we have all kinds of thoughts about the child. Some of these thoughts are positive, and some are negative. We have dreams for the child, for what we want them to become. We try to help them along this road. Yet the child is bound to do something we cannot tolerate. This is when we are tested as parents. It seems so unkind and unfair. Why has this happened to us? We have worked so hard, after all. We have done everything we know how to do. We are baffled.

It is likely someone outside our context would not be so baffled. An objective observer could see how we got the result we did—*even though* we were trying for something else altogether. Sometimes this observer tells us his or her views, sometimes not.

The problems we face as people and as parents occur *within* our own worlds, our contexts. This is the world we know. It is the world we have always known. It is probably the world of our parents, our school chums, our friends and our neighbors. *This is how everybody does it.* We say the world requires it. What could be the problem?

The problem is our worlds are not big enough. They only contain what we know. Everywhere we look we see the same answers. This is how it is in our worlds.

We ask people for advice. They tell us the same things, though each piece of advice is maddeningly different from the next. All this advice and we still don't know what to do. We are like people listening to a jukebox that only has one tune. We have played it a million times, but it still sounds the same.

Some of us have learned to reach out. We want to hear something we haven't heard before. Others of us don't want to hear anything different. What was good enough for our parents is good enough for us.

Researchers have found there is a difference between those of us who were raised in strict father families and those who were raised in nurturing parent families. In the strict father family, one is raised to follow rules. In the nurturing parent family, one is raised to be who one really is. It is the difference between getting it right and getting it real. When one raised in a strict father family reaches out for help, he or she expects to hear rules for how to get it right. When one raised in a nurturing parent family reaches out for help, he or she expects to be helped to find a new solution. In strict father families one is told who one is, or who one shouldn't be. In nurturing parent ,families, one is encouraged to discover who one is.

How we are able to relate to others is critical. This is an issue central to all of us, not just to our children. In attachment theory it is held the interaction between a parent and infant is either secure or it is not. Developed by the British psychoanalyst John Bowlby, attachment theory focuses on what infants need in order to thrive psychologically. Bowlby found that in order for the infant to feel secure, the child needs to feel 1) safe, and 2) welcome. This is not something that can be demanded; it must be achieved. It cannot be given as a medication, nor is it the result of a rule. It is of vital importance how the parents *hold the child in their minds*. If the parents are empathically attuned to the child, there is an open channel established between the parent and the child in which the inner thoughts of the parent are available to the child. When the focus is not on this type of empathic attunement, the focus routinely falls to the infant's behavior. Thus, the response is not so much "How are you feeling?" as "You need to get it right."

Resonant empathy results in children who feel good about who they are. They feel they exist in a world of other people who have thoughts and feelings just as they do. Psychologists call this *mentalization*. Everybody's feelings get to count. Monitoring for correct behavior, on the other hand, results in children who are either overly compliant or resentful of authority. These children have learned that who they are doesn't matter, but instead what matters is what they do.

Entire interpersonal lives can be predicted from childhood attachment patterns. Parent-child interaction patterns as well can be predicted from parents' childhood attachment patterns.

For many of us the family rules we faced when we were children only allowed parts of ourselves to emerge and be articulated. There were, in other words, things we had to keep hidden—as these were punished. We learned it is normal to have a partial *Self*. We were "good" kids instead of "complete" kids, who have both good parts and bad parts. What we didn't learn was that the parts of ourselves that were not allowed to be expressed nevertheless were apparent to others who had learned how to see them. We thought if we denied these parts, no one would know about them. The truth is quite different. It was clear we were hiding things—sometimes huge things. Our parents were complicit in this deceit, as they liked the good child better than the complete child anyway.

It is a life-changing experience to have the parts of ourselves we have hidden (the things we learned were bad) accepted by someone who nevertheless continues to value us. What? Our rotten parts don't result in our being rejected. How can this be?

This is where psychotherapy comes in. It is likely this wasn't an option for our parents, so we never learned it is an option for us. We were taught psychotherapy is something for those who are, you know, sick. It is not for normal people. Not for people like us. Besides, what if anyone found out I was seeing a therapist? They would think I was *crazy*!

None of this is the case. A well-trained therapist is a person who is skilled in creating an environment that is safe and in which one can feel welcome. That is, the therapist is *not* like one's parents. The therapist *listens*. He or she doesn't (simply) dispense *answers*. On the other hand, he or she helps us find our own answers and supports them. When we are seen in a different light by someone seeking to understand us, we are able to find ourselves in a different world from the one many of us have known. It is what was missing in our own childhoods.

In this different context we are able to begin to see things differently. We learn there are other tunes on the jukebox, and we like them. It is this chance to develop a different view that allows us to improve our lives, because for the first time we are allowed to see things differently. This is the magic.

This is also why wilderness therapy is so effective. One is away from one's family context and the behaviors and interactions that work there. One is placed in a context one has not experienced before and must learn how to survive. Resistance and opposition don't work in the wilderness. If you don't gather wood for the fire, you won't be able to cook and obtain heat. This is not a rule established by others; it is simply a fact of nature. If you wish to make a statement by not eating and being cold, that is allowed. Besides, there are caring professionals there who want to hear how you feel and are able to understand.

Compassionate understanding is an experience that is new for a great many of us. We have lived with criticism and negative consequences all our lives. We have thought everyone is critical and has negative views about us. It is what we have known. We have even imported these critical and negative views, so they now operate as a judgmental inner voice that we feel is part of us. Yet this judgmental inner voice is really something that came from others in our childhoods. Our therapist may be the first person who isn't critical of us. When faced with someone who is not interested in criticizing but, rather, is interested in getting to know us—really know us—the world is different. For likely the first time we are able to truly grow.

All it takes is the courage to try.

What does a well-trained therapist look like? A well-trained therapist is an expert at *listening*. He or she wants to hear how you feel—how *you* feel, *not how you are supposed to* feel. He or she will try to find you, where you are. He or she will try to find how it feels to be you, with your history, your dilemmas, your hopes and fears. If instead of trying to hear and find you, your therapist has the right answer for you, find another therapist. The "right" answer will be the therapist's answer and not your answer. This will likely duplicate the ways you were treated by your parents.

Compassionate hearing is actually a different kind of experience than the one we imagined when we thought about psychotherapy. We are not treated as a crazy person who must be fixed. We are treated as a human being who is offered an understanding context in which to grow. How we want to get to where we need to get. The therapist is not a judge.

When therapy goes well, we are able to find parts of ourselves we couldn't find before. We are able to see the world in a new way and find new ways to go about living. In a real sense it is to be able to have a whole new, different kind of life.

We live in a culture that encourages us to "shape up and fly right." This message becomes more important than listening to who people are. But who they are does matter. It matters as much as who we are. Parents who are able to resonate with their child in an empathic way are different from parents who simply require proper behaviors. If I feel my parents truly understand me and value me for who I am, I am able to feel good about who I am as a person. Such an exchange promotes positive self-esteem and feelings of being accepted. In similar fashion it is of vital importance that therapists seek to find ways to empathically resonate with their clients—to "find" them. If I think you "get" me, I will be able to relax and find new ways of living.

Each of us is wired to either move toward things or move away from them. We move toward what accepts and understands us, and we move away from what doesn't. Tragically, all too often, the not understanding group includes our parents and those who say they know "what is best for us." This is also true in interactions we have with our partners and others. We are automatically drawn to those who listen and try to understand. We need to be supported as we consider options in order to see how they fit with who we are. Allowing us the space to find these options is what good therapy is about. When we allow others the space to find these options as well, we function as a good partner or friend. That is, we need someone to help us find our way more than we need someone to tell us what he or she considers optimal.

There is a depth to each of us. Learning how to be allowed into these depths makes for the most profound and important interactions we have. The authenticity found at such levels allows for the experience of life changing interactions and growth—not to mention escape from terrifying aloneness.

II

Dr. Brad Reedy has always been in the business of providing different experiences and outcomes for people. Whether this is in wilderness therapy, intensive weekends, personal psychotherapy, lectures, podcasts, or his writing, he has tried to illustrate a different way to respond to problems and pain. In his own evolution over the years he has learned the importance of struggling to hear what people are saying. This is a process of trying to find and resonate with a person as he or she sees things. It is sad that so few people have been adequately heard. Often the search for answers or wisdom gets in the way of simple hearing.

In addition to seeing his own clients, Brad attempts to help his therapists at Evoke Therapy Programs learn how to listen instead of relying on cook-book techniques. If there is empathic hearing, the client tends to feel safe and welcome. This allows one's physiology to relax enough to explore options. A physiology that is on alert for harm does not feel safe enough to learn. This principle applies as much to adults as it does to children. It applies in the wilderness and in the therapist's office. Therapeutic techniques are fine, but genuine connection is vital. So many people have never experienced this to any degree. It is the most important thing therapy can offer.

A strength in Brad's writing is his many examples taken directly from years of experience working with people. He also uses his own struggles, his own therapy and development in an honest and open way. This helps people find who they are and how to function as a more complete *Self* in the world in which they live.

Not living an authentic life is to live a life that is not one's own.

This is the source of endless misery and failed interactions. Children who have a genuine parent who understands them and feels tenderness toward them are lucky indeed. Improving one's ability to hear and resonate with others improves the lives of everyone around one. It is truly the light in the darkness.

We all need someone who will care about us and help us. Brad has tried to be that person for so many. With these new chapters he continues his attempt to help refocus efforts in a more beneficial way, in order to help our relationships, become more rewarding for us as well as for others. I wish there were more like him.

J.D. Gill, Ph.D.

THE

AUDACITY

TO BE YOU

CHAPTER ONE

ON HUMAN BEING

No matter the story, the heroic journey is always inward.

THE HEROIC JOURNEY

IN MY FIRST BOOK, *THE JOURNEY OF THE HEROIC PARENT*, I began by telling the story of my marital struggles and my journey towards discovering that the problems and the solutions to my dilemma were not solved by staying married or getting divorced but instead the resolution was inside of me. My dilemmas were rooted in my past, my childhood, and its unique story. After reading about my journey, some expressed their frustration that I didn't share the resolution of this story. Did I stay married or get divorced? I don't always finish the stories I am writing about; this is intentional and goes to the heart of this work. The reason I forego the ending of some of my stories is because the answer to "what should I do?" isn't the point. The point is not to give you the answers but instead provide you with an idea of how to discover *your* answer. In that first book, I emphasized "The question is not the question." It is also true that the answer is not *the* answer. Besides, my story is not yet ended; it is ongoing, one-day-at-a-time.

But, for all those that are curious and to make new points, I will begin by telling the rest of the story here.

So, did we stay married? Or did we divorce?

While I was at a week-long therapeutic intensive to decide "what should I do?", I didn't come away with the definitive answer. Instead, I learned that I need to live and speak my truth more honestly and more often. This takes some courage and requires me to resist succumbing to the old scripts that tell me I have to take care of everyone else. This the unconscious obligation I had incorporated from the relationships and unspoken messages of my childhood.

As I practiced and progressed in my willingness and ability to tell those around me the truth about what I thought and felt, it became clear to me who were "my people." Those who could tolerate me, stuck around. Those who couldn't and needed me to be like them, think like them, and live like them, went away. To my wife's heroic credit and as a testament to her hard work, she began to listen, welcome, and honor my truth. It was the sweetest thing I have ever experienced—the experience of being loved just as I am. And along with this, she took more responsibility for her own happiness.

I had been taught and came to believe without question that the only way someone would love me is if I, first and foremost, took care of their needs. My wife showed me something different. She showed me that my *"horrible, rotten Self"* was lovable as is. Over time, as we learned to love each other in this new way, I realized I never wanted to be without her. It is imperative that I underscore that the basis of this new relationship, Marriage 2.0, as we call it, was built on the foundation of each of our individual work.

During our time apart, I realized that the problems that existed in our marriage would be recreated in all of my relationships unless I was willing to address and work through them. As my son pointed out to me at the time, being alone was never easy for me—like many, I can barely stand the few seconds of silence at a stop light without checking my smart phone. Yet, on my own, I noticed I was a better father. Because in the aloneness, my focus could be singular—concentrated on what my children needed versus placating my wife or meeting the ideas that society had about parenting.

To put it mildly, that time was a messy one in my life. Times where we are sorting out what it means to be our true *Selves* typically are that way. It is in the darkest corners, the places we are most afraid to venture, the places that the myths tell us about, where we find the most miraculous treasures. The dreams and ideas I had for my life crumbled and I was left with only myself. There is a kind of freedom in such times of failure and distress. As I *accepted* the idea that I was a *horrible, rotten Self*—for this is the name my guilt and shame gave me for my imperfect, human *Self*—I began to consider abandoning the project of trying to prove to everyone I was good. And with that surrender came freedom, greater clarity and authenticity, and an increased capacity to love *Others*.

My wife and I are together and, while it is a work in progress, we are both clear of our respective projects. We are also clear about the origin of our problems and where they rest in each of us. We continue to work on ourselves and practice loving each other's dilemmas and we are committed to refueling and maintaining a practice of bolstering the *Self* so that we can love each *Other* in the way that each of us need.

THE NEW PROJECT

After finishing my first book, I sat with a team in my publisher's office discussing possible titles. Choosing a title is the most exciting part of writing the book. It feels like some combination of creativity and pragmatism. You want to come up with something that hooks readers and provides them with a sense of the scope of the work. When we landed on *The Journey of the Heroic Parent*, I thought we did just that. The book was about parenting, but it was bigger than that. It was about the journey or transformation a person goes through when someone they love is struggling with addiction or mental health issues. And while it was formed from and applies to the families I have worked with in wilderness therapy, it is really about what it means to be alive on this planet. What does it mean to be in this world and what does it mean to relate to others?

This book is an attempt to expand on the ideas of what it is to be a person or a *Self* in all of our relationships and contexts. I invite the reader to study the stories about parenting or the parent-child dynamic not merely from the vantage point of a parent. These stories are also about *our* stories as children. They are illustrations about what happened to us as children and how we become who we are and how using these new lenses can help in all areas of our lives.

As the *Heroic Parent* book tour began and I found myself describing my approach, I told one buyer, "It really isn't about parenting at all." Maybe that was too far, an overstatement, but what I was trying to imply was that the challenges, the barriers, and the answers to difficult questions were not specific to the task of parenting. The seminal concepts that apply in parenting are common to nearly every relationship. One day, after my own personal therapy session, I remember thinking that how I treat or regard the people in my life— family, friends, and colleagues—has more in common with the ideal way to treat a client than the differences. Renowned psychiatrist Rudolf Dreikurs stated the idea this way, "The proper way of training children is identical with the proper way of treating fellow human beings."

I have written about how I often hear parents say, "You need to be the parent to your child—not their friend," but this may miss the fact that many of the same qualities that exist in a healthy friendship will exist in any healthy relationship: boundaries, a strong and clear sense of one's *Self*, assertive communication, authentic presence, and love. I believe the reason many people misunderstand the similarities between relationships (friendships, couples, children) is because many people misunderstand the core elements of a healthy relationship of any kind. There is no shame in this; it just shows how little we have been exposed to healthy models.

I conduct workshops for families, individuals, and professionals where we use psychodrama as a principal technique. Psychodrama can be understood simply as role-playing with other participants (more on it later). Sometimes we roleplay how others have treated us, or how they might respond to us if we said or did certain things. One thing I often like to do in psychodrama is to ask clients how they would like others—their parents, their spouses, their siblings—to respond. It is fascinating as they consider this ideal. What is most interesting to me is that they often can't imagine an authentic and loving relationship with others. How could they? They have had no example of it. They haven't been taught what it means to be human, but rather they have been taught to be some "good" or "right" thing.

Since there are so few models of what it means to be in an authentic relationship, I often suggest clients attend Al-Anon meetings or CODA (Codependents Anonymous) meetings when they come to me with a struggling child. This is a place where healthy boundaries and focusing on a healthy *Self* are modeled and practiced. Many report back to me and say something like, "I didn't fit in. Everyone else at the meeting was talking about an alcoholic spouse." Or perhaps they'll say, "My child doesn't drink or use drugs, so the meeting didn't apply to us." Further, many of the parents I work with protest to some of the things I and others teach based on details of their situation. Of course, there are unique differences in the decisions we make when considering a relationship to a spouse, young child, or adult child, but the longer I do this work the more I realize that there is much more in common in all of these circumstances than there are differences.

Because we don't know what it means to be human, we don't know how to deal with the struggle of being human. We look for ways to solve what we think are our problems, but no decision is the solution to our difficulties: divorce, staying married, kicking an adult child out of the basement, having your adult child move back in, sending a child to a residential treatment program, quitting a job, asking for what you need to stay in a job, creating, maintaining healthier friend and familial relationships or ending some of those. In all of these decisions, we are looking for peace or a sense of well-being and we think we can find this through these choices. No decision or series of decisions necessarily results in the outcome we desire. We seek advice and answers from wise guides, but we hear so little.

Banksy, the enigmatic graffiti artist, illustrated this dearth of training on becoming human when he said, "A lot of parents will do anything for their kids, except let them be themselves." Relationships are more complicated than any one or any series of decisions. And since we cannot control for outcomes or predict how other people will respond, we must embrace a different sort of *sensibility—a new way of being in the world.*

We must make it our quest to find our truth, and when it is found, our decisions will rise out of that truth.

We prioritize what is most important to us and make decisions that express those values. The peace, in some ways, must come before the decision. We begin to answer questions about who we are and what we want in a relationship and then we make decisions based on these discoveries. Rather than looking at solutions in terms of the decisions we make, I offer the idea of considering the sensibility in which we see ourselves and others. What does it mean to be a human and to be in a relationship? What does it mean to be a *Self?* And how can two selves remain independent while creating a connection?

Joseph Campbell, a foremost American expert in mythology, explained that the purpose of the heroic journey illustrated in our myths is to describe a "transformation of consciousness." The kind of change he is talking about is more than any new skill or tool can provide. This shift is fundamental; it is a *different way of being.* This transformation is even beyond an explanation. It is difficult to put into words or to explain to another person, which is why it is often illustrated through stories or examples. The story (in Campbell's work it is the myth) shows us how it would look and sound if we experienced this change in ourselves. The lessons from the prophets are vertical rather than horizontal. The prophets see different levels or layers of life. They don't offer us, necessarily, a history lesson or a glimpse into the future, they provide us with a deeper meaning to our lives.

I use stories to illustrate the ideas I am trying to put forth in this book. The stories are my stories, stories about my friends and family, or stories about my clients. The story or example *evokes* the sense I am trying to communicate. When I use a story, I am saying, "This is what it would sound like if you knew yourself or if you loved another." I often appeal to the ideal, so we have a sense of where our work lies. I will ask you to consider ideals which may never be fully realized but can become the work of a lifetime.

In church some years ago, a father teaching a Sunday school lesson told us about a dream he'd had in the days leading up to his lesson. His young-adult son had fallen into "worldliness" and was struggling with addictions. "In my dream," he explained, "my son and I came to the edge of a filthy, dirty pond, polluted with all kinds of garbage. I knew the water was toxic, but my son did not. Before I could stop him, he was swimming out into the center of the poisoned pond. I gasped in horror as he struggled and started to sink. I was filled with pain and torment as he disappeared from sight. I couldn't save him, for if I dove into the water after him, I would also die." He told this story, and in the backdrop of his context, he thought the dream explained how his son was trapped and destroyed by the sins of the world. He talked about the dirty pond with disdain and dread. In one way of thinking, his was an accurate interpretation. However, as a therapist, working with young men in similar conditions as his young adult son, I thought of it in a different sense.

His son was swimming into the father's rejected unconscious. Children do this. They signal to us that something isn't working. Their symptoms are the sirens letting us know that something about the context we have created for them is broken. Something powerful pulled his son into it and he was now in the grips of life-threatening addictions. This father had to overcome his fear and his rage to save his son. In a sense, the father and the son *will* die. As the father dives into the work of confronting the unconscious aspects of his *Self*, a new *Self* can emerge. His son needs him to take this risk. The father must confront his fears, go in after the boy, for both to have a chance at emerging as more complete and whole *Selves*. I have seen many brave parents do this for their children over the years and the transformation for all of them is nothing short of magnificent.

This awakening into a new way of being in the world is not simple, nor is it easy. It can be terrifying and painful. We are sure that changing the way we are and the way we related to others will not result in what we want. We are sure that such a change will result in abandonment or annihilation of all we hold dear in our lives as we know them. This is why most of us will not change unless the circumstances are extraordinary: a child struggling with mental illness or addiction, a spouse whose alcoholism threatens our very lives or the lives of our children, or a situation or relationship that poses an indisputable threat to our wellbeing and happiness. Then, and often only then, we will be willing to walk through the fire. And when we do, we may not find what we had hoped for on the other side, but what we will find is a better version of ourselves. This is the death of the old *Self* and the birth of a new one. Campbell stated it this way:

We must be willing to let go of the life we planned so as to find the life that is waiting for us.

With our work, often initiated by some crisis, we can find our truth and learn to operate from it with more and more regularity. At a therapeutic retreat I was running, one woman shared with the group, "In this work, when I discovered that one of my long-held truths was debunked, I realized all of them were up for grabs. It was terrifying."

Over the years, I have noticed a pattern with new therapists that I train, especially those fresh from graduate school and particularly those with a Ph.D. They often cling to theory and to what those in my field refer to as "evidence-based" practices. Understandably, with little experience, good intentions, and a plethora of academic training, they want to provide clients with some version of reliable treatment. One supervisee objected to my approach in supervision. I was focusing on the feelings he seemed to be having with his clients rather than the theory or technique he thought he was employing. He was not the first nor would he be the last to challenge my concentration on how the therapist was *being* with the client. He argued, "What is the basis of your approach? Where is the research that shows that how I feel about the client is critical in terms of outcomes? I," he proudly asserted, "base my work on the most recent research."

Understanding his difficulty, but wanting to challenge him further, I explained how research studies are one way to know truth, but not the only way. Experience also reveals truth. "You would be wise to make use of both what you have read as well as what you have experienced," I told him. "Until you have a significant amount of the latter, listening to others will only enhance your techniques."

What I didn't explain to him is that the experience I spoke of was partly due to my education on effective tenets of therapy and from my practice as a therapist, but mostly it came from discovering my life through therapy as a client. The most valuable things I can offer others stems from my own thoroughly explored struggle. I have been in therapy off-and-on since childhood—somewhere in the range of 30 years—and I have been with my current therapist for more than 20 years. In that process, I have discovered that what my therapist thinks and feels about me is the substance of therapy. Actually, it is everything. My experience has shown me that healing happens when I show up and share my truth and my therapist responds with understanding and curiosity. When clients, children, or others are understood—instead of being seen as something that needs to be fixed—they relax, see themselves and their wounds more clearly, and begin to heal. This perspective is uncommon thinking, even in the world of therapy. To simply seek to understand goes against our natural instincts to fix and to solve, but attempting to understand *is* the key to effective therapy.

The evidence in attachment theory is clear and robust that how we hold the child in our minds is the single most impactful contribution to the child's sense of self and well-being. Thus, therapy can be understood as a kind of re-parenting, but one doesn't usually realize this unless they have experienced it—and it takes years. This process often doesn't sell well when the culture wants quick fixes, simple steps, or easily imitated templates and techniques.

How we hold the child in our minds is the single most impactful contribution to the child's sense of self and well-being.

While this book will cover a significant scope of work, I hope the reader will discover the thread of truth that weaves through each subject—mental illness and therapy, parenting and children, falling in love and getting divorced. I will use each of these areas to talk about the same thing: what it means to be human and what it means to be connected to each other.

After *The Journey of the Heroic Parent* came out, I read a quote from Gandhi that epitomized the essence of this sensibility:

A coward is incapable of exhibiting love; it is the prerogative of the brave.
Projection, fusion, "going home," is easy; loving another's otherness is heroic. If we really love the Other, as Other, we have heroically taken on the responsibility for our own individuation, our own journey. This heroism may properly be called love.

The terrain I would like to explore in this book is this landscape of love and being human. It is my experience that the secrets to life are found as we become most acquainted with the depths of ourselves. Carl Jung explained that in order to understand the darkness of others, we must come to understand ourselves and our own darkness. In the classic tale *The Knight in Rusty Armor*, the knight is led by his mentor Merlin on a heroic journey to find his true *Self*. At a certain juncture the knight desperately calls out for Merlin. When he appears, Merlin responds to the knight's query without being asked. The knight, stunned by this, asks Merlin if he reads minds. Merlin responds, "Since I know my *Self*, I know you."

That is the premise of this work. The discovery of the *Self* is the key that unlocks the door to our understanding of the universe. Our choices and decisions alone will not determine our success in navigating this life; rather, it is the discovery of ourselves and our unique histories that will illuminate the darkness. And when our decisions arise out of this truth, what comes next will be exactly what is supposed to happen for our evolution and enlightenment. It can feel foreign and even terrifying. It is not easy. As one young woman recently said to me in a session, describing the loneliness she felt when challenging beliefs held by her parents and siblings, "It is so scary to stand in my own opinion." It takes a rare kind of courage or audacity. This is a book about having that audacity to be you and what it means to be a *Self* and love an *Other*.

FINDING YOU

"In your longing for your giant self lies your goodness: and that longing is in all of you." Kahlil Gibran

WHAT IT MEANS TO BE A SELF

LET'S START WITH THE SELF, SINCE THE SELF IS THE BASIS of every other relationship. Another reason I want to start with the Self is that I have spent so much of my therapy career emphasizing what we do for others, particularly our children, that I have neglected talking about our right and our responsibility to be ourselves. Sometimes my parent teaching is interpreted as an imperative: that is, "You should do this or that for your child." The fact is that the basis for all relationships, including the relationship with your children, is a foundation of *Self*. We are allowed to be ourselves. We are allowed to have values, thoughts, dreams, and feelings. And it is our job, not our children's, to take care of ourselves. The unlived life of a parent is too much a burden to bear for any child. If we do not make our lives the first project, we will suffer because of it; our partners, children and others in our lives will suffer as well.

From attachment research we learn that our ability to understand ourselves and make sense of what has happened to us in our past is the key to providing our children with adequate attachment. It is not what happened to us, but whether or not we have made sense of things that determines our ability to provide our children with an attachment experience or to maintain intimacy in any of our relationships. This is an important point because you can have a rather traumatic childhood and do the work to heal and unwind it all. Some point to a relatively nice childhood, but if they haven't done the work to understand their childhood, they are less capable of providing children with a healthy attachment or creating intimacy with a partner. It is the work that you do that predicts your abilities in these other relationships. As we learn and become familiar with the landscape of who we are, as we make sense of our experiences, we create the foundation necessary for attachment. From *Parenting From the Inside-Out*, Siegel and Hartzell explain that,

> *Research in the field of child development has demonstrated that a child's security of attachment to parents is very strongly connected to the parents' understanding of their own early-life experiences.*

This is exactly why, when I'm working with a child, I always suggest the child's parents "do their own work," too. Your work is the work of *Self*. This means exploring the depths and discovering the edges of who you are. I agree with Ram Dass who states it so plainly, "I can do nothing for you but work on myself...you can do nothing for me but work on yourself!"

So, what does it mean when I talk about a *Self?* Some philosophies talk about the idea that there is no *Self*. Some cultural messages suggest that the highest form of love is only possible when one is *selfless*. When I talk about *Self*, I am talking about one's authentic truths: what one feels, thinks, likes, prefers, hates, loves, wants, needs, or values. Your *Self* is the naked you; it is your human, fallible, beautiful, scared, imperfect, and perfect you. The *Self* is you without judgment or defense. The discovery of the authentic *Self* must dispose of all the should and should nots we gathered from our parents, our peers, and our culture. In other words, using the word "should" is abandoned when searching for one's *Self.*

Finding one's *Self* can be like trying on a shirt to see if we like the feel and fit. As we begin to look inwards, some of these truths we unearth are profound and stable like, "I value honesty and integrity in friendship." Some are fleeting or superficial like, "I'm hungry and I want Italian food for dinner." When one has clarity of *Self,* they know what they feel and what they want. Confusion results from the voices in our heads arguing over what one should do or shouldn't do. These voices lob shameful insults to keep us in line with someone else's idea of how one ought to feel: "You should go to this charity event. Yes, you are tired, but you will help so many people and sitting at home binge-watching a show is lazy and gluttonous. Think beyond yourself!"

Being right and being a Self are two diametrically opposing projects. If we grow up in a home where our feelings are heard, considered, and valued, we develop a clearer sense of who we are.

When we grow up in a home where the project is to be good and right, we are prone to lose a sense of ourselves. Being **right** and being a **Self** are two diametrically opposing projects. If we grow up in a home where our feelings are heard, considered, and valued, we develop a clearer sense of who we are.

When we grow up in a home where the project is to be right, then we feel we must make a case for everything we want, everything we do. We debate with others, proving the validity of our choices and our preferences. The processes that differentiate the two styles are subtle and more like a continuum than a binary. It is in the air we breathe. I often refer to the way we are raised as "the soup we are cooked in." If we were seen as children, we would have a better sense of ourselves as adults. When we were tired, we would sleep. When we were hungry, we would eat. If we found ourselves in a relationship or situation that asked us to compromise critical aspects of ourselves, we would let the relationship go, or remove ourselves from the situation.

In her book *The Price of Privilege*, Dr. Madeline Levine begins by reflecting on the similarities and patterns amongst her adolescent clientele. Perplexed, she observes that her caseload is filled with young people from affluent families, but the range and depth of their suffering seems profound beyond what their circumstance would seem to predict. Self-harm, eating disorders, addiction, suicidality, depression and anxiety—her clients come from what most would consider "good homes," but their suffering is still deep and profound. So, Dr. Levine sets out on a journey to discover what is happening.

> *The role of a parent is to raise healthy Selves, not good children. Raising a child to be a Self is the most critical thing we do to foster resiliency and provide them with the possibility they may find connection to others.*

In the simplest of terms, she realizes these children are being raised to become good students, gifted musicians, and successful business leaders. But what is missing in the lives of her teenage clientele is support for the healthy development of the *Self*. In other words, they are not allowed to be people. Being a person means that what you feel and think matter even when they don't match up with what others think is the "right" way to be. The enterprise of raising "good" and "successful" children, of course, ensures their failure in the world. A *Self* is whole and messy, sometimes successful, sometimes failing, but a *Self* is always authentic. And since a child's worth is dependent on achieving parental and societal expectations of success, this can result in self-loathing, deep insecurity, and dread.

The role of a parent is to raise healthy Selves, not good children. Raising a child to be a *Self* is the most critical thing we do to foster resiliency and provide them with the possibility they may find connection to others.

How do you feel and what do you want? What is your truth? These may be more important to consider than what is *THE* truth. The former is possible to know, while the latter may be the basis of all the world's wars.

A couple of summers ago, I was at one of our outdoor therapy programs in the high desert outside of Bend, Oregon visiting an adolescent girls' group.

It was midday and we decided to hold a group therapy session. At the outset of the program, parents are asked to write a "Hopes and Intentions Letter" to their child—a letter that spells out why the parents sent their child to the program and what they hoped the child will gain from participation. Gabby had been in the program for less than a week and it was time for her to read her letter in a group. The letter is usually difficult to read and often leads to powerful emotions in the child. As was our custom, we signify the start of group by breaking a stick, exposing the heart wood—the innermost and alive part of the stick and also the most resilient. I asked Gabby to find a stick for us to use for her group. She stood and began to search our campsite for an adequate stick. While we waited, I chatted with the other seven members of the group. After a few minutes, I realized Gabby hadn't found a stick. Wandering about 20 feet away from the group, she was walking in small circles looking at the ground.

Calling to her, I asked, "Gabby. Have you found a stick yet?"

"I can't find one," she said, and she reached down and grabbed one from the hundreds of sticks that lay around our campsite. She looked at me and asked meekly, "Is this one okay?"

"It's your group, so it's your stick," I replied.

One of the other girls reached to her side, grabbed a stick and offered confidently, "Here's a good one."

I looked at the other girl and said loud enough for Gabby to hear, "That's not Gabby's stick. That's your stick." The rest of the girls were quiet and focused on Gabby now.

Reluctantly, Gabby approached the circle and asked again, "Is this one okay?"

"It's not for me to say," I offered gently, "It is your group and it is your stick. What do you think about it?"

"I think it's okay," she said.

"Then it's the right stick, Gabby."

While the above is a simple story, it illustrates how difficult it can be for children—or anyone, for that matter—to find their truth, take hold of it, and show it to the world, "This is my stick!" We risk so much. If we were cooked in the soup of being right instead of being a *Self*, then finding our stick and declaring to the world it is ours may be terrifying. Just sit in any new class of students, of any age, and see how quiet it is when an instructor asks if there are any questions.

In working with a family during a multi-day therapeutic intensive, the teenage son left an afternoon session hurt and angry because he felt judged and criticized by his parents. As the rest of the family sat down for dinner, I went to talk with him as he was standing on the porch by himself, looking at the mountains.

"What do you want to do?" I asked.

"What do you think I should do?" he asked.

"I have no idea what you should do. I can't even begin to tell you what to do. I really just want to support you with whatever you need right now."

Tears began to fill his eyes, "No one has ever said that to me— at least no adult." He told me he trusted me precisely because I didn't presume to know what he *should* do.

His decision to reengage with his family didn't come easy. He had good reason to believe that nothing would be any different from how it had always been. He was sure his parents would tell him why he was wrong and why walking away from them was his issue and not theirs. Eventually, he was able to share his thoughts and feelings, and his parents listened to what he had to say.

When we are raised in the soup or context of "right" and "wrong", *what we feel* is less important. I once had a client share with me that it took six months to convince her therapist that her divorce from her husband was justified. She shared this expert's opinion with me, I would guess, so she wouldn't have to go through the arduous task of convincing another expert of the merits of her decision.

Perplexed, I responded, "It would have taken you less than six minutes with me—in fact, I am not sure I would have had an opinion or felt the need to approve or disapprove of such a choice."

My response surprised her, and she even seemed a little offended by my lack of agreement and acceptance of the rightness of her choice. I explained to her that it was not my job to know her truth and that I could not possibly know what path she ought to take, especially with a decision as profound as marriage or divorce. My job, I told her, was to provide a safe place where she could discover her truth, her *Self*, and in order to provide that kind of space, I would suspend any approval or disapproval as she explored what *she* wanted— what *she* believed she needed to do.

Recently I was conducting a parent meeting where I was explaining about the need for parents to develop capacities to listen and hold their children with love, curiosity, and patience. Two mothers, almost in unison, interrupted asking me the same question, "So then I should just be a doormat to my child?"

I recognized my mistake—I hadn't established the proper foundation for the understanding of a *Self*. I apologized and explained, "No. I am sorry I wasn't clear. And I am sorry I was making it sound like there was a right way to respond to your child. Here is the thing: you get to set limits. You get to say no. You get to say when enough is enough. But the key in doing this is that you do it with the acknowledgement that you have reached your limit, rather than making the child wrong. You own it as in, 'This is what I feel comfortable with or this is my limit.' But, to be able to do this you must have some sense of yourself and a healthy acceptance of who you are." If we remain in the field of right and wrong or good and bad when setting our limits, we have abandoned the work of being a *Self*. And a *Self* is required if we are to love an *Other*. When the foundation is the *Self* and when we can do the thing for the other, we do it. If we can listen to what their anger and insults are trying to tell us, we remain patient and curious and unharmed. When we cannot do it, we don't do it. When our emotional and spiritual reservoirs are empty, we set a limit, excuse ourselves, and fill ourselves up with what we need to reengage at some other time.

Sometimes, the lack of *Self* is illustrated in more mundane examples. For example, a friend shared with me that whenever he is asked to go out to dinner with other friends, he regularly lacks clarity and doesn't know how to respond. The debate in his head rages between the voices that say he should go out because it might do him some good and the voices that tell him he should not go out because he is tired and needs a night in. As he shared his dilemma with me, he confessed that there were only two times in his adult life that he could remember taking care of himself without doubt or regret, and this was after the death of each of his parents. These were the only times in his life when the needs of the *Self* outweighed the guilt that comes from what others might think or expect from him.

Finding the *Self* is a process, and we may never really discover all the edges of ourselves, our wants and our needs. But seeking to do so is a worthy project and we may benefit if we chose to surround ourselves with others who don't know our truth, who don't suppose that they know what is best for us.

THE AUTHENTIC SELF

Jung's assertion that "I would rather be whole than good" is a radical one. He is suggesting that there is some virtue in incorporating what most of us think is abhorrent—the aspects of ourselves contained in what he called the shadow. He is suggesting that those parts of ourselves we are inclined to discard hold some value, some wisdom, that offer great value to the *Self.*

When the project is to be a "good something or other," children come to understand that they need to sacrifice parts of the authentic *Self* to ensure a place in the world. If we behave in ways that our parents cannot tolerate, then we run the risk of being abandoned. The risk of literal or emotional abandonment is too great a threat for the child to ignore. What makes this process more insidious is that the parent has no idea it is happening. They don't experience themselves threatening the child with disconnection or rejection. They merely experience the emotions that come from having a child struggle. Yet for the child, the frustration, disappointment, anger, sadness, or any other disagreeable feeling in the parent signals the fear of physical or emotional abandonment. In response, the child is apt to discard whatever aspect of themselves that is causing the parent to react in ways that suggest that abandonment is around the corner.

This is a universal experience and there is no way to avoid it. It is in our DNA as humans. The variances come in the way we deal with it. Some comply to find their way out of the dilemma. Some defy and fight against it. These "beat the parent to the punch." They give good reason for the parent to be upset by their alarming behavior, seeming to not care what the parent thinks. In either case or anywhere on the continuum, the child is likely to develop some symptomology. The symptom or mental health diagnosis is the real *Self* signaling to anyone that will listen the origin of the issue and an unmet need that has gone unexpressed. As therapists and parents, we have only to develop ears that can hear it for what it is. We can hear it in the young child or in the adult who has not untangled the dilemma earlier in life.

20

A few years ago, my two oldest children let me know they would be spending Thanksgiving with their mother, my ex-wife. I was sad at this announcement, but I knew that she was having some challenges and that my two older children wanted to make sure their mother felt supported during the holidays. When my 22-year-old daughter, Emma, told me this, a few things went through my mind. First, it wasn't the end of the world. We could celebrate either before or after the formal date of the holiday. Second, I began to consider whether I should invite my ex-wife to our house for the holiday. She and I are not adversarial, and if I invited her to my home then my children wouldn't have to choose between us. I could make a sacrifice and they could be taken care of at the same time.

Still, I worried that having my ex-wife over would compromise my time, even if just a little. Would I feel comfortable as myself if she were present? So much of my time is being there for others, so was it too selfish that I just wanted to spend the holiday with people that make me feel the most comfortable? On the other hand, one of my core values is believing that parents should strive to develop the capacity to be there for their children, so shouldn't this be one of those times when I should to expand myself and be there for them so they can be there for their mother?

I brought these questions to my therapist. I knew I was in trouble as I asked her these questions because I couldn't phrase them without including the words "should or "shouldn't."

"Shouldn't I…I mean, isn't it my responsibility, my highest obligation to be there for my children, even if it comes at the cost of some dissatisfaction for me?"

Her face relaxed and she said in the simplest terms, "I think it is your job to be you." So simple and profound, yet so elusive. With my background, it is easy for me to forget this.

Although my reference point didn't come from a religious context or some dogmatic family paradigm, I had fallen into some of the same trappings common to those frameworks. My context was therapy and psychology, and my ideas were about how to be an ideal parent or the ideal *Self*. I had forgotten that I was allowed to be me, to have my feelings, and to be myself.

Plato, in his search for the guiding principles and laws of a utopian society, suggested that in a perfect world there might only be one law necessary: be yourself. The fear for most is that this ideal would lead to anarchy, hedonism, and unbridled urges played out on the weak and the helpless without remorse. However, this is not my experience. When one feels their feelings deeply, they recognize feelings in others and are compelled to respond with compassion. This kind of humanity is fostered in contexts where feelings and the inner world of the child, of each other are considered.

Since the discovery of *Self* does not come when we use words like "should" or "ought to," we must do battle with guilt. In my experience, if we are not battling our guilt, we are not making our way to find our real or authentic *Self*. Shame, and more precisely guilt, are the sentinels that stand guard and hide our real *Self*. Friedrich Nietzsche described the three metamorphoses we may go through in this life and explained that before returning to the original state of being of a child, one must kill the dragon of "Thou Shalt." This dragon shimmers with gold and on every scale the words "Thou Shalt" are written. The dragon represents all our context's expectations, from canonized scripture to today's endless media cycle that tell us how we are to live. In killing the dragon, we do not regress to lawlessness, selfishness, or hedonism. Instead, we act from a place of innocence and pure love, driven by our heart.

Innocence is the child, and forgetfulness, a new beginning, a game, a self-rolling wheel, a first movement, a holy Yea. Aye, for the game of creating, my brethren, there is needed a holy Yea unto life.

THE PROBLEM IS OUTSIDE OF ME

Not all needs in families or relationships can simultaneously be met at the same time, but the mistake many people make is they make others wrong, bad, or selfish when others are unable to respond to their needs. In psychological terms, this is called *projective identification.*

Here is how it goes. If I have a child who is in pain and is crying out in distress, these cries may trigger in me a feeling of inadequacy and can lead me to believe that I am not a good father. This is an uncomfortable feeling, so rather than owning it, I might find it easier to label the child as inadequate or bad in some way and think something like, "He is too sensitive, too dramatic, too needy." Projective identification is more involved than simple *projection,* which is to take unwanted aspects of the *Self* and project them onto others. In this case, rather than owning my feeling of inadequacy and dealing with it, I project it not *onto* but *into* the other person, and that results in the other person—in this case, my child—feeling what I am feeling—inadequate.

The feelings that result from upsetting, disappointing, or frustrating our parents are often interpreted as "something is wrong with me." Or, as Euripides put it, "The gods visit the sins of the fathers upon the children." I do this because it was done to me and it is all I know. My needs went unmet and were too much for my mother and so she responded to them in such a way as to make me feel that something was wrong with me. Instead, if my mother had been more capable and aware, she would have let me know I was okay—I was just being me—that it was she that was inadequate. Due to the shame that results from not feeling like we are enough, owning our limitations is a tall task for most of us. And this inability to own it and the subsequent projection into our children leaves them with a wound. I often tell the adult clients I work with, "This is not your shame. It is your parents. If only we could have escaped childhood with the sense that we were okay, that we were enough, we could have used our resources to give." We can spend our entire life trying to prove to others or to ourselves that we are okay, rather than developing and giving our gifts to the world.

There is hope, however, because parents don't need to be capable of everything. This can be a relieving truth since it is impossible for parents to have unlimited capabilities. But what is helpful is for parents to own their limitations. Otherwise through the process co-created by the parent and child, the child will internalize the parents' inadequacies, limitations, and compromised *Self*. We are human and have limitations and thankfully that is okay and part of being human. If parents were capable of everything, children would not learn to adapt, develop frustration tolerance, or delay of gratification.

We can learn to express ourselves by stating our needs rather than demanding that others change, that others are the problem, "This is what I need. This is what I need to feel okay or comfortable in this situation…" When we are able to own our limitations rather than putting bad feelings into the *Other*, we embark on a heroic journey and offer a great gift to those we love. With this new sensibility, our children are no longer the problem, but just unfortunate to have imperfect, albeit loving, human parents.

My wife has demonstrated this beautifully with our youngest child. Rather than always giving her a time-out, my wife is willing to take a time-out for herself when needed. "I need a time out or I am going to say something I regret. I need time to calm down. I am losing my patience." This way of talking or more importantly this way of thinking makes it about the mother and not about the child. And it has the same effect behaviorally: the child sits alone, without mom, and the escalating behavior is extinguished without the horrible side-effect of the child feeling that she is "bad."

To find the *Self* is to integrate all those things about ourselves others taught us were dark, unacceptable, or horrible. We must learn to embrace the beautiful as well as the parts we think are ugly; Jung called these parts of ourselves the *shadow* because they live or hide in darkness, deep in the unconscious. When we claim these parts of ourselves, we are learning to carry around our own *horrible, rotten, Self.* If we are able to do this, our children and partners won't have to do it for us. Reclaiming these split-off parts sounds like owning our feelings and thoughts like "I feel hurt or tired or hungry or bored or sad." Not owning these parts in the same situations sounds like, "You are a jerk or you don't listen or you are annoying or you are cruel." In the former examples, the *Self* owns the feelings while the latter examples make the *Other* into a problem—they are turned into what psychologists call the *bad object* (the bad mother or father or spouse or child—the bad parts of the *Self* I am not willing to own).

Learning to carry around your *horrible, rotten, Self* is a gift you give to those you love. It takes courage and work; we must betray our parents and our culture. We must regard it as a virtue to be disloyal to a toxic relationship or individual. We must face the monster we think will destroy us and become friends with it. The result of this work is freedom and peace and a greater capacity to love. I often say when you accept that you are the "devil," you are free—free to love and give *Others* love the same way you have learned to love yourself. When you accept yourself, your interactions with *Others* won't be in the service of proving your goodness and worthiness. Instead, you use your energy for loving them.

THE RELATIONSHIP BETWEEN *SELF* AND *OTHER*

We can think of *Self* in relationship to an *Other*. The generic nature of the word "*Other*" emphasizes that the specific characteristics and circumstances of the *Other* are not as important as we might think. The *Other* can be kind or cruel, happy or sad, tall or short, but that the quality of our relationship with them is merely a reflection of the quality of the relationship we have with ourselves.

In another life, when I was a Sunday school teacher but still inclined to use psychology as my lens for viewing phenomenon, I would teach that Jesus's commandment "Thou shalt love thy neighbor as thy *Self*" was less of a commandment about how we *should* be and more like a statement about *the way things are* in the world. Our capacity to love others comes out of the ability we have to see and love ourselves. While some might argue it is possible for one to stem from the other, I argue they are, in fact, one and the same. How we regard others, both their wonderful and difficult parts, is a reflection of how we regard those parts in ourselves. That is why either starting point may make sense and can be effective. Service to others can be getting in touch with beautiful, lost parts of ourselves.

Several years ago, after a colleague had done some hurtful things to me, a mutual friend of ours who witnessed his behavior asked me if I hated him.

I responded, "No. I don't. He was doing it from a place of hurt and fear. I don't like what he did, and it hurt me a lot, but I don't hold angry or hateful feelings toward him."

My friend then replied, "Well, you are better than me. I don't forgive him."

I disagreed with her assessment of me. It was not a moral imperative I was following, and it wasn't even really that effortful. Over the years, I have done a lot of soul-searching through my own therapy, and I have had to look at the many ways I have hurt others—to stare at my own darkness in the eyes. The fact of the matter was, if I hated our mutual friend or harbored some grudge toward him, I would have had the same feelings toward myself. And in wishing him bad things—wishing he would suffer some physical or emotional pain, for instance—I would have had to wish the same for myself. And that burden would have been too great to bear.

As a professor once told me, "What you think about the devil, tells me more about you than it does about the devil."

THREE CIRCLES

In the space where *Self* and *Other* intersect and meet, it is easy for one to lose a sense of who they are. One does this because this is what has been going on for years, starting in childhood when, in order to take care of our parents, we had to split off the unwanted parts of ourselves.

One of my favorite illustrations for understanding *Self* and *Other* is an exercise called "The Three Circles."

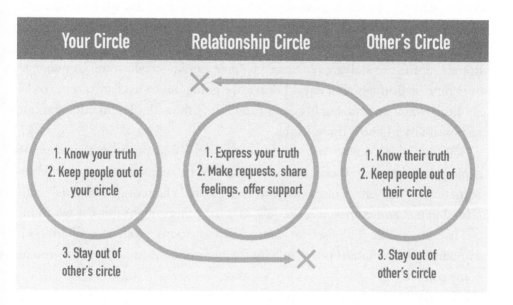

Your Circle	Relationship Circle	Other's Circle
1. Know your truth 2. Keep people out of your circle	1. Express your truth 2. Make requests, share feelings, offer support	1. Know their truth 2. Keep people out of their circle
3. Stay out of other's circle		3. Stay out of other's circle

Imagine three circles on the floor of a room, about the size of a hula-hoop. When I create the exercise, I use a rope and ask participants to move into various circles to illustrate the various concepts. The circles are large enough to fit one person comfortably, while two is a crowd. The first circle represents your *Self*, the second circle represents your relationships, and the third circle represents the *Other*.

CIRCLE 1: CREATING AND MAINTAINING YOUR CIRCLE

In Circle One or "Your Circle" —you have two responsibilities: to know your truth and to keep others out of your circle. Knowing your truth is a lifelong quest. To review what I mean when I talk about your truth and to make it sound less like "psychobabble," it is important to understand that truth isn't mystical but is rather a practical aspect of the *Self.* Truth, in this context, is what you feel, believe, want, like, dislike, or love; it's basically anything that comes after "I" in an "I statement." Some of your truths are profound: "I value honesty above all" Or "My faith in God grounds me." Some of your truths are less fundamental: "I don't like mushrooms" or "I loved the movie Roma." Some are stable over time: "I don't smoke" while some can change over time or throughout a day, "I don't like going out to bars anymore," or "I am hungry and am craving Mexican food." It is the task of a lifetime and our responsibility to know these truths.

Why we don't know our truth at a given moment is also worthy of exploration because these barriers tend to be consistent in our lives. Sometimes it is the voices in our heads, the chattering "shoulds" and "shouldn'ts." Sometimes, it is the fear of what others might think if we admit we like to watch *The Bachelor.* Sometimes it stems from our childhood; sometimes it is reflected powerfully in the present context and in our present company.

Our clarity about our truth is key to our capacity to see others. The clear line we attempt to draw around ourselves, the edges of who we are, is a lifetime's work and if this line is unclear, we are not sure whether we are seeing the *Other* or seeing a part of us.

The important thing is that we recognize that there is no better contribution that we can make to connection and intimacy than to develop a strong and secure sense of *Self.* This is because a clear sense of *Self,* a clear awareness of our truth, is the first ingredient in intimacy.

It cannot be any other way since intimacy is the connection between two *Selves* and therefore the quality of the intimacy will be predicated on the grounded-ness of those two *Selves*. If, for example, we are unclear about what we feel, think, believe and value, we cannot be confident whether what we see in another is them or our projection. "I think my child likes to play soccer, but I wonder if she is just doing it to please me." The emotional and psychological gravitational pull of others is a force we must resist if we are to remain clear about our truth.

Both as a client and a therapist, I recognize the energy required to maintain one's sense of *Self* in the face of fear, the risk of rejection, and the desirable reward of acceptance and belonging. This came to me with great clarity some years ago after a session with my therapist.

> *The emotional and psychological gravitational pull of others is a force we must resist if we are to remain clear about our truth.*

I had just spent the hour sharing some of my truths with my therapist. My wife and I had recently reconciled and there were some things on my mind, some things I wanted to share. The road to reconciliation was hard and I treasured the new level of intimacy we were experiencing, and I feared that sharing some of my feelings and thoughts could lead to regression. After sharing with my therapist and experiencing her warm validation, it was clear that I must share what was on my mind. The thoughts in my head were clear, "Of course I should tell my wife. There is nothing wrong with what I am feeling. If she struggles to hear me, that is about her, not about me." I walked out of the session with great confidence and clarity.

The drive from my therapist's office to my home took about 20 minutes, and as I exited the freeway, my confidence faded and again began to give way to fear. I thought, "There is no way I am going to tell my wife all this." It was then that I realized that therapy doesn't take away fear, at least not completely. What it does do is provide an individual with enough clarity that they are able to walk through the fear. I went home and sat down with my wife and shared what I thought and felt in spite of how it felt. It went fine and I can't even recall at this time what it was that I shared, but what became clear to me is that our fears of how others will react to us is the thing that blocks our awareness.

Someone once told me this phenomenon is called pseudo-stupidity because it isn't really a *not knowing*, it is just that our fears eclipse our awareness. And if we find someone who can hear us and provide a safe place, we can discover our truth. I have had the same kind of experience with many of my clients. Clarity and confidence on a phone call or in a session can evaporate in the moment of truth, the instant they are confronted with the feelings and gravitational field of the *Other*. Deciding on a clear boundary with a child disappears as the child pleads their case.

Keeping people out of our circle means not negotiating how we feel. While negotiating boundaries and decisions is a necessary part of every relationship, negotiating your truth—how you feel, think, and believe—is non-negotiable. But many will try to talk you out of your truth and into theirs instead of allowing you to discuss and set boundaries. I see this with parents and spouses and friends. We try to talk others into what we believe on a regular basis. When *Others* get in our space, try to convince us that what we feel, think or believe is wrong, it is our responsibility to let them know that these are not open for negotiation. "I don't enjoy your friend Tom, but I am willing to have him over if you are okay with me retiring to our bedroom after dinner to read my book." Or, "I don't share your beliefs, but I am willing to go to church to support you."

CIRCLE 2: ENTERING THE RELATIONSHIP CIRCLE

In Circle Two or the "Relationship Circle"—you have two responsibilities: to express your truth and to respond assertively, clearly, and courageously to others' truths. Expressing your truth can be done in a variety of ways: sharing your thoughts and feelings, stating your preferences, making requests, or offering a story from your past. Common errors in the relationship circle are avoiding the issue and repressing or denying one's feelings. Sometimes you don't ask for something for fear that the other one will feel obligated, unable to say no, or be unwilling to take care of their circle. You may fear that if you express your truth, others will respond with anger or disappointment. If you fear being punished and that prevents you from expressing your needs or preferences, you are compromising elements of the *Self*. Most can relate to this type of avoidance.

Using the ropes and circles in the exercise, I invite participants to step one foot into the relationship circle and invite the other to do the same. This sharing of the middle circle is contrasted with examples where we abandon our circle or step into someone else's circle trying to change their mind—change their truth. With this exercise, we can also practice taking people at face value. Many clients worry that shifting into assertive communication and clear boundaries isn't fair to *Others* since those *Others* may not realize the rules of the game have changed. They avoid asking or check-in again and again because they fear upcoming resentments. Repeatedly asking, "Are you sure you're okay?" is a simple example of not responding to others with clarity.

There will be growing pains, but if we establish a pattern of taking others at face value, they will be required to use their words if they expect to be heard.

There will be growing pains, but if we establish a pattern of taking others at face value, they will be required to use their words if they expect to be heard.

In my family, the circles exercise is a tool we use regularly. We invite and remind each other (give permission) to take care of their circle. This front-loading creates clarity and sets the *Other* up for success. My wife does this regularly and adds, "Telling me what you think I want to hear is repulsive—it is not attractive. But, when you tell me the truth and take care of your circle, I am all in." Taking care of your circle or asking if the other feels like you are getting in their circle is a shorthand we use to conjure up all the ideas of this exercise which really are the anatomy of intimacy.

CIRCLE 3: YOUR PLACE (OR NOT) IN THE OTHER'S CIRCLE

In Circle Three or the "*Other's* Circle,"—you have one responsibility: to stay out of the *Other's* circle. Others have the same two responsibilities in their circle that you have in your circle: to know their truth and to keep people out of their circle. Getting in someone's circle is trying to convince them in some way to arrive at a consensus with your feelings, requests, boundaries, beliefs, feelings, or approach to things. We get in *Other's* circle for one primary reason: if we can change the *Other's* mind, we don't have to set and follow through on our boundaries. Trying to convince a child of your thinking behind a rule or trying to get your spouse to stop drinking is classic circle jumping—getting into the *Other's* circle. Shaming and guilting, consciously or unconsciously, are common techniques in circle jumping. They also happen to be very powerful in changing others in the short term. And regardless of euphemisms, circle jumping is a lack of intimacy, a lack of healthy connection—not "loving too much." It is an attempt to violate the sovereignty of another's *Self*.

While the concept of the Three Circles may seem trite, this concept is an analogy at the heart of this entire book: What does it mean to be a *Self*? Who are you? What do you want? And once you develop some clarity surrounding your truth, what would it be like to be in a relationship where each individual's truth is honored and respected? Do your ways of seeing the world align enough so that you want to spend your lives together? Simple as it may be, the Three Circles can remind us of what it means to be connected without being required to sacrifice precious aspects of who we are in the process.

The "Richardsons." The following example illustrates how difficult it can be to maintain one's sense of *Self*, in the psychological-gravitational pull of an *Other*. Sherry Richardson was at a crossroads in her life. With her children out of the home, she wanted to enter back into the workforce. She was trained as a teacher and had set aside her career to raise her children. With all of her children grown and out of the home, she was looking to reconnect with a part of her *Self* that had been placed on hold for more than 25 years. Perhaps she could find a volunteer position or a substitute role; she even considered going back to school to pursue a graduate degree. She had discussed her ideas with her husband, and he was supportive of her goals and wishes, but she still felt uneasy about the transition. She was worried that her husband would still expect her to fulfill all the responsibilities she'd previously fulfilled as a homemaker while she took on her new challenges. They had always had some disposable income and could hire for many of the domestic tasks but had never done so as a matter of frugality and a shared sensibility that a woman's job was to manage the home. Dan was retired, but his day was full of either church-volunteer activities or recreational interests.

The Richardsons didn't come to the couples therapeutic intensive out of a crisis, but to deepen their love and communication as they navigated a critical stage of life transition. How would they be without their children in the home? Would they have enough interest in each other? How would time together be decided since no outside forces dictated the need for either spouse to work? During their

And regardless of euphemisms, circle jumping is a lack of intimacy, a lack of healthy connection—not "loving too much." It is an attempt to violate the sovereignty of another's Self.

session, I laid out three circles on the floor and asked each partner to place themselves inside their respective circle—the one that represented their individual truths. I started with Sherry and asked her what was on her mind—the truth she wanted to communicate to her husband. She began to search for words to talk about the transition into this next stage in life and her worries about negotiating them with her husband. As she meandered from topic to topic, I saw her glancing at her husband. I sensed she was trying to read him—to take his emotional temperature as she began to explore the landscape. Noticing this, I asked Dan to wait in the other room. I wanted Sherry to find her *Self*—her truth—without the distraction of her loving *Other*. After that, we could work on communicating it to Dan and how it would be negotiated.

When Dan left the room, the ideas came much easier to Sherry. I grabbed some index cards to write down the main points she wanted to discuss with Dan. After a back-and-forth, I would write down a sentence or two trying to capture the essence of what Sherry was feeling. "I love you and I want the time I spend at work not to be interpreted as me not caring about you, and I need some help in managing the house in order to pursue this path. Would you be willing to share household chores with me?" We identified five such ideas. After writing each one, I would show the card to Sherry for her approval of my wording. After showing her each card, she would nod in agreement to confirm I had captured her thoughts accurately. Then, we invited Dan back into the room. He stood in his circle and I invited Sherry into the relationship circle so she could share her truths with her husband and handed her the stack of cards. She invited Dan to share the relationship circle and looked at the first card. A long pause ensued. She glanced at the card, at Dan, at me, and back down at the card. "I don't know what this means," she said, her voice shaky and her eyes moist. Her mind was likely racing with thoughts and the anxiety of how Dan might respond. You see, in the presence of her husband, Sherry was not able to hold onto her truths. This is what I mean when I talk about the gravitational pull of the *Other*.

The gravity of his presence pulled at her so much that what she felt, thought, wanted and needed became hidden behind her fears of what her husband might think and feel. When we grow up in a context where we have to read others, predict responses, and conform to what others need in order to avoid painful conflict or rejection, we find holding onto our truths difficult and foreign. It is as though our antennae are so well developed (they had to be because of the context we grew up in) and we are receiving messages from others so loudly that they press on us, imploring at a deep level to fit with whatever the messages are asking of us. Because this ability was required for our survival, its influence over us is beyond our ability to resist. And maybe more importantly, because the messages are invisible and covert, we are unable to see them in our past and we experience this pull as a part of who we are at the core. To resist provokes intense fear and guilt. This is why when people suggest that our fears don't serve a purpose, what they often neglect to point out is that in earlier contexts our fears (and all our symptoms for that matter) served an important purpose in our childhoods. So, by looking at our fears and honoring them, we can discover the wounds that we carry and embark on a path of slowly letting them go.

WHAT OTHERS (INCLUDING YOUR PARENTS) THINK ABOUT YOU IS NONE OF YOUR BUSINESS

If parents need children to feel a certain way about life, a child may forfeit how she or he feels in the service of the parents' needs. The parent needn't ask or overtly require this. It is just a mechanism in the child's development, present in the parent-child dynamic that procures a sense of belonging for the child. As described in earlier pages, a child can often take on their parents' needs at the cost of their authentic and true *Self.* It can become a matter of survival and although that it may not be the case when the child becomes an adult, that hard wiring was set long ago.

This dynamic is why I am *almost* at the point where I want to tell parents this: "Don't ever tell your children how you feel." When I offer this idea many parents (and some therapists) protest. Some state that it is a parent's right to feel and ask, "Shouldn't the child know the natural consequences of their behaviors on others?"

The problem is that a parent's feelings and well-being are often too much for most children to bear. Often, children are not able to hold their parents' feelings and the weight of that is crushing. Children are inadequate containers, and under the pressure of parental disappointment or worry, a child is inclined to compromise their sense of *Self.* Children were never supposed to be the containers for the parent—the parent is to be the container for the child. But few have this model in their own childhood, so this tragic cycle passes down from generation to generation. They will become what the parent needs: a good child, a happy child, a successful child. This inauthentic *Self* can provide a breeding ground for childhood depression, anxiety, substance abuse, cutting, eating disorders, etc. Some children will become angry and rebel. They will lash out at the parent, dismissing every parental value or expectation. To the outside observer, this angry child looks like they have no empathy, no conscience, and have completely rejected the parent. However, the truth is that they are crushed under the weight of the parents' feelings, needs and expectations and rebellion offer the only relief.

Furthermore, a child who is raised to believe that what others (in this case, parents) think and feel about them is paramount, becomes wired for and vulnerable to peer pressure. The brain does not distinguish between a mother or father expressing concern and the sadness of a friend, significant other, or peer expressing disappointment. In other words, parenting by expressing one's feelings as a method for teaching children right and wrong, conditions children to be susceptible to peer pressure.

In other words, parenting by expressing one's feelings as a method for teaching children right and wrong, conditions children to be susceptible to peer pressure.

Many wonder if these ideas are too indistinguishable to grasp for most people— maybe I am splitting hairs. A story about my youngest child and my mother from this past summer may serve to show how even young children can distinguish between boundaries and emotional coercion.

Liv, 11 years old at the time, was spending the day with my wife, my mother, and two of her cousins. It was a warm Fourth of July weekend and they were returning home after a long day at a street festival. On the way, my wife offered to go out of her way to stop by Nelson's Frozen Custard (a Salt Lake City treasure) as a special treat. The wait was long as the drive-through was backed-up. As they got closer to the intercom, Liv and her cousins were rambunctiously playing in the back seat. My wife had asked for their order numerous times and my mother began to grow impatient from their lack of response and turned to scold them saying sternly, "Look. Michelle has spent the entire day driving you around and trying to ensure you have a good time; the least you could do to show your appreciation is to give her the respect of quieting down and giving her your order."

The three cousins became quiet. Grandma doesn't usually raise her voice and this shocked and scared them a bit. After a moment, Liv had something she wanted to say. "Okay. I think boundaries are okay, but I don't think it is okay to shame us." She acknowledged that it was appropriate to set a boundary and remove the opportunity for the special treat unless they quieted down and gave their order, but that it didn't feel right to be shamed.

She paused, "Mom. What do you think?" Not only had Liv made a valid point, but she asked the woman who had taught her the principle to weigh-in. Bravo!

Stuck in the middle, my wife played politics and found a middle ground. "I will have to think about it," she said. When the story was related to me later, I made a point of telling my daughter how happy I was that she understood the difference between a boundary and being shamed.

She has made this observation with teachers and other adults both before and after this incident. And while some might think that children should show greater respect to their elders, I am glad my daughter knows when she is being mistreated and is willing to stand up to it even at the risk of getting into more trouble.

Parents often ask me why their children are so worried about what others, especially their peers, think about them. They lecture children on the need to find esteem by looking in the mirror. What these parents don't realize is that they, the parents, were the ones who taught their children that what others think and feel about them is important.

In Al-Anon there is a saying: "What others think about me is none of my business." I like to add, "This includes your parents." Many of us spend much of our early lives worrying about what our parents (and others) think about us. We were told that what our parents thought about us was the best indication of how we were doing—parental feelings become our moral North Star. Many of us spend the second half of our lives trying not to care about what others, including our parents, think about us.

FROM THE FEAR OF BEING "FOUND-OUT" TO THE RELIEF OF BEING SEEN

Most people are not able to see Others, but rather they impose themselves on you. They do it out of an anxious need, but the insidious aspect of this is they call it "loving" or "caring."

My client, Virginia, was struggling with depression. She told me she felt embarrassed that she felt depressed while living a life that most would envy. She told me that, ashamedly, she often thought of suicide. She believed the world would be better off without her or at least wouldn't miss her. She was a successful businesswoman and caring mother who lived with her husband and their youngest child. The older two children had moved out of the home and were pursuing what looked like meaningful lives. Her youngest was struggling with some anxiety and depression and this client was referred to me for parent coaching. Like most of my clients, it became very apparent to me that the task wasn't about parenting. Rather, it was about this existential point in Virginia's life. As she sat in my office, telling me about her fantasies of death and her guilt for not taking pleasure in a life many envied, I resisted the urge to reassure her with platitudes. I asked her to tell me about her life. Because the threat of suicide is so real, most are inclined (including me at times) to ward off that threat, but in this moment, I just wanted to listen.

She told me she really didn't feel like she had any friends or any real connections. She shared that she loved her husband and children, but she had no safe space to share her inner turmoil. Any time she tried to talk about it, people would, as she put it, "Tell me I was wrong—that my feelings were wrong."

She explained that it wasn't just the big things, but it would happen in conversations about movies or interpretations of her interactions with others. "No, you're overthinking it," her friends might say to her. "They didn't mean that. You would do well to give others the benefit of the doubt—assume they have good intention." These exchanges, of course, left her feeling hopeless, isolated, and as if something was fundamentally broken in her.

I replied encouragingly, "I am so glad you are noticing how dismissed you feel. You are right!" Most people are not able to see *Others*, but rather they impose themselves on you. They do it out of an anxious need, but the insidious aspect of this is they call it "loving" or "caring." I told Virginia, "The only thing I would offer to you is that it's probably happening much more than you think and for a lot longer than you have noticed." At that, tears filled her eyes and she said that it had been a long time since someone heard her.

This experience is prolific. I often illustrate this with a simple example that most of us can relate to. I say, "You know, I am in my 50s now, and to this day, I am not allowed to have an opinion about something as simple as a food preference without someone trying to talk me into trying it again." It goes like this:

Other: "You have to try this dish."

Me: "Oh it looks like it has mushrooms. I don't like mushrooms."

Other: "You can barely taste them," or "just try the dish with butter on it" or "try it the way my mother used to prepare it and you will love it."

The iterations are endless, and if at 50+ years old I am unable to state a food preference without the high probability of someone trying to talk me out of it or give it another chance, we can be confident that when it comes to career choices, relationship choices, or other more profound and personal expressions, these subjects will often be met with opinions intended to change us.

Such comments from mushroom-lovers have led to a shorthand response for me and my close family and friends illustrated here. When trying to convince a friend of an opinion I held to be an absolute truth, he simply stared back at me and stated, "I don't like mushrooms." First, I scolded him for using "me" on me. Then, of course, I acquiesced and just let him be him. You can share this idea with yours. Then, when someone is trying to get you over to their side of an opinion, you can simply say "I don't like mushrooms.

When I was in college, I heard a story where Bob Dylan was asked about how he felt about his son Jakob's success. Jakob was the lead singer in a band called The Wallflowers, and they had a hit album out. The way I remember it, Bob replied by saying, "How I feel about it is irrelevant." When I heard the story, I thought it was just Bob being Bob. He is famous for not liking the media and replying to reporters with disdain. But as I have thought about it since then, I have come to appreciate it more and more. I have come to a place in my life where I try to have less and less of an opinion about my children's paths. Some might interpret this as abdication, but I see it as a necessary condition for healthy attachment and the development of a child's *Self*.

I remember the first time I told a client about this idea. He was a heroin addict and carrying enormous amounts of shame for the relapses and for the betrayal and pain he had inflicted on his parents over the course of his addiction. I told him the story about Bob Dylan and followed it up with something like, "If my son got into Harvard, I wouldn't be proud of him. I might tell him it is something he could be proud of or I might be happy for him or impressed by the effort he put into reaching such an accomplishment, but I wouldn't feel proud of him. The other side of the equation is that since I am not inclined to be proud of my son, I am also not inclined to be disappointed in him. I try to remain curious, and if he is struggling or makes choices that some might regard as disappointing, the feeling I would have might be something closer to sad or maybe a bit concerned." Dylan's example deepened for me when I found out that he initially failed to accept the Nobel Prize and the nearly 1 million dollars that came with it. His sense of *Self* and his capacity to see his child, beyond the behaviors, accomplishments and failures, is a bright example of the kind of sensibility for *Self* and *Others* we are talking about.

As I shared these thoughts his eyes rose to meet mine and he said with conviction, "Yeah, well, no one thinks that way."

I told him that I used to think that as well until I found a therapist who did feel that way and it has made all the difference in the world. I remember one session almost 20 years ago where I told her I knew how to make people like or even love you. "You just need to take care of their needs first," I told her. She looked at me quizzically and said, "I think it may be possible to just be yourself and have someone love you." I thought she was joking or stupid or just playing some trick on me, but since then, through years of experience, I have come to find out she was right. It is possible to be one's *Self* and to also be loved, although it may be an exceptional experience and can only be found when you find yourself in the company of someone who has done a mountain of work on themselves. When we learn to express and value our truths, we may lose friends but the ones who stick around are the right ones.

This experience of sharing with clients the idea that who they are is okay, that they could be who they are and still be loved, and that people, including parents, who believe that they know what is best for them, has been a common experience in my practice. This imposing of oneself onto a child or an *Other* is not love and realizing that can be profound. It is not "loving too much," but rather, it is born out of anxiety. The fact that many try to convince us that it comes from a place of love adds weight to the feeling that something must be wrong with us. It often leads a person to think, "If they love me and I am hurting them, I must be in the wrong, or even further, I must be wrong."

When considering parents and children, I think that many of the greatest challenges start with the lack of *Self* in the parent. For instance, many think that an entitled, narcissistic child is the result of indulgent parenting. While that may be present in the dynamic, it is really the lack of *Self* in the parent that is the core issue. And like everything I talk about, there is no shame in this. It is true of all of us to some extent. The *Self* of the parent is the foundation for the child's development. It allows the parent to see the child clearly and respond to their needs instead of asking the child to take care of the parent. Indulgence, then, results from having few boundaries and no sense of *Self*, so that the child then reflects back to the parent that the parent is good. If we, as parents, have enough of a sense of ourselves, enough of a sense that we are okay, we can respond with the limits and boundaries that require our children to consider what it is like to live with an *Other*. It is not about perfection—that is impossible. But, in having a *Self*, the parent can more aptly provide an adequate experience for the child.

THE AUDACITY TO BE YOU

Near the completion of writing this book, I had the privilege of seeing the musical *Hadestown* on Broadway. It is a beautiful portrayal of the story of Hades, Eurydice, Persephone, and Orpheus. After his love, Eurydice, is taken to the underworld, Orpheus sets out to get her back. After receiving instructions for the perilous task of retrieving her, he begins his journey into Hades. And as he starts, the fates whisper in his ear, "Who are you? Where do you think you're going? Who do you think you are? Who are you to think that you can walk the road that no one ever walked before?"

These are the same voices we hear in our minds when we dare to show up as we are: naked and our *Selves*. Who do you think you are to get that promotion? Who do you think you are to deserve compassionate love? Who are you to think you can be happy doing what you love? Who do you think you are to think that you can write a book? But, with some healing, in the form of someone seeing us and being okay with us, we can develop the audacity to be our selves.

This is a book about therapy and how that process can quiet those voices, but it cannot replace therapy. To heal and repair, we must take the risk to show up in therapy; we must tell the truth about ourselves. We must take the risk to tell the therapist how we feel about them when they hurt or upset us. And when we do that—when we tell the truth like that—we risk getting the reaction we have received in our previous contexts: from our parents, our teachers, our peers, our *Others*. That is really the best way to see if you have an adequate therapist: tell them how they messed up, hurt you, didn't understand, whatever you didn't like, etc. If they apologize and ask you to help them understand so they don't do it again, you know you have a good therapist. But many can't do this. It's not their fault. They were never taught or shown it, so they don't know how to do it.

The reaction we received in our earlier contexts is that we were not allowed to feel or think certain thoughts. But the tricky thing is that our parents didn't say it like that. They said

"You misunderstood me…
I had good intentions…
Let me explain myself to you…
You are crazy, too sensitive, narcissistic, anxious, etc."

Because of this, their well-masked shame, they told us we were the problem. They couldn't allow for it to be about them. And the worst thing of all, is that they often called it love. So, we walk around with these wounds: these wounds of not being enough or being too much. Too much of this or that. We are a burden. And we learn to hide very well. We cannot imagine that we will be tolerated just as we are; we have to earn love. I spoke recently about how most parents gaslight their children on a regular basis. Gaslighting is sowing seeds of self-doubt and trying to convince the *Other* they are crazy to protect an insecure *Self*. Some took issue with my use of the word "most" and some thought applying the term to parents was too heavy-handed. While gaslighting may speak to a more conscious process than the above examples suggest, it is essentially the same dynamic. The narcissistically wounded parent (the wound of not having been seen resulting in a compromised *Self*) makes the child feel crazy so the parent doesn't have to own and carry around their own *horrible, rotten, Self*. Regretfully I have done this more than I would like to admit. It is precisely this experience in our childhoods that makes us susceptible to gaslighting later in our lives; it is why we struggle to get out of toxic relationships.

But, if we stumble into therapy (or something like it) and sit with someone for a long while who has the capacity to see us as we are and not shrink away in disgust or pity or gasp in fear in the face of us, something changes inside. We begin to imagine the unthinkable; we begin to think that we are okay. This is how it is done. I don't know a better way. I am sure there are other ways. Mindfulness and meditation are practices that seem to have this same project in mind and seem to have the similar results, but if that doesn't fit for you, sit with someone who can see you and accept all of you.

In a way, therapy is a kind of mindfulness with two people. You may know about sitting-mindfulness practices or silent meditation. You may have heard about eating or walking mindfully. Therapy can be thought of as *talking mindfulness*. We share what we think and feel with another and they are charged with seeing it, or simply holding space for it—for us. And we begin to discover we are enough—we have the audacity to be who we are.

KILLING THE *SELF*

Many clients I have worked with have shared with me that they came to understand the qualities of God's love by learning what was required when we love someone who is struggling with addiction or mental health issues. Sometimes we learn about grace-filled love when we are on the receiving end and sometimes, we learn about it when we realize what is asked and required of us by those who hurt and betray us. Even if faith wanes or doubts arise when we watch someone we love struggle or maybe even lose their battle with addiction or mental illness, there is nothing more powerful than the love that is asked of us in the face of such exquisite pain.

Many years ago, while I was struggling with some significant depression and anxiety, I would spend my days fantasizing about dying. I wasn't suicidal, but the idea of not waking up gave me some relief. I told myself I would never kill myself. It was so final, and I would not want to do that to my children, but the weight of my life at the time seemed overwhelming and there seemed no way out that didn't come with more pain. As I shared these thoughts and feelings with my therapist, she said to me,

The suicidal impulse is correct. The mistake that most suicidal people make is that they think they have to kill the whole Self. But rather, for many, they just need to kill a part of themselves and they will be free. And for many, this part of the Self is caring about what others think of them.

I had never thought of it this way and while it may not be true for everyone, this idea gave me hope. It didn't remove all the darkness or solve all my problems, but it gave me a project to work on and that project gave me hope. My project was to find and express my truth. I would discover what part of my *Self* I needed to get rid of, and I would learn how to get rid of it. In the course of doing that, I would continue with my therapy. And eventually I discovered that for me, it was indeed what others thought and felt about me that was in the way of my freedom. I had to kill that part of me that thought that I was responsible for what others thought and felt, and as I did, I also discovered what love was.

Developing and discovering your *Self* is a worthwhile project. Out of this will come all the other things you are looking for. It is not indulgent. It is not "self-centered." It is the secret to the universe and the secret to loving. As I go through this book, I will expand on this idea and discuss what barriers stand in the way of you discovering your authentic *Self*. But you may have to experience the presence of an empathic *Other* who doesn't know your truth, over and over again, for it to begin to take root and I suspect the journey will last your lifetime.

CHAPTER THREE

FINDING OTHERS

"Boundaries are the distance at which I can love you and me simultaneously."
Prentis Hemphill

BOUNDARIES, SELF-CARE, AND CONNECTION

IRONICALLY, WE CANNOT HAVE A CONVERSATION ABOUT connection without talking about boundaries. Boundaries allow for connection, otherwise the relationship is comprised of two compromised selves and lacks essential ingredients of intimacy.

When I talk to people about boundaries, they often ask for tools and skills. While tools may help us on our path towards a more meaningful life and more meaningful connections, they do not do the work for you. Tools merely assist us in the work of developing a *Self* and a connection to *Others*. A meaningful relationship is like art: techniques can help, but you will not paint a masterpiece by learning the techniques alone. Tools can, if followed, either help you towards a different way of being or reveal that although you know what to do, there are forces in your psyche that resist or reject the use of such tools. For example, taking a time-out when you are escalating is a simple tool that most anyone would agree to be useful in a conflict, but many resist using it for a variety of reasons: the

46

anxiety of walking away without reassurances, the unwillingness to own that one needs a time-out—that one is not in control of one's *Self*, and confronting the vulnerability that comes from realizing one has limited capacities.

Boundaries are one of those concepts that are elusive to so many. We want to know the formula for success, but we often measure success by whether someone else changes in ways that removes our suffering. Parents often ask me, "What is the boundary I should have with my child to prevent this or that behavior? How do I respond when she does X, Y, or Z?" Spouses ask me, "What should I do? My husband won't stop ignoring me," or "my wife won't stop nagging me," or "my husband is drinking too much," or "my wife works too much." The problem with the answer to any of these is in the question itself; the problematic premise is in the belief that tools are for changing other people. We need to shift a fundamental idea underlying our understanding of boundaries from changing other people to taking care of ourselves.

We need to shift a fundamental idea underlying our understanding of boundaries from changing other people to taking care of ourselves.

During a casual conversation, a colleague asked me, "How are your boundaries?" I sat for a moment and thought about the many arenas in which I have varying degrees of success. Better with my parents. Mixed bag with my wife and kids. As I paused to consider his question, he perceived a lack of clarity about the question so he pressed, "For example," he continued, "if a client called you on a Sunday morning, would you pick up the phone, or would you let it go to voicemail to make sure they understand that they would have to wait for regular business hours if it is not an emergency?"

Then I understood more about his question and responded, "I don't set boundaries to teach someone else a lesson or to change them. I set boundaries to take care of myself. So, ideally, I would take stock of my resources at the time and make the decision based on how I felt. If I was feeling full and capable and the schedule ahead wasn't daunting, I would take the call. If I needed the break, I would let it go to voicemail. It is still a work in progress for me, but this is how I try to think about it."

Again, the shift here is that our boundaries aren't about changing other people. Boundaries are about self-care. They help us identify what we need to feel okay in a given situation. With this metric, it is less about figuring out the right thing to do and more about paying closer attention to what we need in a given moment or a given situation. Even with children, this kind of thinking can be applied. Instead of saying, "You can't stay at Darcey's house for a sleepover, you are too young," or "Clean your room before you can play. You need to learn that work comes before play," we might say, "I am not comfortable yet with you having a sleepover," or "I may be old fashioned or a little neurotic, but I need you to clean your room before you can play." Or with a partner we may say, "I don't want to have sex at this point in our relationship." More important than the words themselves is the sensibility these examples illustrate. The more we own the boundary as our need—our truth—the less we worry about who is "right" or "wrong."

If you don't want to be in a marriage where there is heavy drinking, you are allowed to get out of it. Following this principle, the husband who decides to leave his wife because of her drinking and all the problems that stem from it doesn't divorce his wife to get her to stop drinking. He does it to take care of himself. He might even say, "I can't get you to stop drinking. God knows, we have had a thousand fights about that. It's not even my business to determine whether you are an alcoholic. You can keep drinking; I just can't have it in my life."

The shift here is dramatic and subtle at the same time. The husband in this scenario takes a courageous stand for his own self-care. He takes the risk of being alone, of being wrong, in his attempt to live and express his truth. Parents often struggle with this because of their responsibility to care for and guide their children. Yet, at its core, setting boundaries with your children is the same project as setting boundaries with others in your life. You make your decisions based on what makes you feel okay. It is helpful to do this with the help of therapy or a support group, as in a 12-step group, so that you have clarity about what you're feeling and where it is coming from. Our fear and anxiety about our struggling children may be honest and those feelings can signal something important, but we may need to go to therapy or a support group in order to take care of ourselves so when we show up with our children, we are there for them rather than the reverse. When those we love are struggling, we take care of our feelings so our interactions with them, especially our children, can focus on responding to their needs and not our needs.

"Well," some might argue, "if my decisions as a parent are based on what I feel comfortable with, aren't I just asking my child to take care of me?"

No. You are taking care of you. And yes, it impacts them, and they have to deal with it, but you are operating from a place of "I will take care of myself, so you don't have to." They will resist and like most relationships will put some pressure on you to change your boundary. If you are able to resist that pressure, which usually comes in some form of "you're a bad parent," or "you're being unfair," you further demonstrate that you are not relying on them to take care of you. You are saying, "I hear your anger and your sadness. I am sorry it is so hard. But this is my best guess. I am not sure if I am right or not, but this is my line. I will continue to look at myself so that I may gain clearer insight into how I can support you." Obviously, you might not use these specific words, but they are my attempt to capture this way of thinking.

When those we love are struggling, we take care of our feelings so our interactions with them, especially our children, can focus on responding to their needs and not our needs.

BEING RIGHT VS. BEING A *SELF* IN RELATIONSHIPS

I sat with a single mother recently during her visit with her son, in an inpatient treatment facility. He was there for substance abuse and other dangerous behaviors. He had been showing great progress and was pleading with his mother to return home early. "I am ready," he begged. Several of the parents and the staff in the support group were offering suggestions and support in the form of rationale for the mother to follow the clinical recommendations that were suggesting the young man to stay until the end of his course of treatment.

After listening to all of this I offered an alternative response. I asked the mother for permission to speak for her and to correct anything I said along the way. I looked at her son and said, "I think your mother misses you terribly. I think she may stay up late at night, with great self-doubt, about her decision to keep you here. I think she may be tempted to convince you of the rationale for your continued treatment here, but the fact of the matter is that it is only her best guess based on all the information she has. She knows, deep down in the most honest recesses of her *Self,* that she might be making a mistake, but this is just her best effort." As I finished, I looked at his mother to see if I had misrepresented her. Tears were streaming down her face, and she nodded in agreement.

The mother then turned to her son and said, "It is true. I am doing the best I can, and I don't know if it is right, but what I do know is that I cannot go back to this—to debating and justifying my parental boundaries. I can't do that anymore. What I can do though, is tell you the truth."

Most people don't think feelings are enough. They think they have to be right, to prove themselves in a virtual court with the *Other* sitting as judge and jury, but the reality is that our feelings and our best guesses are all we have. Anything else is a paper tiger, something we try to use to influence the opinion of others that we are right. But, in fact, boundaries are not about being right, they are about being a *Self.* In this way of thinking, you don't get to be right anymore. But you do get to be a *Self.* And being a *Self* is so much better.

In this way of thinking, you don't get to be right anymore. But you do get to be a Self. And being a Self is so much better.

In the book *Addictive Thinking: Understanding Self-Deception,* author Abraham Twersky shares, "It has been said that the difference between psychosis and neurosis is that the psychotic says, 'Two plus two equals five,' while the neurotic says, 'Two plus two equals four, and I can't stand it.'" Similarly, many people, when asking about boundaries do the same thing.

They ask the therapist, "What can I do to help my struggling child, or my struggling sister or spouse?"

In the early stages of growth, if the therapist responds to the patient by saying something like, "First and foremost, work on your *Self.* Go to some meetings. Continue in therapy. This is the path for finding your answer," the client may get angry or impatient with the therapist at this.

It is like the client is asking, "What is 2+2? But please don't say 4." It is understandable that a person would have this response when a loved-one is suffering. For example, coming to terms with the reality that you cannot prevent a child's suffering is often too heavy a burden to bear for most any parent. But we

There is a great difference between loving someone and trying to get them to feel love. One you have control over and one you don't. The former comes from a place of giving and the latter is from a place of needing something from the Other.

are not saying this work doesn't have benefit for the child, it's just that you can't think about that when you are setting boundaries. If you do, you will miss the point. The best and most positive impact and contribution you can have on those you love is knowing your *Self* and learning to express your truth and set the subsequent boundaries. Most likely you will have to do battle with some internal voices that feel bad (like guilt, failure, and shame). But the battles are worth it. Knowing the battle offers some relief but does not erase the inner-conflicts that vex us—it just provides us with the peace that comes from knowing where to put our energy. And you will model for those you love what it is like to work on the development of a *Self*.

Some find this work easier or harder with their spouse, family-of-origin, children, friends, or even with strangers. There are many small brush strokes we could explore that would illuminate why some contexts present a greater challenge for us, but a core component might be our need to be good: a good son or daughter, a good spouse, a good parent, a good friend or a good person. The quality that you most value or that you most want others to see in you will present the greatest challenge. This is especially true if you have doubts about yourself in that area. Overcoming the feeling of needing to ensure that others see you as fair, good, patient, or understanding will be your most difficult challenge, your Achilles heel. This is where the ghosts haunt you and others might access your insecurity or your need to "be good." They may knock you off your center. It is what many refer to as "pushing your buttons."

Trying to be a good "something or other" is the enemy of growth, connection and love. There is a great difference between loving someone and trying to get them to feel love. One you have control over and one you don't. The former comes from a place of giving and the latter is from a place of needing something from the *Other*.

We will explore more on this in the next chapter, but suffice to say the need to be a good "something or other" will get in the way of honesty, authenticity, and love.

YOU DON'T GET TO WIN

Early in my career, I was introduced to the borderline personality disorder diagnosis. Suffering from fractured attachments, these clients are constantly pushing and pulling. "I hate you, get away from me," they might say in one moment, but in the next, "don't leave me." One day you are their hero, the next you are the enemy. Dramatic attempts to gain attention through self-harm, suicide threats, and other dangerous ways of acting out are common. All is a test to see if you love them and just when you think you have succeeded; they change the rules and sabotage. In many ways, they have an unconscious drive to get those others around them to feel as hopeless, confused, scared, and powerless as they feel. The game is rigged. The game is "you lose"—end of game. Sharing this with my supervisor, she offered a different way out. She suggested, with people who suffer with borderline personality traits, you don't get to win. You get to *choose* how to lose.

Hearing this, the clouds parted, and I could feel sunlight coming through. What's more is that I realized how universally this perspective could be applied. When setting boundaries that allow us to keep a sense of *Self* and maintain the chance for an intimate relationship with the *Other*, we must often accept the maxim, "You don't get to win. You get to choose how to lose." Obviously, not everyone I know in my life qualifies for the diagnosis of borderline personality disorder, but this same rule can apply. Setting boundaries or sharing one's truth is not guaranteed to change those around you. You don't get to win by changing them. However, if we express ourselves

When setting boundaries that allow us to keep a sense of Self and maintain the chance for an intimate relationship with the Other, we must often accept the maxim, "You don't get to win. You get to choose how to lose."

courageously and accept that we may lose the battle of trying to change the *Other*, we can win the war of maintaining our sense of *Self.*

HONORING SOMEONE'S TRUTH

One of my roles at work is to supervise and train therapists. Being a supervisor offers an amazing vantage point of learning and perspective. Sitting in the Utah desert, I sat with a new and promising therapist (we'll call her Melissa) as she talked with her adolescent clients. One client, (we'll call her Bella), had a significant history of attachment trauma. Her mother was a drug addict, her dad was out of the picture, and her mom's sister and brother-in-law were her custodians. During her visit to the desert the previous week, Melissa had provided Bella with an extra therapy session, but Bella was still not satisfied. The mere fact that Melissa went home, even after meeting with Bella for a second session, provided Bella with evidence of rejection; this echoed the abandonment she experienced in her childhood.

We met with Bella early in our list of sessions that week with an awareness she had been harboring ill feelings towards her therapist. The days between the therapist visits had been dark ones, with Bella fighting off feelings of suicide and self-harm. She had been on arms-reach safety-watch the entire week and her time was filled with voicing to the staff her feelings of rejection, hurt, and anger towards the therapist. As we sat with her, her therapist asked her about these feelings. Bella was eager to share. "You left me," she said. "You don't care about me. I just asked for a little more time with you and you got in your car and left. I saw you laughing with the staff right before you left, and I know you were laughing about me."

"I do care about you, Bella." Melissa told her. "I met with you twice last week."

"But the second meeting was like five minutes," Bella shot back.

"No. It was more like 30 minutes Bella, and I had to go." Melissa's tone was encouraging.

53

"You don't care about me," Bella repeated. "You were laughing with the staff before you got into your car."

"I don't remember that, but I am sure it had nothing to do with you." Melissa gently argued.

"Why don't you just leave me alone? I know this is just a job for you. You just do it for the money." Bella was crying and her head hung low, eyes staring in her cross-legged lap.

"Listen, Bella, I do care about you. I do this job because I love it. I love working with you girls. I love helping you. I remember being your age and how it felt, and I just want to give you what someone never gave me." I could feel Melissa's empathic misery and her earnest desire for Bella to feel loved and cared-for. "What can I do to show you I care, Bella?"

There it was. I finally heard it. I interjected, "I am not sure you can do that for her." I spoke directly to Melissa. "I think what Bella needs is for us to hear how it has been for her. The people who were supposed to look out for her and never leave her did exactly that. Why would we be the ones that change her fortune? Besides, even if she is here for an extended period of time, we will not be in her life forever." I turned to Bella. "I think that we need to just hear what it is like for you." There is often no solution to these situations except to listen—in other words, hearing and sitting with someone's painful story is the solution.

Bella raised her gaze and looked at me. She visibly relaxed. She didn't say much, instead she just looked at us both knowingly or rather with a sense of being known. There was no solving this. We couldn't bring back her childhood. We couldn't bring back her parents. We couldn't instill in her, in a handful of sessions, the feeling that she was lovable. And any attempt to try to get her to feel something other than what she currently felt only reinforced her feelings of aloneness. Any attempt to solve it would trivialize the immense pain and sadness she felt.

Bella didn't change that day, but she had a moment of being seen and understood. It is really easy to do therapy when you are not the therapist and you are not the target of the transference (Bella was projecting her feelings and experiences from her parents onto Melissa). Her parents weren't there to hear those feelings—that would have helped some. But *we* could be there to hear them. We just had to let go of the idea of winning. We had to let go of the need to accomplish something. Melissa had to let go of the idea that she had been a good, caring therapist.

A supervisor once explained to me, "To understand and truly hear someone, sometimes you have to lose your mind." We have to get out of our world and what we need in order to understand the *Other*. Melissa's context had taught her that the important thing was to be *good* and the best way to do that was to make others feel better. To know and understand and ultimately help Bella, Melissa had to leave those ideas behind; she had to learn to sit with Bella in her pain.

In a way, Bella was fighting for her *Self*—for the boundaries that surround who she is. She was saying to us, "This is my truth. This is my story. This is how I see the world and don't try to talk me out of it." It wasn't a boundary as in "You can't treat me this way," but the same core elements were present—we wanted to change her feelings and her reaction. "This is my experience in life and don't come in here and try to take that away from me or talk me out of it." It was only in our willingness to lose our goal of trying to fix things, that we were able to provide the space for Bella and her truth.

Our instinct to fix can cause us to lose contact with the *Other*. Early in my career, I worked with young children who had suffered serious abuse. I was supposed to use play therapy since play is the language of children. I was terrible at it and my poor supervisor was exasperated by me. I kept trying to fix and teach, but the children just needed to tell their story. My supervisor would tell me, "Stop intervening. Just assess!" But I couldn't hear him. My impulse to teach and redirect their play left us all frustrated. The therapist's model or agenda can eclipse the client and prevent the therapist from seeing the client altogether.

THE MYTH OF "LOVING TOO MUCH"

In an episode of NPR's *Invisibilia*, "The Problem with the Solution," the host shares how individuals suffering from severe mental illness are cared for in Geel, Belgium. In the episode, differences between how the villagers in a small-town magnanimously treat strangers suffering from mental illness versus how they treat their own children (who may or may not be struggling) is explored. They uncover how parents' "overconnected" language triggers the same kind of fight-or-flight responses that shape angry, critical, or shaming messages. Communication that most people would find nurturing hijacks a child's higher-level thinking and shuts down their ability to reason or accept guidance or direction from others. An example of the type of language they discovered:

> *It breaks my heart to see him suffering. I'd do anything for him if it would help. There's nothing I wouldn't do for that boy.*

Researchers explain how such expressions present a threat to the child. "This kind of comment or even just that yearning…oozes out of a person… and works to trigger relapse in the person they're thinking about. Which is odd and noteworthy because that kind of response sounds so supportive compared to hostility and criticism…The reason that we believe it is associated with relapse is because from the part of the patient, they're just feeling too monitored. They're feeling too cosseted…They feel stifled." It is common to conflate love or "loving too much" with anxious attachment. "Loving too much" is a euphemism for the unhealed attachment wound and its expression in an anxious parent. The problem is not "loving too much," but rather not enough *Self*.

Anxiety and worry may be natural and well-deserved, but the child is not capable of "holding" this energy. It is the parent's job to deal with and manage their anxiety, perhaps in therapy or in an Al-Anon group setting, so that when they approach the child, they can be there for the child's needs rather than vice-versa.

I remember years ago when I was working in a co-ed wilderness group, a mother wrote a love letter to her young-adult daughter. The first week's letter described the daughter's behavior that led her parents to enrolling her in the program. The mother knew her daughter was suffering. She had low self-worth and was sexually acting out for attention and affection, she was cutting, and she was issuing threats of suicide. All of this indicated her daughter's vulnerability. The mother decided at the end of her second letter to write a list of "The 50 Reasons I Love You." We read the letter in session and at the conclusion, I asked the young woman how she felt about the letter. She hesitated and responded, "It was nice."

It is common to conflate love or "loving too much" with anxious attachment. "Loving too much" is a euphemism for the unhealed attachment wound and its expression in an anxious parent. The problem is not "loving too much," but rather not enough Self.

Something didn't feel right to me and I sensed the same for this young woman, so I offered, "The letter feels a little anxious and needy to me, like she is trying to convince you of something."

The girl looked at me with clear eyes and said, "Me too. I guess I thought I was supposed to be grateful for it, but I'm not. It kind of leaves me feeling empty."

"That is probably because the words don't match the feeling," I said, "Your mom is scared and sad. She is in her anxiety. She wants you to feel okay, and she thinks this will help. But I will talk with her and help her to understand what you need. You need to be understood. You need to tell her how you feel, and she needs to be able to hear it without fixing it." The young girl nodded.

When I recounted the story on the weekly phone call with her mother, she agreed without any hesitation. "You are totally right," she said. "I would have never thought of it, but the truth became obvious as soon as you said it. It was all my anxiety." This was a powerful, open woman who was willing to look at herself more honestly and courageously, and because of that, she was willing to stretch and grow into something so she could be a more capable giver to her daughter.

BOUNDARIES DON'T SOLVE PROBLEMS

Setting boundaries isn't the solution to a problem but arises out of our truth. Boundaries are the courageous expression of our truth and the great challenge is that things may not always turn out the way we hope. That is why it can take surrender and the willingness to let go of outcomes, to be able to tell the truth. When therapists recommend boundaries to parents or partners, they often don't have the effect hoped for by the client, because many believe that serenity, contentment, and happiness is an outside job. You've probably heard the saying, "To have a child is to see what it feels like to have a heart beating outside of your body." While this is a sweet and romantic idea, it also destroys healthy attachment between a child and parent. The old adage that says, "You are only as happy as your least happy child" is an insane notion. Again, it's romantic, but it sets the child up to be responsible for the parent's sense of well-being, and few children can bear that burden.

While setting boundaries may not change others, it does impact the people around you. Those that honor you, stick around and those that don't honor you, tend to leave. In parenting, boundaries aren't for teaching children lessons, but they do have that effect. Even in parenting, more than changing children, boundaries can implicitly communicate what it means to be a human with a *Self* and how we relate to other humans.

This is why the establishment of boundaries is built on the foundation of finding your *Self*. To express, enforce, and make requests in the service of your truth, you must first find a clear sense of it. But if someone else needs to change, to be different in order for you to be okay, you are violating the core idea of a boundary. You are in essence extending your sense of *Self*, expanding it so that it overlaps with the other person.

It might be helpful to note here again that while I am talking about the parent-child relationship, it is not only for readers who are parents. Many of these examples are for the child in you and have implications for your current relationships with partners, friends, and other family members. We were all children once and understanding the invisible and unspoken dynamics that existed between us and our parents helps us to understand our inner workings. We can discover the origins of our need to make others feel good even when feeling sad, hurt, or anger is warranted. Understanding what happened to us as children can help us start to unwind the crippling guilt we feel when we hurt other people, even when we have done nothing wrong.

In my previous book, I told the story of how setting a boundary with my 70-year-old mother led her to seek counsel with a therapist and return to me with a capacity and a willingness to show up in my life in a way that I needed. What I didn't mention, however, is that around that same time, I set a similar boundary with my father. The specifics of the discussion were different, but the expressed boundary was essentially the same. My father was asking for me to have conversations with him about what I was going through. He framed it like this: "I want to be there for you. It will be good for you to talk about it." Analogous to the conversation with my mother, I told my father what I needed, and he has never, to this day, been able to respond in a way that I needed. Consequently, we don't have a relationship to speak of and may never have one. This wasn't an isolated incident with him. It was just that the intensity of this moment highlighted what had been the pattern between us. Throughout my life, he has consistently been unable to respond to me in ways that I consider acceptable.

Many parents have come to me over the years with questions related to their adult children. When their children express difficult feelings or set a boundary, how can we respond to them with love and capacity? One mother asked, "My son told me he doesn't trust me. He says I don't listen to him, but I do listen. What should I say to him?"

Another parent shared, "My daughter told me that she can't be around me. She tells me that I am overwhelming, and she often feels horrible after our interactions."

Both of these matters have many elements in common when it comes to boundaries. Both have difficult truths. It is not easy to hear your child or any loved one express hurt and pain directed at you and your behavior. Most of us struggle with the urge to be good—to be a good friend, a good spouse, a good parent. Therefore, feedback to the contrary challenges us and may trigger shame and guilt within us. My answers to such questions focus on responding to the child according to their needs—their truths. To the first parent, I simply offered that she might respond, "I am sorry I have hurt you. I am glad you are telling me that.

If there is something I can do to earn your trust or listen better, you can let me know. I can talk to my therapist about this and see what I can do better. Thanks for being willing to tell me how you feel."

To the latter I would offer, "I am so sorry you feel this way. I am glad you are willing to tell me how you feel. I want to be there for you in a way that leaves you feeling okay. If you are willing to tell me, I will do my best to listen and respond in the way you are asking. If you want to go to a therapist so we have a mediator, I would be willing to go with you. If you need space, I will give you the time you need, and I will work with my therapist to see what I can learn about being with you in a way that might help you to feel okay."

I often tell people that if my adult children came to me and said that being around me left them feeling bad, not okay, or not safe, I would tell them to take care of themselves. Ten times out of ten, if a client tells me that someone, even a parent or another loved one, makes them feel unsafe, we will talk about ways that could help them feel safe, even including and up to cutting that person out of their life. The irony of the suggested response above and the idea of supporting someone's boundary and the underlying truth that informs it is that nobody would want to leave someone who would honor their truth in that way. If someone had enough ego strength, enough *Self*, to honor my truth even if it included my experience of them hurting me and my need to take some distance, I would want that person in my life. I would never want to lose them.

I don't take losing a friend or a loved one lightly. In fact, one of the earliest things my therapy taught me as a teenager is that I could be loyal to a fault. That is, I was (and sometimes still am) inclined to give someone too many chances. I find that to be true for the majority of my clients. What I also find is that many of us are willing to compromise core, important parts of ourselves in order to find acceptance. Being alone, for many, is the most intense fear or threat. Many of us also have the experience of being told that our truth is wrong or told that we have to prove our truth so that we are inclined to doubt ourselves. If you grow up and are cooked in the type of soup that honors your individual truth, you are lucky. You are less susceptible to someone talking you out of your truth or causing you to doubt it. You are less inclined to stay in situations and relationships where you are continuously being erased, ignored, dismissed, or hurt in some other way.

As this chapter's epigraph states, "Boundaries are the distance at which I can love you and me simultaneously." We stay in proximity when we can be kind, loving and patient without feeling erased or battered. If we find ourselves becoming cruel, impatient, or manipulative, it may be a sign that we need some distance. This idea of loving when we can and taking space when we need to is at the heart of this work. I will often say to people in high-conflict relationships that the acrimony you feel towards your *Other* is a symptom that needs your attention. You don't want to be unkind to your *Other* and you don't want to expose your *Self* to unbearable pain. Sometimes people think (when I speak of holding or containing others) that they hear me suggesting they deny or repress feelings of hurt. I explain to them that if you do it in the way I am describing, it will not hurt. Their anger will go through you and it won't feel like it touches you. But, if it does, you may need to take some space; you may need to set a boundary to ensure you can still be loving. And this will take some courage on your part, but it is worth it for all involved.

ENMESHED OR DISCONNECTED: TWO SIDES OF THE SAME COIN

Salvador Minuchin and Murray Bowen are two of the pioneers of Family Systems-informed Family Therapy. They had slightly different ways of describing the same phenomena of boundaries between *Self* and *Other*. Like all the pioneers of Family Therapy, they were more interested in the stuff that happens between and amongst people rather than looking strictly at the individual alone. Both subscribed to the premise of Family Systems encapsulated by the maxim, "The whole is greater than the sum of its parts."

Boundaries Scale			
Boundaries	Rigid	Clear	Diffuse
Relationship Style	Cut-off	Healthy	Enmeshed

Minuchin thought of boundaries as a continuum. On the one end, boundaries are diffuse. People who have diffuse boundaries are considered enmeshed: reactive, dependent, essentially overlapping selves. They need agreement and consensus. They look at themselves through the other person's eyes and say, "What you think and feel about me is who I am." This response can be highly conflictual, violent, and combative, or conversely, it can capitulate and become what the *Other* wants. They lose themselves in the *Other*. They have no separate space. They are the reflection or the extension of the *Other*.

The other end of his continuum describes *rigid* boundaries. On this side of the equation, individuals are said to be *disengaged*: uncaring, unresponsive, apathetic, inflexible, quick to reject and abandon. In the middle, between diffuse and rigid, we would have clear boundaries. Balancing between the two extremes, individuals with clear boundaries are warm, kind, and loving, and they also respect and value the individual. They are capable of asserting their own needs in such relationships without threatening the relationship. This is a very simple model, and much of the vernacular is intuitive. Minuchin's structural framework has been helpful for me to diagram relationships for couples and families for years.

Bowen had a slightly different way of describing the concepts. His model posited the two opposites, enmeshed and disengaged, as similar and differing only in their style. Both were the absence of relationship. Instead of enmeshed and disengaged, he referred to them as fusion and cut-off. Bowen suggested that while they are stylistically different, the substance is the same: they lack a balance between *Self* and connection. He defined *differentiation* as the balance between honoring the *Self* and connecting to the *Other*. One does not erase or threaten the other. Differentiation is intimacy and, as we discussed earlier, intimacy is the connection between two *Selves*. It is not fusion or loss of one's *Self*. Fusion may look dramatic, dependent, or weak, and cut-off may look cold, harsh, or uncaring, but both are fundamentally the same—different sides of the same coin. Both are undifferentiated.

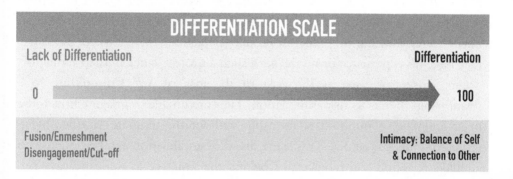

Early in my career I was working with a teen with a substance abuse disorder that illustrates the similarity between the two styles operating in relationships. Towards the end of her stay in treatment with us, she shared that she feared going home because she thought she wasn't strong enough to resist drinking. In my experience, it was and is rare for teens to admit to such things, for fear that their treatment time would be extended. But this was exactly what she was asking for. Her father was coming for her graduation from the program the following week and she feared sharing this with him. "I am afraid he will freak out and just walk away." She shared.

"You think your father is that fragile?" I asked.

"Fragile?" she responded surprised. "My father is not fragile! He is a rock. He is absolutely, unapologetically unforgiving."

"Right." I explained. "But what I meant was that he lacked the capacity to be in a relationship. I know he has the appearance of a rock, but that just masks his inability to be flexible and engage you or others in more flexible and human ways. He looks tough, but like many things that are rigid, they tend to break rather than bend when pressure is applied."

So, we see that on one level things may look very different, but on a deeper level, our relationship challenges are the same: maintaining *Self* and connecting to the *Other*. The boundary is the substance between *Self* and *Other* that defines this dynamic. Individuals accused of a fear of commitment are often afraid that once in a relationship they will not be able to maintain their sense of *Self*. They may have no experience or model with such a project, since in their family-of-origin, closeness came at the cost of the loss of *Self*. Committing to a relationship then is to risk annihilation. They are unable to imagine how to be in an intimate, committed relationship without the ultimate sacrifice being required—the loss of *Self*. This same dread of annihilation can be underneath a child's rejection and rebellion or behind their motive to run far away. Yet, unless the issue is addressed, they will run right into the arms of a partner who mirrors the same level of differentiation found in their family-of-origin.

When we think the solution to the problem is to run away, we fail to recognize that the issue is not solved, and the monster is only temporarily kept at bay. Leaving a relationship (or joining one) is not the solution. The solution is the discovery of *Self* and our truth and determining if the *Other* is able to connect to us in a meaningful and supportive way.

THE SOUP WE ARE COOKED IN

Bowen had a name for the soup that we grew up in. He called it *ego mass* (I prefer calling it "soup"). He said that families operate in such a way as to unconsciously and repetitively communicate a certain level of closeness or differentiation. It is not in the spoken rules but in how they function. Does Dad use his anger to try to tell the children how they are doing? Does Mom's anxiety communicate to the children whether they are doing well? Is Junior allowed to have his feelings and be mad or sad without being told he is being too sensitive or to get over it? How much is each person's *Self* honored and held while at the same time remaining a separate *Self* from the others? Bowen illustrated his model using numbers along a line starting at 1 (undifferentiated) and ending with 100 (differentiated). (see the figure above).

Imagine, for example, if your family's ego mass (the emotional closeness or differentiation) was a 65 on the differentiation scale. This model suggests then that each family member will be somewhere around a 60-70. All were cooked in the same soup, so all have the same flavor. When someone from this family goes out in the world with a 63, they will only be comfortable with people around their same level of differentiation. A 63 will only enjoy 58-68s. Forty-fives will seem dramatic and immature. Eighty-fives won't make sense to them either as they will seem cold, uncaring, and unwilling to change who they are to fit what the 63s needs, feelings, and beliefs. Sure, 85s will say all the right things; they will use active listening skills and offer empathic gestures, but those will feel hollow and inhuman to a 63. The 63 will say to the 85, "Stop using that psychobabble. Be a real person!"

When teaching this to a group recently, one person asked, "It is not fair to change the rules on people. Can't we explain to others if we move up the scale, so they understand what is happening?"

I replied, "First, 90s don't explain themselves. And second, even if you tried to explain it, it wouldn't make sense. A 90 cannot explain the way of being to a 55 in a way that it will sit right."

Leaving a relationship (or joining one) is not the solution. The solution is the discovery of Self and our truth and determining if the Other is able to connect to us in a meaningful and supportive way.

We can move up on the scale and grow with work: therapy, self-help books, and other growth-producing experiences. And under extreme stress or trauma, we can regress. The work is arduous and slow-going. If we move up on the scale and others don't, whether they are friends, spouses, or other family members, we may not have a place for them in our lives. We may need, in these circumstances, to lovingly let go and say goodbye to old relationships and situations. We must grieve these old connections to honor and make a place for the new version of ourselves, but this is tremendously important albeit painstaking work. This is what therapists are often talking about when they say, "You married your mother." It's not the details, the way she looks, her profession, or the specifics of her family background. Instead, it's about her fundamental way of being: her number or level of differentiation.

Tian Dayton explained, in *Emotional Sobriety*, that children absorb the emotional climate and distance invisibly communicated in limitless interactions. "Children live in their unspoken and sometimes unfelt emotional world. Our children drink us up like little sponges... we are showing them who we want them to become..."

The study showed, in this instance, attachment trumps pain. We are attracted to contexts and relationships that feel and operated like those of our early attachments. So, if our early contexts were chaotic, we seek chaos; if our early contexts were enmeshed, we seek enmeshment.

There is a study from attachment theory that powerfully illustrates how difficult it can be to choose something other than what we learned in the "air we breathed as children." Researchers conducted experiments on baby mice that give some illumination on the roles of attachment and associated trauma. The studies, though simple, suggest something quite profound.

They took baby mice and separated them into two groups. The first group were in cages by themselves while they were shocked; the shocks were paired with the scent of peppermint so the mouse would associate the pain and shock with the odor. The second group of mice were also shocked, and the shock was paired with the scent of peppermint. The difference with the second group was that they were kept with their mothers and would be shocked while nestling with their mothers. Then, sometime later, both groups were introduced into a maze with various scents at the end of each maze or tunnel. The mice that were shocked by themselves avoided the peppermint scent. But the mice that were shocked while with their mothers strongly preferred the peppermint; the trauma was present with and paired with the primary bond. This study shows how attachment operates on the top of the hierarchical level of needs—attachment trumps trauma. Since it is most important that we not be alone, even when our primary attachment contexts were mixed with a certain type of trauma, we seek after attachment experiences that remind us of those earliest relationships. The study showed, in this instance, attachment trumps pain. We are attracted to contexts and relationships that feel and operated like those of our early attachments. So, if our early contexts were chaotic, we seek chaos; if our early contexts were enmeshed, we seek enmeshment.

We may seek out attachment styles (similar types of boundaries and differentiation) that feel like those of our family-of-origin. The type of context where we were once offered the only sense of comfort and safety we could ever know is now the context we seek. Tottenham's study with mice is not proof of this idea, but it is a point of reference that illustrates this concept that resonates with us.

BOUNDARIES: TELLING OUR TRUTH

In March of 2014, I was driving from Philadelphia to New York with a friend, a songwriter that I admire. I took the opportunity to pick his brain on the subject of song writing. I have written some poetry but have never had the courage to show it to many people. I even dropped out of a poetry class in high school when it came time to share our poetry with the class. I asked him, "How do you write lyrical poetry? I have written some poetry and was wondering the difference."

His response was immediate and has stuck with me ever since, "I just tell the truth."

I had no follow-up questions.

I think of that statement often. I have used it with clients in many fields of practice and in many different situations. It is the work of boundaries to discover and express the truth of that discovery. I have even shared this with actors and other artists whose craft is that of pretending or creating something out of nothing: just tell the truth. People often think when I invite them to focus on intent and one's truth and to let go of outcomes that they hear me advocating for passivity in relationships. On the contrary, one who practices healthy and courageous boundary-setting is absolutely assertive.

Honest expressions of a need, a feeling, or a truth take courage because there is no guaranteed outcome. The *Other* may respond with anger, rejection, judgment, hurt, or any other undesirable response. Telling the truth is a simple way to understand boundaries. Most of us lie and say something like, "I can't go to the event this weekend; my kids are sick," so we don't have to set an honest boundary. Saying, "I need some time to myself, so I won't be coming to the event this weekend" does not come as easily. No one can argue with the former and the latter example is starkly honest without any attempt to justify the truth or the decision to cancel plans to attend the event.

People often think when I invite them to focus on intent and one's truth and to let go of outcomes that they hear me advocating for passivity in relationships. On the contrary, one who practices healthy and courageous boundary-setting is absolutely assertive.

Our first task is to find our truth even when it is hidden behind the myriad of voices: voices from our childhood that were invisible and imperceptible to our young minds, voices from our peers, voices from our teachers, voices from our culture. My experience is the best place to discover that truth is in the presence of an empathic *Other*. Gill said it this way:

Part of the business of psychotherapy is to discover and create alternate experiences for thoughts, feelings, attitudes, and beliefs. This is undertaken in the service of freeing people to be able to re-experience themselves in a safe but different context. The virtue of talking to an empathic and accepting person who has a different base is that it quickly illuminates one's own. What was automatic and unconscious is noticed and discussed.

This is the connection between the previous chapter and the current chapter. *Self* is necessary for connection and the extent to which the *Self* is developed is the extent of the capacity for connection. The foundation of boundaries is one's unique truth, and the discovery of that truth is a heroic endeavor that lasts our lifetime. Many think you can skip or ignore the first step and move right into setting clear boundaries. That is like learning to throw a ball at a target while diving at the same time or learning to play the piano by starting to learn one specific song. Neither of those endeavors is impossible, but without the foundation and the fundamentals the learned skill only applies in one specific instance. The moment the equation changes, you need to throw the ball into the catcher's glove from the pitcher's mound or to play another song on the piano, you are back to square one.

Boundaries, or any tools for that matter, are not the thing. They are the extension of one's truth into the world of relationships. Boundaries aren't the solution, but they may be part of the solution. Divorce isn't the answer, but it may be what comes out of the realization that you cannot accept certain behaviors in a partner anymore. Sending your child to treatment is not the solution, but it may be the expression of the place that many parents arrive. "I cannot support this experiment anymore. I am not willing to stand by and do nothing. I am worried that my child is not getting what they need here, so I am going to send them there."

And we crave to be right. This craving, ironically, robs us of our truth. Being right says the truth is out there rather than the truth is in me somewhere. This is, in part, why we named our wilderness therapy program "Evoke"—we believe it is our job to *evoke* or draw out the truth that is present in every client, child, parent, or spouse and to support them in giving it the voice it deserves. That is what our myths and our stories do for us and what the examples from my clients do for us in this book; they *evoke* the sense of what it means to be a human and to love an *Other*.

CHAPTER FOUR

LOVE THAT MAKES A DIFFERENCE

For love to be meaningful, it must go beyond feelings. Love as affection can best be described in its fullest as passion. This kind of love can lead to control, possession, and anxiety. For love to be meaningful, it must have the capacity born from self-awareness and arrives at kindness and supportive energy for the Other.

MEANINGFUL LOVE

L ET'S START WITH WHAT LOVE IS AND WHAT IT ISN'T. I HAVE worked with couples and families for years who have used the word *love* to justify behavior toward each other that is far from ideal. I have heard clinicians suggest that boundary violations, parental anxiety, or attempts at control are simply *too much love*, as in, "You love them too much." If we understand what love is, we would understand that *you cannot love too much*. To understand love, we must separate anxiety, fear of rejection, and the need for control from love—those have nothing to do with love. I have heard people justify others' behaviors toward them by attributing it to love or some other some benevolent intent, as in, "I know they meant well, but what they did hurt." I have heard parents and partners passionately express love even though they demonstrated overt physical and sexual abuse. Frankly, if those kinds of behaviors can happen under the cover of love, then love itself loses its meaning.

I think most people think of love as a feeling—a deep and profound affection for another person. Again, if love is merely a feeling, then it is of very little value. Unless there is something in the definition that suggests action, love is worthless. We would be best to call love without action infatuation or obsession. To further look for a meaningful definition of love, let's take the quote from Gandhi introduced in chapter one and break it down point by point.

"A COWARD IS INCAPABLE OF EXHIBITING LOVE. IT IS THE PREROGATIVE OF THE BRAVE."

Love is brave because it asks people to see beyond themselves, and seeing requires capacity. Love requires us to confront our fear and shame rather than living in subjugation to them. It asks people to recognize where they stop and where others start. It asks parents to see their children as separate and love asks partners to realize there is no guarantee, no control that can prevent pain.

Once, during a group therapy session, a young man, Zach, was sharing with his teenage peers the shame he felt. He talked about how his parents were embarrassed by him—his drug use, his arrest, and his multiple treatment placements. To him, it didn't feel like they loved him as much as his sibling who was a successful student and always seemed to do the right thing. He told the group he could see the difference in his parents' eyes when they introduced his brother to their friends contrasted against the slightly deflated way they looked when they introduced him. After listening to these feelings, the boy sitting next to him said, "I know your parents love you or they wouldn't have sent you to this program." This wasn't the first time someone had defended Zach's parents. They are warm and caring people and prominent in their community. People looking at the family from a distance aren't always aware of each family member's private journey.

I interjected, directing my thoughts toward the young man who was trying to be encouraging. "I am not sure you hear him. I know his parents a bit. I have had several sessions with them. And I have no doubt that they would step in front of a train or take a bullet for Zach. But that is not what Zach is talking about. Zach is telling us that his parents don't know how to hold him or what to do with him. They are not unfeeling towards Zach; rather, they lack the capacity to love him in the way that he needs, without condition. They don't celebrate him the same way they do his brother, and this communicates that they don't love him in the same way they love his brother because their shame is in the way." With this, Zach's eyes filled with tears and he gave a small nod to indicate he had been heard.

When I supported my adult children to attend a therapeutic intensive, I knew that they would spend at least some of the time focusing on me: how I hurt them, how I failed them, and how I fell short in loving them. My oldest daughter, Emma, was the first of my children to attend. I nervously joked with her as I said my goodbye. "Good luck," I said. "I hope they help you see how we screwed up."

Upon her return eight days later, we went to the back porch to unpack what she had learned. I again, anxiously kidded as we sat down. "So, did you figure out how we messed you up?"

"I didn't really talk about anyone else but you," she replied solemnly. Her words shocked me. I was ready to be *one* of the bad guys, but not *the* bad guy. What about her mother or her stepparents, I thought? Surely, they have some culpability.

The worst part was that I let these thoughts escape me and said them out loud, "What about your mom, your stepdad, or your stepmom?" I asked. "I know you have stories about them too." I was looking at the ground as these words came out of my mouth. I was actually counting with the fingers on my hand the other possible topics and targets worthy of her work. When I looked up, I saw that she was crying, and I realized my mistake. "I am doing it right now, aren't I?"

She nodded.

"I am sorry. I will try to do it better if you give me another chance," I said.

We sat for a couple of minutes before she started talking through her tears. She told me about times she didn't feel seen or understood by me. She told me about times she didn't feel safe, times I should have protected her from others in the family. She told me about times she didn't feel love from me. This last one was the hardest to hear. But I did what I knew she needed me to do: I kept my mouth shut and listened. After a half hour or so, she told me she was done. Then I asked her how I did. "How did I compare to the roleplay of this conversation at your program?"

"The person substituting for you didn't say a word," she told me. I nodded and told her I loved her and was grateful that she was telling me these things. We hugged then took our separate spaces.

I felt a heavy weight that evening. I remember going to bed early. I felt defeated. I felt a sense of failure. Academically, I knew that all parents are imperfect and wound their children, but her singular focus on me left me feeling sorry for myself. The next morning, I also slept in late. It was a Sunday morning, and as I lay in bed feeling sorry for myself and feeling resentful of the other parents who weren't put under the microscope, a thought came to me: who cares? Who cares what she thinks and feels about the other parents? That is none of my business. My job is to show up for my daughter and when I fail at it (which is not an uncommon occurrence), to listen and welcome her expressions of hurt.

When I confessed this disaster of a conversation to my therapist later that week, she reassured me, "It is okay and maybe even good that you screwed it up with Emma. She is so used to you getting everything right that making a mistake like this can be helpful. Just apologize and show her how to own your horrible, rotten *Self*. I did do that with Emma, and she has shared with me that when I messed it up so badly, it was validating of the many hurts and injuries I had inflicted on her before.

Recently she told me, "If you had responded perfectly, I would have doubted myself. But when you, the author of the 'heroic parent' failed, it made everything a little easier."

One more thing came out of this experience. I told the folks running the program she attended not to mention my name or that they know me. My daughter knew I knew the people that ran and facilitated the program, and I wanted it to be her space. But I didn't get the message to everyone.

Immediately after one of her pieces of work about me and our relationship, her group was taking a break in the break room to grab some snacks. One of the administrators of the program, a good friend of mine, bumped into my daughter in the lounge. "Are you Emma Reedy?" she asked.

Emma nervously nodded.

"I know your dad," the administrator said. "He is an amazing guy." The comment was without malice and only meant to offer Emma a sense of connection, but instead it robbed her of her own unique experience. Several of her group members overheard the comments, and she felt embarrassed, humiliated, and erased. How could her feelings of pain and disappointment about me be true if I was an "amazing guy?"

To love a child is to see them, to hold them with compassion and curiosity. And these capabilities rest on the ability to courageously look at one's *Self* and to recognize the line between *Self* and *Other*. And, as in the instance above, your healing and evolution can expose the emotional immaturity of your parents.

While our obligation and position with our children is unique, the same thing can be asked of us in friendships and partnerships. In our adult relationships, we take turns seeing each other, and our greatest challenges come when both participants in a relationship are needing to be seen. This is where therapists and others from our support system can play an important role.

"PROJECTION, GOING HOME, FUSION IS EASY. LOVING ANOTHER'S OTHERNESS IS HEROIC."

It is easy to love someone who thinks and behaves like you. It is easy to fall in love with the familiar. That requires very little capacity. As a father, I have found the greatest challenge is to provide a container adequate enough to hold my children and their unique differences. At work, the project is easier, but at home, it requires transformation. I believe it to be a worthy project because I want my children to become themselves, not some version of me.

The same is true for couples. Learning to see each other and love each other despite differences takes some work. The most common challenge comes when both partners need support, and neither is in a place to give it.

Another challenge some have is they see validating the *Other* as a threat to their perception and sense of *Self*: "If what you think and feel and the way you see the world is valid, how can the way I see the world still be okay?" For these people, early family life had limited resources and each member was fighting for a sense of *Self*. In such families, one or both parents were not seen by their own parents and thus were trying to work out their sense of value while raising children. A zero-sum-game is when members of a group or family see things as a win-lose. If I win (+1), then you lose (-1). If you win, then I lose: +1 and -1 = 0. If we grew up in a family where differences were seen and treasured, then the task will be easier, but these families may be rarer than we imagine.

As I mentioned earlier, one of my jobs at Evoke is training our new therapists. A few years ago, we hired Mikey, a slight, quirky, self-diagnosed oddball with ADHD to be our newest therapist. He had years of field experience in our wilderness program as a former field guide and we knew him to have great rapport with teenage boys. After some time in his former role, he returned to school to become a therapist, and my business partner hired him with great confidence. My first impression didn't leave me with the same opinion. He was so different from me— "goofy" is the best way to describe him. But I trusted my partner, and I was to shadow him for the next several months.

Our first week, instead of going out to one of the adolescent boys' groups, we drove around the field area and got to know each other. Mikey, nicknamed "Chief" by the boys, told me about the time he got pulled over by the St. George police while he was working as a field guide. Upon encountering him (scraggly haired, shabbily dressed, and a truck with a camper shell with all kinds of junk in it), the cop was sure he would find drugs. As the officer rummaged through and emptied his truck, he came across a banana costume and tossed it on the ground next to Mikey. So, like any normal person getting searched by the cops with a banana costume in their truck, Mikey got up and put on the costume. My business partner drove by to see this spectacle only to learn later that it was one of our field guides.

Mikey told me about his ADHD and how his mother, a teacher herself, asked for special accommodations for Mikey from teachers at school. She asked that they allow Mikey to stand in the back of the class and even to pace while listening to lessons. He told me how his father had cleared out the back of the station wagon so the boys could wrestle on long car rides or how his father would drive the frontage road on long trips while Mikey and his brothers ran alongside the car for miles. To describe Mikey as an avid runner wouldn't do it justice. He runs to live. Morning runs are a necessity for him. They help with his ADHD and provide him meditation time for the rest of the day. Needless to say, Mikey and I could not be more different in so many ways. So, it was as clear as ever, that my training had to focus on Mikey being Mikey, not some version of Brad.

We spent the next six months together. I would often tell Mikey, "You have wisdom—not from the same sources I have—but you have it just the same.

When a boy is struggling or a mother is anxious, share YOUR story. Draw on what you learned as a punk-rock garage-band guitarist, or what you learned as the son of a state champ track coach. It won't sound like me, but it will be compelling—authenticity always is." To this day, Mikey needs an assistant to help with paperwork, and he is likely to get lost on a morning run in a new city, but the parents and angry young men who work with him would tell you how much they love him and how much he has helped them. Most importantly, they would tell you how good they feel when he is around.

After many months, Mikey's success was well-established, and referral sources were consistently asking for him—not an easy accomplishment for a young therapist. I asked him what made him so successful so soon. He said it was when he was given permission to be himself rather than having to conform to someone else's idea of what he or any therapist should be. That's when it all worked for him. He thanked me, and I told him I was just doing for him what others had done for me: my Great-aunt Katherine, whom I met once; my fifth and sixth-grade teacher, Mr. McKechnie; and my therapist, Jami Gill. All of them saw me and that made all the difference in the world."

Some years ago, I was working with a mother who had done tremendous work around her codependency. Before this work, she thought it was her job to raise her children in her image—to raise them in the right way to be or the way she had been raised. But her daughter's eating disorder and the family work that went with it lit something inside of her and she grew beyond the limits she had been told to fear crossing.

During a session a few years ago, as she talked about the growing pains in her ability to see her children, she came up with an idea. She would buy each of her adult children something special that showed them that she saw them. What was unique about each gift was that it was an expression of the differences between her and them. For her oldest, she bought nice beer mugs (she was a non-drinking person and even suspected her son might have a problem, but he was adamant it wasn't a problem). For her middle-son she bought a book on Yoga and another book on Buddhism. She was raised in a strict Catholic family, so these gifts acknowledged her son's interest in exploring Eastern philosophy as an alternative to the family's religious ideas. For her daughter, she bought a gift certificate to a spa and some expensive skin-care products, since her daughter identified as one who battles with the guilt that comes with self-care. As each child opened these gifts on Christmas morning, they recognized the significance of the gesture. These gifts were symbolic of the kind of love we are talking about here—the kind of love for an *Other* that requires that we yield and surrender to each person's uniqueness.

Often my client reflects on the gift of her daughter's eating disorder. The work that she has done at the invitation that such a problem asks has been lifesaving. She would tell you that she is a better mother, wife, and friend than she would have ever been had she not been required to take this journey.

TO BE LOVED IS TO BE SEEN

In my 40s, I realized something related to this business of seeing people and being seen and having an adequate container. I had spent most of my life trying to prove to people that I was okay, that I was worth something, that I had value to offer. I did this because as a child, I was told I was *too much*. I was too sensitive, too dramatic, too needy, just too much. Because I upset and frustrated my mother (and others), I thought something was wrong with me. These kinds of reactions and messages from others sank into me as a child and they became part of me and my inner voice. I spent decades trying to be something others would value, admire, and love. It wasn't until my 40s, after more than a decade in therapy, that I realized if I had just known I was already enough, if I knew that I was okay, that I could have spent my time and resources on giving my gifts to others, rather than trying to prove I was valuable.

The effect of *seeing* someone cannot be overestimated. This is true for our clients, our children, our spouses, our partners. Being seen is a recognition from the *Other* that gives us a sense that we are okay. Unfortunately, most people's instinct is to fix those things in the other person that cause us discomfort or anxiety. This energy, often not completely visible, leaves the other person feeling *wrong* or *bad*. What is horrible about this is that it is unspoken, and the words often seem loving, "I just want the best for you. I am worried about you. I just don't want you to suffer." Rather, if we develop the capacity to see an *Other*, we can discover their story and the meaning of their symptomatic and anxiety-producing behaviors. Then, they can heal the wound that lies beneath the defense that is protecting them.

Famous psychologist D.W. Winnicott went even further to suggest that to be seen is to exist. I have had the thought that the reason some don't remember much from their childhood is because they weren't seen. When someone is truly seen it is as if their life is recorded. It happened. When someone takes an interest in you, really cares about how you think and feel, it has the effect of "Yes. There I am."

It is so hard to watch someone we love struggle. This is precisely why we need to go to therapy, to Al-Anon, or some similar kind of support group, in order to deal with our anxiety and our need to fix and to gather resources to be there for the other person. If you find yourself in one of those meetings, there will be no strategies on how to fix your anorexic daughter or your alcoholic spouse. The work will be you: on developing the capacity to love and the clarity to draw a clear boundary for yourself. You will discover why such things have eluded you as you listen to others tell their stories. You will discover how it was not okay for you to be you as a child. At first, the notions will sound strange and may not seem to apply to you, but if you stick around long enough, you will make it past the sentinels of guilt, shame, and filial obligations and discover the wounds that led to you losing yourself. According to Freud, this is the primary purpose of therapy: to free us from unconscious obligations.

The reason that defining and discovering the *Self* is the primary project is that unless we have come to know ourselves, we have little ability to see the *Other*. Of course, no one can completely know themselves, but it is important to know that this is the first project, and we will be limited in our ability to see and to connect to others to the extent we don't know ourselves. Relationship problems with other people are essentially relationship problems with ourselves; every problem we have with others stems from a problem we have with the relationship to the *Self*.

Inner-child work is where you imagine your young *Self* in the third person. It is as if you could travel back in time and sit with your younger *Self*. You imagine talking to your young *Self* and listening to what they are feeling and thinking—you hear their fears, their hurt, their shame. You can learn to listen to them, welcome their story and offer your patience and presence.

Relationship problems with other people are essentially relationship problems with ourselves; every problem we have with others stems from a problem we have with the relationship to the Self.

I do this kind of work with others in guided meditation and in psychodrama (role plays where one enrolls another in the role of their inner-child). With the practice of therapy, you can begin to hear what your inner-child has to say. In reality, your inner-child is just you—the parts of you that were present before someone told you that you were wrong, needy, making excuses, weak, or selfish. It is the part others have told you to discard, the part of you that thought you needed to get rid of in order to fit in and belong. They may not have used these words, but their exasperated, frustrated, disappointed, anxious reactions communicated to you that something was wrong with you. It isn't true, of course; the inadequacy was in the other person, but children are unable to draw this conclusion. Children absorb and incorporate those feelings into themselves and become what some refer to as *the bad object*.

When we find a therapist who has the capacity to listen to us and to the story our inner-child has to tell, we discover that nothing is wrong with us. We are just who we are. As we discover this truth, we become more capable of listening to others, to their stories, to their inner-children. This is how the relationship we have with ourselves becomes the foundation for the relationship we have with every other person. We learn to welcome the child in the *Other*, rather than respond with should and shouldn't as in, "Stop blaming your circumstances on your parents. It is time for you to take responsibility and stop whining."

When I do inner-child work with people, I can see clearly how they regard themselves. They are often quick to instruct or even rebuke their inner *Self*, "You don't need to be scared. It will all be okay. You just have to stop making such a mess of things."

More subtly, they will try to put the child at ease by offering comforting suggestions. Sometimes even these comments can be dismissing. If I sense this is the case, I ask the individual to just sit and consider what the child is feeling—just acknowledge it and sit with it. For most, this is counter intuitive, but inevitably the simple act of listening and understanding leads to healing. "Of course, you feel scared. Of course, you feel alone. How could it have been any other way, given your story?" Such a response invariably relaxes and soothes the child. But since we had so little experience with such empathic resonance, we don't know how to do it with ourselves. And when we learn to do it with ourselves, we will be more able to do it with our children and the *Others* in our life.

Recently, while teaching a new employee about this concept of inner-child work, she asked me this question, "Sometimes my poor-single-mother *Self* shows up. When I was raising my kids, there were many lean years and it was a frightening time in my life. That part of me is scarcity and fear based and can cause problems in my life today. When she shows up, should I just tell her she doesn't have to be afraid anymore?"

"No," I explained. "Tell her you understand. It was a scary time and she did a great job raising and protecting her children, on her own. Tell her you understand her and why she was so afraid. Tell her you love her and will sit with her." This type of exercise or practice is built on the foundations spelled out here—and it takes some practice and a great deal of time to learn how to do it.

"IF WE REALLY LOVE THE *OTHER* AS *OTHER*, WE HAVE HEROICALLY TAKEN ON THE RESPONSIBILITY FOR OUR OWN INDIVIDUATION, OUR OWN JOURNEY. THIS HEROISM MAY PROPERLY BE CALLED LOVE."

The reason that loving another's *Otherness* is heroic is because we have accepted the invitation to journey inward. This means we work to know what we think, feel, believe, want, value, prefer, and love. We explore our history, our trauma, our resources, and then we have a sense of the vastness of what we don't know. But most of us are afraid to look inward. We are afraid of what we will find. We might worry that it will feel overwhelming; we may be loyal to some idea that to look into our past is a search for excuses and for people to blame (imagine where that message may have come from!). Yet the journey inward is the heroic journey. In storytelling, dark caves, ominous forests, closets, deep oceans…all metaphors for the heroic journey are inward. And as Joseph Campbell tells us, "The cave you fear to enter holds the treasure you seek."

In *The Knight in Rusty Armor*, the protagonist is seeking to shed armor that has become impossible for him to remove. He meets Merlin, and the wizard tells him he must travel the Path of Truth and pass through the three castles in order to be able to shed his armor. Each measure of his journey leads to a tear-drenched experience, and it is these tears that cause his armor, piece by piece, to rust and fall away. On the way to the first castle, the Castle of Silence, his visor falls off with tears he shed when he realized that his son did not know him because his armor was in the way. "Tears from real feelings will release me from this armor," he discovers, and he starts to see the world more clearly. He recognized that the birds were not all alike, and he can see the smallest sunlit particles in the trees. His guide, a bird named Rebecca, explains, "You're starting to see the differences in other forms of life because you're starting to see the differences in yourself."

To discover what is within us is what gives us the capacity to see others. I run men's groups for therapy professionals in my field and when I invite someone to join a group, invariably they express some trepidation at the thought of sharing some of their innermost thoughts with colleagues. And these professionals are in the business of inviting others to look inward and take the risk of sharing what they find with them. I share with each person I talk, "I know it seems scary and there is a risk. There's a risk that you will be judged. There's a risk that others might lose confidence in your work because they catch a glimpse of your darkness. It is the same risk that we ask our clients to take. But what I can tell you is this: after doing this for several years, I have found that instead of others losing confidence in you, others will come to trust you more. I have learned that while there are differences in our stories, everyone's underbelly looks essentially the same. This is my experience with these groups over and over."

As I mentioned earlier from the *Knight in Rusty Armor*, at a desperate moment in his story, the knight calls out for Merlin, and as he had promised, Merlin immediately appears and responds to the question on the knight's mind. Dumbfounded by this, the knight asks, "How could you know I was going to ask you that?"

Merlin answers, "Since I know myself, I know you."

This is why I tell therapists I train, "You can be a successful therapist if you read and study and listen to good teachers, but you will never be a great therapist unless you do your own work. Most of what I know is from sitting on the client's couch, not from a classroom or a book or from sitting in the therapist's chair. Having a sense of why I do what I do, what I feel, and what prevents me from being my authentic *Self* gives me the greatest clue about *Others* and their dilemmas."

I talk with many parents of adopted children who discover that the notion that "love will heal all" is shattered as the child begins to struggle with mental health and addiction that may or may not be related to attachment trauma. Many of these parents struggle due to the chasm that exists between them and their children. The child's *Otherness* is profound and obvious due to differences in temperament or physical traits. These differences make it hard for these parents to connect and provide support in a way that makes sense to them and offers the child what he or she needs. And this sense of *Otherness* is not exclusive to adoptive families. Many parents I talk with seem to be in a perpetual stage of "Why is my child like this?" or "I don't even know them anymore."

While this feeling is typical and makes sense, it is indicative of the situation, and I tell parents, "It is okay to ask these questions, wonder these thoughts, and seek for answers, but not if your question of 'Why?' is masking a shameful message which communicates to the child that something is *wrong* with them. Your child needs you to understand them. And understanding them will require some work on your part."

I came across this simple and profound quote recently,

> *The first thing you should know about me is that **I am not you**.*
> *A lot more will make sense after that.*

The spiritual teacher Ram Dass has a beautiful way of talking about the differences in others and how we can transcend our inclinations to judge or even have an opinion by comparing people to trees in the forest.

> *Some of them are bent, and some of them are straight, and some of them are evergreens, and some of them are whatever. And you look at the tree and you allow it. You appreciate it. You see why it is the way it is. You sort of understand that it didn't get enough light, and so it turned that way. You appreciate the tree.*

> *The minute you get near humans, you lose all that. And you are constantly saying "You're too this, or I'm too this." That judging mind comes in. And so, I practice turning people into trees.*

Celebrating your child and their unique *Self* is evidence of this capacity. Their unique journey, with all the twists and turns, is a gift to the parent who is able to love another's *Otherness*. I have had many children who have come out to their parents as LGBTQ+, and many of their parents have struggled to celebrate their children's unique *Self*. They say things like, "We love you anyway," or "Even though you are gay, we still love you." Some parents have gone farther in their disapproval and have recited an often-quoted motto, "Love the sinner, but hate the sin." The problem with this is that what you call "sin," the child experiences as an expression of who they are, so the sentiment doesn't land the way the parent thinks. I saw a Jewish father surrender to the reality that his adult son was not going to follow in his footsteps. The father baked a cake for his estranged son's birthday and offered it as a gift with a card that read, "This is for you and Maddy to enjoy on your birthday." (Maddy was the live-in girlfriend). At this, the son responded by reinitiating contact with his father, and small steps towards rebuilding a relationship began to sprout in the wake of this gesture—the gesture of loving *Other* as *Other,* born from this father's willingness to let go of the version of a son he wanted.

As I stated above, if love is simply affection or warmth, it is meaningless. But if love is measured over the long run as a spouse's, a friend's, or a parent's willingness to take on the work of their own project, then the impact is profound. To take responsibility for your own journey and your own differentiation is to courageously explore your own mind, your history, your wounds. It is to take the risk of walking into a support group or a therapist's office and telling the truth about who you are at the risk of again experiencing what has previously happened to you. In times past, the person with whom you shared your real *Self* became upset or anxious and these feelings spilled over, making you feel somewhere deep down that who you are is not okay.

In *Parenting From the Inside-Out,* Siegel and Hartzell share in their research that the key to healthy attachment, "loving *Other* as *Other*," is based on the parent's ability to sort through their own story. Their study interviewed mothers using the Adult Attachment Interview (AAI). The amazing thing they found is that it is not the quality of the childhood that determines whether the mother can provide a secure attachment for her child, but rather it's based on whether she has dealt with and incorporated her story adequately. The ability to tell her story, to unravel her wounds and her childhood, predict the attachment she has with her child with 85% accuracy. Rarely do social science studies show such high correlations. They concluded, "Here again, the important point of the AAI is that it is *not what happened to an individual by itself that matters, it is how that person has come to process those events*" (italics added). The ability to meaningfully articulate your experience is more important than the actual quality of the experience.

A couple of summers ago, during a clinical meeting, one of the therapists asked if she could present a case. She talked about a young woman, in the seventh week of our wilderness therapy program (the average length of our program is nine weeks), who continued to show significant struggles. One of the staff pulled the therapist aside after the weekly staff-change group to share her thoughts, "I was here her first week and from what I just saw, she has made virtually no progress whatsoever."

To take responsibility for your own journey and your own differentiation is to courageously explore your own mind, your history, your wounds. It is to take the risk of walking into a support group or a therapist's office and telling the truth about who you are at the risk of again experiencing what has previously happened to you.

The therapist didn't feel much different than the staff and was losing hope. The client was not only resisting anything that the therapist tried, she was sabotaging the group process and causing a strain on the entire system. Some of the therapists in the consultation offered suggestions and interventions or assignments that sought to topple the client's resistance.

I asked the therapist on the case to tell us a little more about the client's history and diagnosis. She flipped through the file and told us about the death of one parent with the other parent serving a prison term. Grandparents were doing the best they could, but nothing seemed to make a difference. The therapist concluded with the diagnosis one would expect with such a background:

Reactive Attachment Disorder—a diagnosis caused by stress in early childhood due to neglect and mistreatment. Those affected have difficulty with and avoid or sabotage emotional closeness and often battle with authority figures.

After listening to various suggestions from the clinical team, I said, "Well, I like all your suggestions. They are all creative and thoughtful, but the arrangement here is that we are supposed to lose. And of course, not much has happened in weeks. The kind of stuff in that file doesn't go away in two months. Those wounds are with you for a lifetime. Instead of trying to fix her, I would suggest you go back out to the group and tell her you are sorry. Tell her you are sorry because you have been trying to fix her and you realize how insensitive this was. Fixing her symptoms in some short order would be erasing these deep and primal wounds. Tell her from now on, you just want to understand her. We should look for another placement, one that will continue this work and can keep her and others around her safe, but in the meantime, with the time we have left, let's try to understand her." The longer I work with young people, the more I realize in a certain sense, they are right and we (those trying to fix them) are wrong.

How does one develop the capacity to be there in the way a struggling child, friend, family member, or partner needs? Years ago, at a parent group I was running, a father stopped me to ask an honest, simple question. "So, if I hear you right, you are saying that the challenges in parenting, the blocks and the barriers to more effective parenting...the roots of these are found when we look back into our own childhood experiences?"

He asked it so plainly, I almost let out a laugh at its simplicity. "Yes. That is exactly what I am saying."

When Alice Miller explained,

Experience has taught us that we have only one enduring weapon in our struggle against mental illness: the emotional discovery of the truth about the unique history of our childhood, she gave parents, partners, friends, all of us a blueprint for unraveling the layers that block us from our wisdom and clarity. It is this journey, the journey toward our own differentiation, the journey to discover the origin of the voices of self-doubt, fear, shame, and guilt, that lead us to our liberation. This journey is not a search for excuses. It is a search for explanation and understanding.

Henry Wadsworth Longfellow wrote, "If we could read the secret history of our enemies, we should find in each man's life sorrow and suffering enough to disarm all hostility." I believe he is right because I have seen it in myself and with my clients who thought they were unlovable because of what they had done and who they had hurt. Often, I think what is most interesting is not *what* we don't know, but *why* we don't know it. If we believe what Miller is telling us and what my experience in working with clients has taught me, the answers will be found as we explore our own inner landscape.

If the job of the therapist is to know, see, and understand the client in order to provide healing, we can extend this idea to our roles as parents, partners, and friends. One of the young men I worked with asked me many years ago, "You say you care. You say you love us. How can you love us if you are paid to do it?"

I told him this, "I don't get paid to love you. I get paid to find you, to understand you. And when I do find you, loving you is easy."

LET GO OF OUTCOMES & FOCUS ON CHANGING YOURSELF

We talk about codependency in the context of a loved one's addiction. The problem with doing this is that codependency is present in many cases where children or spouses or other loved ones aren't demonstrating overt mental health issues. Codependency, like mental health and mental illness, is a continuum and we are all on it somewhere. "Codependency" is a pop-psychology term; it is not in the diagnostic manual. In more descriptive psychological theories, we would refer to codependency as the lack of a *Self* and the subsequent relationship dynamics that are created when there is that lack of *Self*. Codependency speaks to the quality of the attachment.

Professionals in mental health and addiction talk about healthy detachment in contrast to codependency, but they are really talking about healthy attachment or *proper* attachment. Healthy attachment, in clinical terms, is synonymous with pop-psychology's concept of healthy detachment. Thus, the *proper* amount of letting go is present in healthy attachment and in healthy relationships with our partners.

When you have a loved one struggling with addiction or mental illness, inevitably you will be required in the course of treatment to ask yourselves different questions about your relationship with the person. They will tell you hard things: ways you've hurt them or times when they felt erased by you. You will learn about boundaries and communication. And in the case of tragic conditions of your loved one's disorder, these questions and exercises may stir up strong feelings of guilt and shame for you. We all have work in these areas. It's not that your faults are particularly rare or profound, it's just that for your loved one, these dynamics are wrapped up with their disease.

Recovery from codependency, as some suggest, is not about simply setting stricter boundaries. It's about setting better boundaries.

Here's how the idea of codependency and non-blame can come together. In my experience, many addicts are medicating to numb or escape from the wounds of trauma and fractured attachments inherent in the codependency—the poor attachment. To be in recovery from codependency is to get out of that cycle. It is to heal and create a foundation for healthier connections to others, including with our loved one's suffering with various addictions. We learn what it is to be human and we learn to love and connect to the *Other*—and while it is not simple cause and effect, this connection can contribute to their healing.

Recovery from codependency doesn't cure anyone else's addiction. Professionals would be wise to avoid teaching or implying that recovering from codependency will resolve anyone else's problems—that is one of the initial problems with the codependent's thinking. Recovery from codependency, as some suggest, is not about simply setting stricter boundaries. It's about setting *better* boundaries. Better boundaries refer to their quality: the intention and idea behind the boundary. The boundary's purpose is to separate and distinguish people's emotional lives from one another so each can be connected in a healthier way. Recovery from codependency means different boundaries and the difference is rooted in each person's differentiation and love.

Recently, a mother asked me about letting go. She was struggling with her son and was trying to get some clarity on her boundary setting. Letting go is one of those principles that is hard to explain because it is a feeling and a way of being rather than a set of behaviors. If we interpret letting go incorrectly, we think it means not caring or doing nothing. The letting go is in the intention. It is in the relationship we have with the *Other* and their struggles. So, when I am asked, as I was by this mother, "What should I do? How can we be most helpful to our son?"

I answer it this way. "If your arrangements with the other person (providing them money, staying married to them, providing guidance or other support, etc.) causes you to regress into a relapse of your codependency, you may choose to extricate yourself from those circumstances. You may choose to stop paying for their school or get a divorce. Or you can choose to go deeper into your recovery in the face of such stress. This is a different way of making decisions: whether you set a boundary or continue providing them with the support… it is not to change *them*, but it is instead for you and your own recovery—your self-care and wellbeing.

Sometimes I suggest people play a little game in their heads and pretend they don't know what someone else's journey should look like. If they practice this often, they may even start to believe it. This is a practice I have to go back to again and again with my wife, my children, and my clients. I am often triggered, and I regress to my old ways of thinking. Then I have to apologize to the person and go back to my practice. This practice does not make me a great husband, father, or therapist. But I think the fact that in the end I know the work lies in me makes me tolerable.

LOVE IS A GIVING THING

I was directing a psychodrama with a client, Darcy, where she was having a conversation with her wife. She had been unfaithful and with the support of a therapist, decided to confess her indiscretions to her spouse. She hadn't been caught but wanted to work on what she had identified as a love addiction, and this was a part of her recovery. She was lucky enough to be married to a strong woman who showed a strength that allowed for the healing process. They had two children together and loved each other, and the betrayal brought them to the edge of what both thought possible. With the help of therapists and sponsors, they walked through a fire that few are willing or able to do. Their marriage was in a much better place, but ghosts still haunted them both. Due to the gift of grace her wife had offered her, Darcy felt perpetually indebted, so much so that she was often unable to advocate for herself since she had been the recipient of so great a gift. During the therapeutic exercise, as she was trying to express her limitless gratitude for the gift of forgiveness from her wife (through the person playing the role of her wife), Darcy broke character and turned to me and asked, "Is it okay to need someone?"

"Of course, it is," I replied. "We need people in our lives. We cannot do much of this on our own." As she nodded in acceptance and turned back to the role play, I added, "But that is not love. Don't confuse the two. Loving is a **giving** thing and needing is a **taking** thing. We can love the same people that we need, but it is critically important that we recognize and acknowledge the difference between giving and taking."

A few years ago, we helped to create an off-Broadway play based on wilderness therapy. Part of this project included having a reporter from *The*

New York Times visit the field for a day. A photographer and another one of the writers also came out to the field. During the visit, we sat in on a spontaneous group therapy session. One of the boys was angry and complaining about his experience. At this, one of the visitors decided to chime in. He offered the boys some of the wisdom from his life experiences, and as expected, the teenage boys just waited for him to stop talking. The therapist, on the other hand, listened deeply and empathically and restated back the things he was hearing to make sure he understood what the boy was saying. The therapist offered no lesson or advice, instead, he offered a safe place, a container for the boy to express himself.

After the group I sat with the reporter to talk about the group she had just experienced and the reason for our involvement in the project. I said, "One of the things about therapy is that if you don't know what it is, you can't see it. The lesson and advice that the writer was giving the boys wasn't therapy. The therapist's listening was the therapy. The boy was needing to be heard, and the gift that the therapist was giving him was in not saying much back. He didn't state the need overtly, but it is implied in the sharing of difficult feelings. Advice or lecturing are easy—anyone can do that. The hard work of therapy is what you don't say. That is the difference between most people and a master therapist."

Learning what people need and what they are asking of us is part of the process of becoming more aware of what we need from others. Parents and partners justify their unwelcomed attempts to help others with advice or lectures. They even call these things love. But these attempts are more to meet the needs of the one expressing them than they are for the one receiving them.

Many expressions of love are really requests for something. Asking for a loved one to tell you how they feel may be your need rather than their need. Asking, "Are you okay?" may really be a request for reassurance. I see you are not okay, and it is making me anxious. Please tell me something so I can feel less anxious. Often anxiety is hidden behind verbal expressions of love. An "I love you" can really be a request for a response...as in "Do you love me too?" Talking **tends** to be a taking thing. Listening **tends** to be a giving thing.

Talking or sharing our feelings means that we are asking the *Other* to contain us. Sharing something with someone can be an expression of love or giving, but very often we need something from them. One way to know whether it's giving or taking is that if you get cut off during your sharing, take notice of how it feels. If being cut off results in hurt, anger, or some other painful emotion, then you were needing

*Talking **tends** to be a taking thing. Listening **tends** to be a giving thing.*

something from the *Other*. If after being interrupted you are able to let it go easily, then you didn't need something in the exchange.

On the listening or containing end of the equation you are being asked to listen or contain and that is why the listening can feel so draining. It is not uncommon in an exchange between my wife and me that the person who has just unloaded feels relieved and an increase of love or intimacy, whereas the person doing the listening feels distance or discomfort.

Understanding what is happening, what it being asked and who is giving and who is taking can give us some clarity. We can assess whether we are up to the task of listening or containing, and we can realize that when we are sharing with someone, we are really asking for something that takes emotional resources and capacity. People often naively imagine that when they are sharing, they are giving something that leads to intimacy when, in fact, they are *asking* for something that can lead to intimacy.

Love asks, "What can I do for you? What do you need from me?"

Need asks, "Can you give me this or that? I am hurting or scared, unsettled or anxious and need something from you."

Both are perfectly okay. It is when we confuse the two or conflate the two that we get into trouble.

THE ASK IN INTIMACY

Rather than sharing something vulnerable, the more difficult task in intimacy may be seeking to understand the *Other* and holding space for them. When the *Other* is compromised, hurt, or struggling to connect to us, do we have the bandwidth to recognize and honor their struggle? Or do we sit righteous in our supposed attempt to open up to them and declare their inability to connect as an indictment on their intimacy-impaired personality.

I ran a therapeutic intensive with six alumni parents a few years ago. Each participant had a child struggling in some similar and some unique ways. As the week progressed and we started into the role plays, it was as if each participant was building on the previous parent's insight. As a group, they were beginning to see the project of parenting a struggling child with greater and greater clarity.

As the last role play ensued, a father pulled a letter out of his pocket to read to the person standing in for his struggling daughter. He had seen others lose track of what they wanted to say and so he stayed up the previous night and crafted his best letter. He told his daughter (through the person playing the role of his daughter) that he loved her. He told her how he was worried about her and gently listed some examples of why that was. He told her he would support her in the ways that he could, as long as they didn't violate his core values or feelings. His reading the letter brought many in that room to tears. As is the custom in these exercises, I asked him to reverse roles and play the role of his daughter. I told him, "Now respond the way you think she would respond if she could access her deepest truth."

In the role of his daughter, he began, "Thanks Dad. I know you love me…" But it was flat. He stopped and looked at me and said, "I think that is what she might say, but it is not the deepest truth."

"What is the truth then?" I prompted.

He paused and gathered himself. "Dad. I love you. I am struggling with some pretty severe anxiety and I am not sure I can deal with yours on top of mine. I love you but I may have to take some space for a time. I am not mad; I am just overwhelmed with carrying my struggle and yours. I am afraid this will hurt, and I don't want to hurt you, but I need you to know this." He looked at me and my eyes were spilling over with love and gratitude for having witnessed this courageous and profound expression of love.

He reversed roles again and simply responded to his daughter, "I understand. I think I know what that feels like and I can give you the space that you need. I will take care of myself."

Again, love is a giving thing and intimacy asks us to share our truth, but also to welcome difficult truths from those we love in order to create closeness. And this father, standing on the shoulders of all of his co-participants, demonstrated these qualities to all of us. He was able to see that he was asking something of his child that she could not give. She had plenty of her own struggles and adding her father's grief and anxiety on top of that was too much. He was able to welcome her feelings, and with grace, he embraced her need for some distance.

The above exercise again demonstrates the dynamic between children and parents that I shared earlier in the book that has led me to tell parents that I am almost at the point where I don't want parents to tell their children how they feel. When I suggest this, parents and others often scoff at me and ask, "What about parents? When is it their turn to share feelings? Shouldn't the child know how they are affecting their parents?"

It may seem like a strange notion to suggest that it may be a bad idea to share our feelings with others—sharing one's feelings seems to be at the heart of most approaches to therapy. However, if the goal in sharing one's feelings is to get the other person to change, we would be wise to reconsider. It is critical in our relationships that we get clear about who is responsible for our feelings. If the sharing of feelings comes with the implication or the overt suggestion that others are responsible for our feelings, then all we are doing is asking them to take care of us and using a therapeutic language in an untherapeutic way. This is true in all relationships but is most dangerous with those over whom we have power, like our children.

The problem with parents sharing their feelings is twofold. First, in the vast majority of the cases I have observed between parents and children, parental expressions of feelings are motivated by the parent's desire to change the child or their behavior. In essence, they're saying, "Please stop doing this or that and feeling this or that, and/or please start doing this or that instead so I feel good in some way." Even in the rare cases where a parent has no intent on influencing the child's behavior, it is still almost impossible for a child to resist taking on the task of caring for the parent's emotions. Even if we frontload the expression to our children, they are inclined to believe that what we feel and think *is* about *them* and not about us. And they are all too willing to compromise and sacrifice their true and authentic *Self* to take care of their parent. It is a survival instinct because the risk of not taking care of the parent (upsetting them too much) is that the parent will abandon the child.

A few years ago, my family was at the mall near Christmastime participating in our family's ritual of buying stocking stuffers. This was a few years before the earlier recounted Thanksgiving story. We would break up into pairs and go around the mall to get little presents for others in the family. During our first meet-up, my 18-year-old daughter shared that she and her older brother would be spending the entire Christmas holiday with their mother and stepfather. Prior to this, the holiday was alternated every other year with us taking Christmas Eve and their mother taking Christmas Day—this was part of the arrangement we had since the children were young. Now that both children were over 18, they could spend holidays wherever and with whomever they wanted. My daughter said, "Our cousins are in town and my mom has bought a bunch of crab for Christmas Eve."

My instant, insane thought was, "I have more money than their mom and I will buy more crab." Luckily, this thought passed very quickly, and then I was left with my grief and sadness. My two older children were grown. Legal agreements couldn't dictate where they would spend holiday celebrations. I acknowledged the news from my daughter, and we left in pairs to go back to shopping. As I shopped with my youngest, I couldn't shake the feelings I was having. We still had the rest of the evening together, and I was having difficulty concentrating or pretending to enjoy the activity.

During the next meet-up I thought I would share how I felt. My intent, as I considered this, was to let everyone know how I was feeling so I could move through the feeling and so they would know why I might be acting a little off and so I could let go of it, "Hey," I said, "before we pair off again, I just want to get something off my chest. You don't have to do anything about it, but I think I need to say it so I can move on. I am sad that you two won't be spending Christmas Eve or Christmas with us. I know we can celebrate before or after, but I am just struggling a little to adjust."

Emma, in her sensitivity and inclination to take responsibility for how others feel, responded. "It's okay, Dad. We will tell Mom that we will spend Christmas Eve with you."

Even though I had front-loaded it and was sure I wasn't hoping for them to change their plans, her instinct to take care of me trumped anything happening in that moment. Children carry the feelings of their parents whether their parents intend to hand them over to them or not. And in my experience, parents *do* hand their feelings over to their children. This is why I tell parents to try and consider not sharing their feelings with children and if they do, to be very intentional about the purpose of doing so as parental feelings load too heavily on children's shoulders.

After hearing Emma's offer, I playfully responded, "You're not invited anymore." I then went on to explain that they didn't have to take care of me, of us. We would be okay. In fact, I felt a little better already after having shared. But I realized in that moment the weight of a parent's feelings on the shoulders of a child. Whether it is pride, sadness, worry, or happiness, the child is inclined to think that a parent's feelings are about them and it is their responsibility to do something about those feelings.

The love project is about developing capacity and garnering needed support and resources. Loved ones, children, and spouses who struggle may require us to stretch and grow. They ask the hardest things of us. They ask us to lose our minds. They ask us to give up old ideas and old beliefs. They ask us to stretch far enough to see them, even when they are hiding. If we are willing to do this, if we have enough love that we are willing to do this, then love is the difference. But, if love is just loving what we already know, the familiar, then it will not be enough.

I have had the privilege of working with parents and partners who have shown the willingness and capacity to support their *Others* after tragedies, catastrophes, betrayals, and heartbreaks caused by mental illness and addiction. And while it is a long and painful process, they have expressed gratitude that their dreams did not work out the way they'd initially planned. They allowed their lives to be changed and transformed through this suffering and what they found on the other side was a richer, more meaningful and more fulfilling life. They found out the meaning of love, how to give it, and how to ask for it.

CHAPTER FIVE

MARRIAGE, DIVORCE, AND PSYCHOSIS

"Love is a temporary madness. It erupts like an earthquake and then subsides. And when it subsides you have to make a decision. You have to work out whether your roots have become so entwined together that it is inconceivable that you should ever part...Love is not breathlessness, it is not excitement, it is not the promulgation of promises of eternal passion... That is just being "in love" which any fool can do. Love itself is what is left over when being in love has burned away, and this is both an art and a fortunate accident." Captain Corelli's Mandolin, Louis de Bernières

MADLY IN LOVE

"You complete me."

"He is my everything."

"She is my world."

"He is my best friend, my lover, and my biggest supporter."

"She is my better half."

All of the above might sound wonderful and may express, in a poetic sense, the powerful nature of romantic love, but these statements can also reveal a fundamental misunderstanding of what it means to be in a healthy, mature, and intimate relationship. The idea of two becoming one, in a psychological sense, may be the seed of later problems in marriage.

Robert Bly describes the development of a *Self* and the transformation into marriage using the image of a ball of light. Children are born as a bright ball of energy, a 360-degree personality. "But one day we noticed that our parents didn't like certain parts of that ball….to keep our parents' love, [we] put [those parts] in the bag." Next, teachers and peers have their say, telling us what is unacceptable. Bly describes this process using the imagery of a bag that we drag behind us—we put all of those parts of ourselves in the bag to keep from being alone. In middle school, high school, and college, the process accelerates, and our stuffing of the bag fills it up larger and larger. Then,

…out of a round globe of energy the twenty-year-old ends up with a slice. We'll imagine a man who has a thin slice left…and we'll imagine that he meets a woman; let's say they are both twenty-four. She has a thin, elegant slice left…They join each other in a ceremony, and this union of the two slices is called a marriage. Even together the two slices do not make up one person.

While many imagine the fusion of two into one romantically, it can also be a condition of psychosis—a severe distortion of reality. The phrase "crazy about you" may be an accurate depiction of the early stages of romantic love. As the relationship grows, fissures are exposed and later with time and pressure they may become chasms. If we look close enough, we will inevitably discover that the early experience of love was flawed.

The most interesting thing for me when a couple or an individual comes to me as divorce is being considered is that most often the roots of the divorce were present in their courtship. In other words, the dynamics present in a couple considering or traveling towards ending the relationship were present as the two fell madly in love, when they found each other's company enough to sustain them, so they didn't need food or sleep. In the early stages of romantic love, life seems complete and holes are filled that give partners the sense that all is finally right with the world. The commitment to spend the rest of their lives with each other was the expression of the intensity of these feelings.

So, where do things go wrong? In my exploration, they went wrong from the beginning; it is only the betrayal of the unconscious contract agreed to during their courtship that is causing the dissatisfaction. What follows is an exploration of the landscape of how intense, romantic love turns into infidelity, discontent and in some instances, hatred.

Because children are required to navigate their parents' defenses to survive childhood, they develop in such a way that they end up relating to people who are the same shape, size, and color of their parents. In other words, we become shaped by a certain kind of compromised person, and as we grow up, we are inclined to relate to those same kinds of people. The shape of our wounds predisposes us to fit with others who mirror, in some ways, our original contexts. The work then is to come to know this by unraveling our childhoods—good, bad and in between—so that we make friends with ourselves. And if we are lucky, we find a partner who is willing to travel a similar path that is their own.

MAKING EACH OTHER HAPPY

The mistaken idea that falling in love is about making each other happy often leads to anger, shame, and ultimately dissolution unless it is corrected. Two people meet and find each to be attractive and appealing. For the sake of easily identifying the landscape, I am going to refer to a man and a woman, a husband and wife. The dynamics are similar in same sex couples and the roles that each partner plays are not limited to their gender or their orientation. This scenario is not meant to suggest stereotypes of men and women being masculine and feminine, but rather the archetype they represent.

For the man's part: let's call him Sam. Sam is attracted to his girlfriend. Let's call her Jess. Sam adores Jess. Sam sees his role as provider, fixer, and rescuer. He provides Jess with a sense of safety and security. Sam's mother may have been overinvolved, absent, anxious, or otherwise unavailable to him. All human parents are limited in their capacity to provide children with their needs in their totality. This left a chasm in Sam and he has a limited sense of *Self*, a limited sense of his "okayness." As he meets and dates Jess, his ability to soothe a partner and receive positive feedback from her gives Sam something he was not able to achieve with his mother—the sense that he is good, enough, and worthy of love. This feeling cannot be underestimated—it is intoxicating. It is the accomplishment and longing of life, to find a sense through another person that we are lovable and desirable. During the falling-in-love stage of the relationship, Sam neglects other relationships and obligations, so intoxicating is the feeling. He loves the feeling he has when he is around Jess as they talk late hours into the night. When their sexual union further reinforces the feeling that has been absent all of his life, the feeling that he is desirable, he feels *home* for the first time.

Sam calls his feelings "falling madly in love." As James Hollis, author of *The Eden Project*, explains,

> *This is what happens in projection. In the most rabid stage of being in love — and rabid is by no means too strong of a word — one is unable to do anything other than obsess on the Other. One is caught in a projective identification with the heart's desires, the boundaries between Self and Other dissolving again, as they did for the infant.*

It is a kind of madness, a kind of psychosis. It distorts his reality and temporarily gives him a euphoric bliss. He has the experience for the first time of being whole—of being "completed." Why wouldn't he desire this feeling for the rest of his life? He has finally found "home," or, more accurately what home should have felt like long ago. Alice Miller explains, "We then realize that all our lives we have feared and struggled to ward off something that really cannot happen any longer; for it has already happened, at the very beginning of our lives while we were completely dependent."

Jess too suffers from some unsettled feelings: she feels uneasy and incomplete. The ground beneath her feet never feels quite solid enough, and she longs for a sense of safety and security. She learned in her childhood that the thing that assured her place in the world was to fit in, to provide others what they needed. Yet this security was tenuous and dependent on her ability to always meet others' needs. Jess sacrificed her authenticity for the comfort of belonging to someone. Then, when she meets Sam, he seems to provide her with the sense of safety and security that she longs for. He is attentive, adoring, and capable of soothing her fears. The sparkle in Sam's eye tells her she is wanted, and his promised constant attention tells her she will be safe. She feels whole and completed by this fusion of two partial selves and reflects back to him that he is good, giving him the sense that he has come home.

The dance of filling each other's emptiness is exhilarating in its infancy and can be exhausting as it matures.

The dance of filling each other's emptiness is exhilarating in its infancy and can be exhausting as it matures. No one has enough energy or resources for it indefinitely. Because individuals in couples think that the project is to make the *Other* happy, they romanticize with such euphemisms as, "You are my everything. You are my best friend. And moreover, you are the one primarily responsible for my happiness, joy, and serenity." Any failure in providing the partner with these feelings either directly or indirectly can lead to turning the inadequate partner into the bad object. If it is direct, it is easy to spot. "You are a selfish, self-centered, uncaring slob of a human." If it is indirect or subtler, it will look like the hurt one sharing feelings, over and over, with the implicit implication that it is the partner's responsibility to fix those feelings.

Years ago, in an attempt to achieve greater cohesion and unity in our business partnership, my partners and I enlisted the services of a business consultant who also had experience as a marriage therapist. Those of you who have started businesses or have business partners know well the parallels between that and marriage. In our first session, the consultant made the comparison overt by asking the four of us, "What is your responsibility in a marriage?" All of us were therapists, three of the four trained as marriage therapists, so we had spent some time considering the roles and duties of marital partners. Each took a turn describing what he or she thought were the primary obligations of a romantic partner. We agreed upon mutual respect, showing kindness, providing support, reflectively listening, and many other sensible ideas. After we were finished, the consultant asked another question. "What if the answer was that it is your job to enjoy your partner? How do you think you are fulfilling that obligation?"

His notion differed from all of our ideas by some distance. His suggestion was fundamentally different. His was not an action aimed at trying to cause the other person to feel or experience something. His suggestion placed the onus of marital satisfaction on each of the partners. *It is not my job to make my partner happy; it is my job to find happiness.*

This idea flies in the face of most people's concept of marriage and what a committed-shared journey and relationship "should" look like. The idea that it is a spouse's job to make the partner happy is an almost ubiquitous idea in our society. The notion that happiness is one's own responsibility differs from the way we were raised. We were raised to think that when Mom was happy or proud of us, we had done something right or well. If Dad was anxious or disappointed, he would make that known to us in the hope that we would realize we were off track. In other words, we were raised to believe what others thought and felt about us was about us, that their joy and serenity were our responsibility. But this just isn't true. The old adage I mentioned earlier that says "you are only as happy as your least happy child" goes unchallenged, yet it is madness for everyone in that relationship. And it is this madness that leads us to look for a partner who can make us happy, who can give us the unreachable response we sought after from our parents.

A friend recently sent a video clip of the actor Will Smith talking about marriage and the evolution he and his wife, Jada Pinkett-Smith, have experienced. In it, he explains that you cannot make someone happy. That this project is impossible.

Whether or not a person is happy... is utterly out of your control. We came into this false romantic concept that somehow when we got married, that we would become one and what we realized is what we were two completely separate people on two completely separate individual journeys and that we were choosing to walk our separate journeys together. But her happiness was her responsibility and my happiness [was] my responsibility...we decided that we were going to find our individual, internal, private, separate joy and then we were going to present ourselves to the relationship and to each other already happy.

The worst part is that in the early phases of courtship and dating, we temporarily experience the elusive experience of making someone happy and them making us happy. Author Alain de Botton explains that success in marriage is something that is accomplished after the couple works through the early ideas of romantic love, "Compatibility is an achievement of love; it must not be its precondition."

THE TWO PROJECTS IN MARRIAGE

In many of our interactions, there are two projects. One is to tell the truth, no matter what. The problem is that many of us learned the cost of telling the truth: rejection, judgment, abandonment, loneliness, and being told early in our lives that (because sharing our truth made our parents or others feel inadequate) something was wrong with us. Our exploration into new relationships and risking our vulnerable *Self* is like the old Peanuts cartoon where Lucy convinces Charlie Brown to kick the football, assuring him that this time will be different. This time she will let him kick it. Of course, he is reluctant at first. Nothing in his experience tells him things will be different this time. But with his child like trust and optimism he eventually makes a go at the football. And, of course, like all the times in the past, Lucy pulls it at the last second and Charlie Brown falls on his back.

The other project is to be a safe person, as best we can. To be safe means we learn to respond to the *Other* with understanding or curiosity. This receiving of the *Other* is called *containing*. If we gasp with fright, frown with frustration, or retreat with disgust, we may justify those reactions as the reactions of a caring person only concerned with the well-being of the *Other*. But the truth is that those reactions are evidence of our lack of capacity and our inability to provide the *Other* with a safe person. There are several variations of this, many of which take on more subtle forms like fixing or telling people not to worry about it, but invariably they all tend to generate the same experience for the *Other*, "Oh, this person is not safe. I don't want to have to take care of them. I need someone who can be there for me. I will hide this part of myself and go and talk to someone who can listen."

To get out of this trap, each person must take responsibility for their own happiness. They must come to the marriage with an internal ability to be happy so when they show up for the *Other*, they can support them from a position of abundance rather than need. It is important to develop a network of resources so both partners can have their needs met when one partner is unable or unavailable to respond. When I talk about this idea to couples, one or both of the partners responds, "What? I didn't get married so that I can get my needs met by other people. What is the purpose of our marriage if I go outside of it to get my needs met?" The person asking this must be willing to deal with their fear of abandonment in order to change their approach. They worry that such a path will lead to separation and the dissolution of the marriage. When we embark on the journey toward our own differentiation, because such a process was never modeled for us, it will feel wrong. It will feel terrifying. Differentiation feels like a gulf to us because what was modeled for us, the soup we grew up in, was fusion. But in order to love, we have to learn to confront this fear and let go of the old ideas of what it means to be in a relationship with an *Other*.

I don't really know what other people "should do" nor do I give advice—I just know what has worked for me. Both my wife and I went to therapy for years before our separation, and we continued to go during our time apart, as well as after we reunited. Most of the work was in individual therapy, but there were some couples sessions. We don't go to therapy only in the context of a problem or a crisis. We both go to weekly therapy and we both believe we may never stop. It is not a problem-solving endeavor for me—it is just where I go to rediscover myself each week. For one hour every week, I am in a room where I am okay no matter what. I try to carry that feeling into the world, but it is hard for me to do, so I return each week to my therapist's office. These days, we rarely, if ever, have couples sessions, but a lot of work that happens in our individual therapy applies to our marriage. This is because the relationship problems with other people are just relationship problems with our selves.

For example, during our separation, we both went to a lot of individual therapy. We had the good fortune to have access to a talented therapist who had the capacity to see us both individually and as a couple. We also both went to a therapeutic intensive during this process (a week-long therapeutic experience that looks into your family-of-origin). When I completed my intensive, I didn't want to reconcile—that was not the problem nor was it the solution. The problem was that I wasn't living my authentic *Self* in the service of trying to make my wife happy. She was trying to control me because she thought by doing so, her anxiety could be resolved. This may be oversimplifying, but my work was on telling the truth more courageously and my wife's work was on being a safe person, and by that I mean her work was to take responsibility for her own happiness and not need me to be a certain way for her to feel okay and not anxious. The biggest takeaway for me in my work is that I have to tell her the truth no matter how she reacts. Prior to this realization, I was always trying to control her (I didn't think of it that way but that's what it was) by trying to make her happy so I could be okay (un-anxious).

A few years ago, I was finishing up my week's work in my home office on a Saturday afternoon. I had just finished leading a multi-day therapeutic intensive. It is satisfying work but requires significant emotional resources. As I filed the paperwork, my wife came into my office, "You have a second?"

"Sure. What's up?"

"I know you are probably exhausted and just got off work, but I want to talk to you about something. It's okay if you can't; I can call Dawn (her closest confidante) and talk to her, but I would prefer to talk to you if you have the energy," she said kindly and clearly. I could sense she was heavy with emotion.

This was the moment of truth for me. I could say "yes" and do my best to give her the attention and space that she needed. I wasn't sure the content of the issue, but I could tell it had some weight. I thought it is probably about me or the children. But there was a risk: I was exhausted, coming off an emotional week, and I would have limited energy. If I tried to be there for her, and the energy required was significant and more than I had available, we might end up in a fight. Even if I was able to make my way through it without leaking, I would probably feel resentful for having to hold space for her when obviously I was spent (something I thought she could see plainly enough, and she shouldn't be putting me in this position).

I could launch an offensive attack and shame her for asking something substantial of me after I had clearly just finished a significant work week. If I wanted to add some icing on the shame cake, I could mention that I was doing this work to provide for her and the kids. With this as my pedestal, I could accuse her of being selfish or needy or weak. "Do you really need me now? I could ask. "You're so insensitive. You know what I have just been through and you don't give me even one minute to unwind! You say you love me, but if you really did, you would give me a little more slack and some appreciation for what I do for the family. I feel like I do all of this alone!" In short, this would all amount to me saying, "You are a bad wife."

But in reality, she was just being herself. There was nothing wrong with her request nor was there anything wrong with her expectation that it was *my* job to take care of myself and say "no" when I am at my limit. She showed she was resourceful and capable of finding other sources of support when she needed more than I could give. She was not alone and was not threatening me with abandoning her if I needed to take care of myself.

I could say no and risk a fight like the ones we used to have. Many young couples have these kinds of fights, and they go something like this: "You know, you spend all of your time helping other people so that when you get home you have nothing left for us. I wonder what your clients would think if they saw how little you are able to give your wife and children while you preach having the capacity to love those closest to you." In plainer terms, she would be saying "You are a bad husband."

But we have worked hard on ourselves. I have worked hard on telling the truth and she has worked hard at tolerating it.

So, I took the risk to the tell the truth, "I think I am too spent. If you wouldn't mind, I would like to relax the rest of today. I should be rested enough that I can talk tomorrow."

And what did she do? First, she has worked hard to structure her life so that I am not the sole source of her comfort. I relish that role, but I cannot be solely responsible for providing her comfort and a listening ear. Her good friend Dawn, also a therapist, is an excellent listener. My wife's therapist is also a pillar in her life. And in past years when her life felt more unsettled, she also had a sponsor on whom she could rely.

Rather than turning me into the *bad object*, she warmly said, "I understand. Thanks for telling me the truth. Thanks for taking care of yourself. I will call Dawn, and if there is anything left over, and if you have the energy, we can talk about it tomorrow."

As she left my office, the significance of this interaction filled me with gratitude. We have worked very hard to change the project in our marriage and this was the fruit of that effort. When we do our work, we change the frame from turning the *Other* into something bad to seeing the *Other* as simply a human being.

When we do our work, we change the frame from turning the Other into something bad to seeing the Other as simply a human being.

I wasn't a bad husband; I was just a human husband with limited capacity. Often, one of the most vulnerable things for me to do is to admit something is beyond my capacity—especially when it is something in support of my wife or children. She wasn't a bad wife; she just needed something I couldn't give. Our work in therapy allows us to abandon the idea that was taught to us since birth, to let go of the notion of trying to be good. When we give up on trying to be good, we allow ourselves and others to just be a person. We learn to own our own feelings, such as inadequacy and insecurity. Rather than project them onto others to make them feel responsible and bad, we have a foundation that allows us to own them, sort through them, and integrate them into a whole self.

My wife and I call this kind of interaction an illustration of "Marriage 2.0." It is not perfect. It is a work in progress. But we have exchanged the old clichés, the old arguments, and the old software for a new project. The ongoing project is working out our issues with our selves rather than making the other person responsible for our sense of well-being, serenity, and our life's satisfaction.

No chapter can adequately discuss love or marriage or the parent-child relationship. The purpose here is to explore a few ideas that give a sense of what it means to be a *Self* and love an *Other* in the context of a marriage or a committed relationship. When we come to understand this, it can have an effect on all our relationships: our children, our partners, our friends, and our colleagues.

DIVORCE AS AN OPTION

When I work with couples who tell me that divorce is not an option, I respond by saying, "It has to be an option. If is not an option, there can be no love. If divorce is not an option, then you will spend your days beating on each other and demanding that the *Other* conform to your idea of what a husband or a wife should be. Divorce must be an option, or the two choices left are to serve out a prison sentence or for one of you to abandon yourself in the service of the union. But like all important life decisions, divorce is not the solution either. Neither is staying together." The solution is not in important life decisions. The solution is to find yourself, your truth, and your capacity; out of that comes all the important decisions.

The solution is not in important life decisions. The solution is to find yourself, your truth, and your capacity; out of that comes all the

Like with parenting, the seeds of our challenges are found in our history. It is so much easier to believe the problem and the solution is out there, outside of us, in the *Other*. Then we spend our focus and energy on trying to change the *Other* into something that fits what we think we deserve. We try to change them into the perfect parent we never had. We nag, plead, recruit, beg, intimidate, ignore, punish, or employ any manner of behaviors, including therapy and communication skills, to get our partner to change into something that will make us happy. We keep a ledger. Marriage becomes a constant battle of, "Who is right and who is wrong?" Spouses withhold sex because their partner doesn't listen or talk. Spouses cheat, either sexually or emotionally, justifying their behavior because their partner is cold and inattentive to their needs. Each partner punctuates the cycle, positioning the other's bad behavior as the cause, so that it justifies their position further. They retreat to their corners and the distance is either tolerated as a new normal or something brings it to a head where the couple dissolves the marriage or addresses the dynamics that have been present all along. Children, especially struggling children, can prolong this process since they provide the couple with a shared project—another person besides each other where the problems and the solutions are "out there."

The solution to improving your marriage is not in *what not to do*. It is easy to identify the problem and commit to not doing it again, but this will likely lead to a cycle of acting out, then feeling guilt and shame, and then acting out again. The solution is not...*don't yell, or don't lie, or don't nag, or don't cheat*. Those all come *from* the deeper work, the more profound project.

If you can learn to make happiness your project instead of making the problem out there and external, if you can learn to find yourself and tell the truth or learn to create a safe container for your partner by stretching, transforming and developing new eyes and new ears. If you are willing to look inward, then you have a chance of success. Couples therapy can help with this project as long as you are willing to look at yourself.

Often couples therapy is reduced to each partner trying to put the evidence on the table and build a case for the therapist, "If you can just change this idiot, all of *my*...excuse me, all of *our* problems will be solved." I am often asked if couples should go to therapy before they decide to separate or divorce. My answer is that the best time to start therapy was ten years ago. The second best time to start therapy is always now. I think couples could benefit from going to therapy long before there are any problems—even when they are in the early stages of romantic love. Couples therapy helps partners to share in the journey and build a common understanding of the landscape of how their wounds fit together. Shared language and tools can build a bridge between partners so each can come to a better understanding of the *Other's* dilemma. This understanding creates deep compassion and reduces reactivity since the *Other's* behavior is understood as an indication of who *they* are rather than who *we* are. Regardless of whether partners participate in couples sessions, individual therapy can be the foundation for a better relationship with anyone. You can be sure that the

Falling in love is profound when we can be ourselves in a relationship and who we are is tolerated, even welcomed.

work I do each week in my therapy is aimed at making me a better father, husband, friend, boss, or therapist.

Regardless of circumstances, separation, divorce, or staying together are not the solutions of the deepest issues at play. The solution is becoming a more authentic *Self* and being able to provide your partner with what they need to move forward on their journey (without sacrificing your core needs). That doesn't mean it will feel good along the way. Letting go will feel wrong and scary, but leaning on someone else (a therapist or sponsor) for what you need in the meantime can help. If partners change the project, they can create something that neither would ever want to lose. Falling in love is profound when we can be ourselves in a relationship and who we are is tolerated, even welcomed.

But if either partner is not allowed to be themselves, or if one of the partners requires the *Other* to be something they are not so that one partner is okay, the marriage may wilt and die. Authenticity, honesty, and being seen is compelling. Joseph Campbell explains,

I think one of the problems in marriage is that people don't realize what it is. They think it's a long love affair and it isn't. Marriage has nothing to do with being happy. It has to do with being transformed, and when the transformation is realized it is a magnificent experience. But you have to submit. You have to yield. You have to give. You can't just dictate.

In my phone, my wife's contact information used to read "My Everything." I thought that was the goal. I thought she was supposed to be my best friend, my partner, my lover, my confidant, my closest advisor, my therapist, my *everything*. We spent years trying to make this paradigm work for both of us. However, we both became angry, we both tried to control the *Other*, and we both retreated into shame. Then our deeper work really started. Thankfully, we both were willing to work to kill the old idea of marriage, the idea that is perpetuated in romantic comedies and in the stories our culture and our families tell us. At one point, I fell out of love and I thought it would never return. But in our separation, I discovered a more authentic version of myself and mustered the courage to tell her the truth. And she developed the capacity to hear it and see it, to hear me and see me. As a result, I fell back into love, into Marriage 2.0. I discovered when you find someone who can tolerate your truth, you never want to leave.

Kahlil Gibran explained it this way:

> *Let there be spaces in your togetherness, and let the winds of the heavens dance between you. Love one another but make not a bond of love: Let it rather be a moving sea between the shores of your souls.*

Now, if my wife calls and you look at my cell phone to see what name appears, you will see it reads "My Favorite Other."

CHAPTER SIX

KNOWING MENTAL HEALTH

"It took me awhile to figure out the difference between the staff and the patients in a mental hospital I worked in. And then it came to me. The staff have keys." Jami Gill

WHAT IS MENTAL HEALTH?

ONE OF THE REASONS WHY I WANT TO INCLUDE A CHAPTER as general as "mental health" is that we have so little experience with it. It is rare. Mental health and mental illness is a continuum and we are all on it. But we can imagine some ideal, and by imagining it, we have a sense of the depth and scope of our "work." In the distance between the ideal and where we are lies our work.

My wife had an exchange with her father recently over the phone. Her father is confined to a wheelchair and is not able to travel. His sister recently passed away and he felt great sadness that he could not attend her funeral service. He called my wife and asked her to go in his place. He suggested that she speak at the funeral and even offered some examples of the stories she might use. After some of this, I listened to my wife calmly explain, "I am not sure I feel comfortable doing that. I don't even know if I can go to the service. There are some things here at home with the kids that are pressing, and I am not sure I can get away. Also, I loved my aunt, but we really weren't that close." She held firm and remained calm. She told me later that her father was a bit flustered and seemed upset, initially putting up somewhat of a fight when she set this boundary. This wasn't the first time.

After she hung up, she told me, "You know, ten years ago, I don't know how I would have responded to that conversation, but I think I would have felt obligated to do it for my father. I would have been anxious and uncomfortable and wouldn't have been able to be so clear. At the very least, I would have been confused because I would have thought the right thing would be to do it for him, but I really wouldn't want to do what he was asking. I would have assumed I was the problem." We talked about how so many things like this simple exchange were a part of our childhoods. We couldn't hear the unspoken messages, so we think they weren't there, but as we grow and become more aware of mental health, boundaries, healthy relationships, and our own sense of *Self*, we hear them so clearly. Much of our abuse and trauma, the mental illness of our family and context growing up, is not overt abuse—it is much more subtle and therefore much more insidious. We only know that we develop a sense of "something is wrong with me" rather than understanding "something happened to me."

This is why, when a new client tells me they had an ideal childhood, I respond with "Therapy can fix that."

This is why, when a new client tells me they had an ideal childhood, I respond with "Therapy can fix that."

We look to our past, to our roots, not for excuses but for understanding. And when understanding is found, there is a grace that comes. We don't look back and get stuck there; we look back so we can move through it all. We look back so we can heal and live.

WOUNDS, DEFENSES AND DIAGNOSES

Some years ago, as a young man was enrolling in our wilderness therapy program, I scheduled separate calls with his parents. Jack, the father, was a successful businessman, a CEO for a Fortune 500 company. His ex-wife, Dana, was successful in her own right. She had a thriving acting and modeling career before the children were born and subsequently spent her time between parenting and philanthropic activities. Their only child, Jacob, was a 15-year-old suffering from anxiety and esteem issues. Jacob was bright, sensitive and prone to oscillating depression and anxiety. He struggled in school, often refusing to go or avoiding schoolwork to the point that he was asked to leave. He had been to several of the nation's top boarding schools and he was spending the summer at our program to see if he could return to a mainstream school or if he needed the additional support a therapeutic boarding school would provide.

From my first session with Jacob, I knew there was severe acrimony between his parents. They had divorced a few years prior after a high-conflict marriage. So, with this knowledge, I asked the office staff to schedule separate calls for the first week, and we would then go from there and later decide if I would hold joint calls with his parents.

Jack was my first call. He began by saying, "Jacob's mom, my ex-wife, is crazy. She is "Borderline" (Borderline Personality Disorder) and manipulative as hell. No matter how hard I try, she is able to turn a discussion into a fight. The divorce was hell, and, in the end, I gave her everything she asked for. It was either that, or she was going to use Jacob as a pawn. She was committed to hurting me and didn't care whether he was hurt in the process. I hope you are savvy. She is able to put on a good mask. I hope you're not fooled by her. Some therapists have been, but I have a report from one that confirms everything I am telling you." I listened without judgment to his description of his ex-wife. I could hear the pain, the helplessness, and the anger. Our first call was mostly about his ex-wife, although I was able to spend some time updating him about Jacob's first week.

A few hours later, it was Dana's turn. She said, "Some of my therapists have diagnosed Jacob's dad, or Jack, with Narcissism, but I think he is really a Sociopath. He can be charming and put on a good act. In his personal and work circles, he uses money to buy your agreement or at least your silence. He thought he could do that with our divorce. I think, in the end, he was hiding money. My lawyer told me he had never seen such a complex portfolio and wasn't even sure if all of it was legal, but I didn't want to go down that road or it would just hurt me. He is a womanizer, an alcoholic, a liar, and a cheat. Don't get fooled by him when you talk with him. Many have before."

"I already had my call with him," I told her.

"Were you able to see past his B.S.?" she asked. "Please tell me you saw it. Do you think he is a Narcissist or a Sociopath? I have a report from a psychologist that confirms what I am telling you."

"Well," I started, "I am not really thinking about it that way. I am inclined to see beneath the diagnosis. I know everyone has their defenses and patterns and when these patterns are organized, we call them diagnoses. But I prefer to see his woundedness." The brain is changed over time and it is said to have a chemical imbalance. We come with predispositions to these imbalances and our wounding or our attachments solidify chemical patterns over time. They become recorded with the chemistry and wiring in our brains. We use a diagnosis as a kind of short-hand to communicate the patterns the symptoms display. The idea can be stated simply with this flow chart.

Wounds, Defenses and Diagnoses			
Genetic Predispositions ⟶	Events, Wounds ⟶	Defenses, Coping Behaviors ⟶	Patterns become Diagnosis

My explanation seemed to satisfy her enough. As long as I wasn't buying what he was selling, she would trust me. I never read either of the reports that their psychologists provided to confirm the diagnoses, but those discussions crystalized for me some ideas on mental health and mental illness. In this way of thinking, compassion increases, and we are left to wonder, "Aren't we all innocent by reason of insanity?"

THE WALLS WE BUILD TO PROTECT US

Last summer, we sent my son on a wilderness and service adventure. Part of it was to get him outside and away from screen time, and part of it was to deal with the some of the anxiety he was battling. In the course of his 30-day experience, we were asked to exchange letters at the direction of his counselor. In the first letter, we were asked to share our hopes and intentions for sending him on this trip. Here is a passage from my wife's letter where she eloquently and generously acknowledged her contribution to some of the issues:

> *It's not lost on me...the irony that we sent you on this trip to have you remove some of the walls, some of the defenses, that you put in place to protect you from us and from how we hurt you.*

The walls we build to protect us from real or perceived threats shouldn't be ignored. These defenses are doing important work and the style in which they are organized begins to form a diagnosis. If these patterns reach certain levels, it can be categorized at a clinical level. When I teach, I often use this explanation to illustrate the idea of mental illness: "If you built a wall around yourself to protect you from threats, and someone approaches you with a hammer and chisel, a jackhammer, or any other tool used to break down walls, what would be your response?"

No one has ever gotten the answer to this question wrong. It is universally intuitive. "You would build the wall higher or thicker to reinforce it. You would run away for safety, or you would mount an offensive attack." However, when faced with the wall, instead of respecting it as the defense it is, we attack. We ram our weapons against people's walls. We try to shame them out of their defenses or intimidate them with consequences and we miss trying what we already know works in such situations: laying down our weapons of destruction, taking off our armor, and honoring the defense. That is, listening to the defense and showing compassion for it and the wound it is protecting.

In our efforts to break down the walls of those we care about, we tell ourselves it is for their own good. We call it love or caring. We tell them the walls they built to protect them have become their prison. Yet, no matter how we see things and what we call it, the walls they built are to protect them from threats. Our attempts to knock them down will only lead to the reinforcement of the defense.

A short time ago, my wife, also a therapist, entered my office and began to vent her frustration towards me and my recent co-parenting. When she entered my office, I was writing, so I was in a conceptual mindset. After her initial complaint, I responded calmly, "You are feeling inadequate and instead of owning it, you are projecting it onto me, and it won't stick to me. This is projective identification, and you know it." Regardless of the level of accuracy of my assessment, you might guess that this didn't deescalate the situation. It is so tempting to attack the defense, but when we do so, we also bear some responsibility for its subsequent reinforcement.

Many parents, therapists, partners, and friends are inclined to confront people who they feel need it. They imagine this as a valuable aspect of therapy and a quality of a good friend or partner. I have reflected on this idea of intimacy and the supposed value that confronting others on their stuff demonstrates some sign of closeness. The older I get and the more experience I have as a therapist, father, and husband, the more I see the value in honoring the defenses or the "stuff" rather than attacking it by calling it out.

I learned long ago the need to allow children their dignity. As a trained therapist working with adolescents, I once prided myself in my ability to cut through nonsense with surgical clarity. I thought it brave to point out my observations. I looked through the defenses and did not consider the experience on the other side of the equation. It took years for me to learn and to hear from my own children of the anger and even humiliation of that kind of experience. I thought that by cutting through things, I had found some sort of shortcut to honesty, awareness, and accountability. After hearing my own adult children talk about their experience of me as their father, I realized how cruel I have been with others.

In our efforts to break down the walls of those we care about, we tell ourselves it is for their own good. We call it love or caring. We tell them the walls they built to protect them have become their prison. Yet, no matter how we see things and what we call it, the walls they built are to protect them from threats.

I also learned from experiencing my therapist's patience and compassion. Things that I am sure were obvious to her—mistakes and defenses—were met with curiosity and understanding. If she gently offered an idea and it was met with a defense, she would back off effortlessly and wait for my ability to see it to develop. There were things she gently suggested 20 years ago that I rejected, that now are plainly obvious to me.

There is no great wisdom, no great secret in calling someone on something or confronting them. It is the easiest and crudest form that could be considered "helpful" in aiding someone to come to some awareness or epiphany. The real talent is listening in order to understand.

I would like to share two examples—or, more specifically, two mistakes—that illustrate how we can see someone's mental illness without contributing more shame or resistance.

I once worked with a young man, Nick, who was especially resistant to therapy. Nick was smart, savvy, and seemed capable of holding his emotional breath long enough to outlast anyone's patience. In my arrogance, I saw this as a challenge—I was going to crack him. I would try challenging him verbally as well as using behavioral consequences to smoke him out of the cave he was hiding in. Even as I write this, I shudder at missing the opportunity to consider why he was hiding.

I once prided myself in my ability to cut through nonsense with surgical clarity. I thought it brave to point out my observations. I looked through the defenses and did not consider the experience on the other side of the equation.

Our first several sessions led to confrontations with me sending Nick off to timeout. One time, while the parents of another boy were visiting our wilderness group, Nick laughed when the other boy made mention of a drunk blackout. Infuriated by this (mostly embarrassed in front of the parents who I was trying to impress), I yelled at Nick. "You think it's funny? He could have died! I don't want you in this group until you are willing to take it seriously. Take a seat over there by the tree. I will let you know when I am ready to talk to you and what you will have to do to earn your way back into the group." Later, Nick would tell me he was scared, but he was able to mask it well that day—the darkness of his cave hid everything from anyone poking around.

Nick's parents were some of the nicest people I have ever worked with. They were kind and conscientious, asking me for more and more assignments. They worried about Nick and his increasing isolation, his escalating drug use, and his cold, unending, silent anger. On my first call with them, just 24 hours into Nick's enrollment, they said, "Give us assignments and don't go easy on us. We are open. We love him and we will do whatever it takes to help him. We are not afraid of finding out we are a large part of the problem." This is in contrast to some families that want to keep an arm's length from their child's situation or fear any contribution to the issues because they see any connection as an excuse for their child's behavior. I thanked Nick's parents for their openness and willingness and encouraged them "not to work harder than their son."

As the first few weeks rolled by, I gave them updates on the progress, or lack thereof, and their son's exceptional capacity to emotionally stonewall the process. They felt validated. They shared that they had explored several options at a relatively young age, to find a way inside their son's mind, inside his struggle. In the search for answers to his mental illness, they had taken him to therapists for psychological tests, to family therapists, and had even had brain scans performed to see if they could literally use x-ray vision to look inside their son's head for answers, whether he was willing or not. They felt validated by my lack of success as they shared the several ways they had used to try to see behind the curtain.

As they told me this, particularly as they told me about the brain imaging, it hit me: Nick was trying to keep everyone out for a reason. His well-intending parents, rather than asking why, were simply pushing forward and violating his well-built defenses. He was keeping them out to maintain his sense of sovereignty. And his parents and I were trying to drill through his barriers without considering the reasons why he had created such formidable walls. I shared my realization with the parents. I told them I would apologize to Nick on my next visit. Since Nick hadn't written a letter in weeks, I told them to wait until my session and I would report back before they wrote their next letter.

I was excited to see Nick. I couldn't wait. When I arrived in the high desert that evening, I masked my excitement but selected Nick for the first session for the week. I told the staff that I wanted to meet with him alone rather than the usual procedure of having a staff member present. I didn't want an audience for this. I wanted Nick to feel my sincerity and not to wonder if I was performing for others.

We sat by the fire, flames flickering, and I turned to him. "I am sorry Nick. I have failed you. I have been unkind and arrogant." He looked up at me, his eyes moving from the ground where he usually stared. "It is my fault and I will do my best not to do it anymore. I talked with your parents during my weekly update call and they shared with me all the interventions and testing and even the brain scans. It seems that they, although framed in love and concern for your well-being, have been trying to get into your head for some time and I followed suit. I will not confront you. I will manage my frustration and anger. You don't even have to talk. I will need to keep some boundaries in place if you create an unsafe environment for the group, but it will not come from an angry place. If you want to talk, great. If not, we can just sit and enjoy the fire tonight. I am sorry. I wasn't considering why you had built such sturdy walls, but now I think I am starting to understand."

Nick's face relaxed and his eyes were wide and clear. We sat in silence for a few minutes before he said, "Why do you want to do this job?" Students usually never ask me that question. He was letting me in. I shared my motivation for getting into this work and told him it came from my own struggles as a child. I told him I was angry as a teenager too and it took years for someone to show me that my anger was justified. Mostly, they just told me to get rid of it.

In the weeks that followed, Nick opened up more and more. He continued to relax, and our relationship grew. His parents joined in, apologizing and acknowledging their mistakes—prying their way in without considering the cost. It wasn't perfect. He had some struggles, but we kept in contact for several years after he graduated from our program.

I reflected on the job of the therapist: it wasn't to fix this young man; it was to find him. I said, "Rather than fixing him, and there is a lot of pressure on you to do that, let's talk about what you can do. I think it is your job to find his story and tell it for him.

He finished high school, went to college and we have since lost touch. I try not to forget the lesson he taught me, though it can be difficult. People have their mental illness, their barriers, and their walls for good reasons. If we are to be of service, rather than ramming into those walls or using some sort of clinical acuity to see through their barriers and call them out, we would do well to listen and try to understand.

While in my own individual therapy session, I was sharing with my therapist the challenges in my marriage of the previous week. My therapist has a deep understanding of both my wife and me, and as she explored the landscape of my wife's behaviors, something came to me with a great clarity: to fall in love with someone is to fall in love with their dilemma. That means we understand them deeply, including their wounds and the ways they seek to protect those wounds. Jami taught me,

It is important to recognize the defense is doing important psychological work… Ripping away defenses does not improve the situation. Taking them away before the person is able to tolerate what the defenses masked leaves the person worse off than before… Both cruel people and inadequate therapists are famous for a desire to destroy defenses without considering the consequences.

If we have the ability to see anyone beyond their behaviors and their symptoms, they can be found. Our job, as therapists (and loved ones) is to try to see these most important things. If we are distracted by symptoms and behaviors, then those defenses are doing their job. For the job of a symptom is to mask, confuse, and distract from the wound—Jung's idea of the "legitimate suffering." For if the wound is discovered and unearthed, we are left to feel it and that can be an agonizing thing to bear.

Seeing with compassion past the defense to the *Self* gives the *Other* the *experience* of being okay. If we truly see a person, we will give them a sense of themselves. They will carry an internal copy of this throughout their lives. So many times, I hear my own therapist in my head, and she is telling me I am okay. Many of my clients have told me that they ask themselves, "What would Brad say here, in this situation?" If I have done my job well, they will imagine me communicating expressions filled with compassion and understanding until it is incorporated into their *Selves*.

In another example of a child struggling in our program and carrying deep and profound wounds, a therapist brought his case to the treatment team meeting. Like one of the previous examples, this young man had lost both of his parents. His grandparents and home therapist had enrolled him in our program several months prior and he demonstrated significant growth before his departure. After struggling for some time in another setting, he was reenrolled in our program in the hopes of capturing some of the previous magic. But this time did not go like the last time. The staff and peers were becoming exhausted by his inability to work within the expectations of the program and the group. They had tried all sorts of creative interventions, including an extended trip with two staff—we call this a "Walkabout"—where the focus would solely be on him and his needs. The Walkabout was temporarily successful, but his return to the group resulted in a return to chaos, turmoil, and conflict with others. The therapist was feeling the pressure to recreate the success he experienced in his first stay with us. The grandparents and the home therapist added weight to this by saying that they had never seen more growth at any point in time as they did during his last stay with us.

As I heard the therapist lay out the case and the challenge she faced under the weight of the countertransference (her feeling that she had to perform a miracle), I reflected on the job of the therapist: it wasn't to fix this young man; it was to find him. I said, "Rather than fixing him, and there is a lot of pressure on you to do that, let's talk about what you can do. I think it is your job to *find his story* and tell it for him. Tell it to the staff, to his peers, to his grandparents, and to his home therapist. If he can't tell his story, you tell it for him. And in this story, we will find two things. First, in his story, everything he is doing and has done will make perfect sense. In some context, no matter how crazy it seems, everything we do makes sense. Second, in his story, there will be requests from others. There will be things he needs from you, from the staff, from his peers, and from his grandparents. Each will decide whether they can give him what he is asking for, what his story tells us he needs, but in any event, it will be clear. That is the task. His story will explain why his first time with us was so successful and why this current time with us is so difficult. Hopefully, his story will also help to create an empathic response in those around him."

Mental health and illness are found in each of our stories. Shame and fear keep those stories hidden—shame is what our walls are made of. It is in a context where we feel safe that we manage enough courage to find and share our stories, and then they don't feel so crazy. They just feel like our stories.

In *Motivational Interviewing*, Miller and Rollnick lay out a model and the research behind it that helps us effectively find others' stories and thus to find healing. More than a gimmick or set of techniques, they describe "a way of being with people" that changes them. They suggest that our "purpose is to understand the life before you, to see the world through this person's eyes rather than superimposing your own vision." As we develop "accurate empathy, an active interest in an effort to understand the other's internal perspective, to see the world through her or his eyes," we invite others and their stories out in the sunlight to heal.

As I began my studies to become a therapist, I remember learning about the origins of human feelings, our cruelty, our *good* and our *evil*. I learned that "What we do to stay safe, wounds others." Could it be that simple and that beautiful? I remember thinking the explanations offered by our culture and by many religious traditions seemed to be inadequate and two dimensional. Those explanations also posited the problem as outside of us and that's why I think that version of things has such widespread appeal. The more I learned about what psychology taught us about what motivated us, the more compassion and understanding I developed for others and for myself. And unlike what many feared, my understanding and compassion for the cruelty that people could inflict on others didn't lead to an amoral ideology. On the contrary, it led to a morality rooted in love. And such an understanding of the origins of what drives us needn't rob anyone of their boundaries. We could, for example, understand the roots of mental illness, child abuse, or alcoholism and still respond with boundaries and limits. The difference is that these boundaries are rooted in love rather than judgment. They are rooted in the idea of *Self* rather than in the ideas of right and wrong.

Kahlil Gibran explained it so eloquently in his poem, "On Good and Evil,"

Of the good in you I can speak, but not of the evil.

For what is evil but good tortured by its own hunger and thirst? ...

You are good in countless ways, and you are not evil when you are not good...

In your longing for your giant self lies your goodness: and that longing is in all of you. But in some of you that longing is a torrent rushing with might to the sea, carrying the secrets of the hillsides and the songs of the forest.

And in others it is a flat stream...

Many times, I have been asked by clients to reconcile therapy and psychology with religious teachings. I do believe that the themes illuminated by the science of human behavior can be found and beautifully supported by religious stories, teachings, and scripture. Yet, in the end, I must answer that I am a therapist. My lens for looking at the work is psychology. I am not a priest, rabbi, cleric, or pastor. I am a therapist. My job is to understand why someone is doing something and to offer a compassionate reflection back to them and also to discover the scared person hiding in each one of us. This search and journey are painful and beautiful. If I have any success in this endeavor, I also get to witness walls crumble, revealing injured children who were lied to about their story and told to hide it because it was too much—too ugly or unacceptable.

As I was approaching the end of marriage with my first wife, I met with a clergy member. This was required as I attended a private university with a requirement that each attendee receive a letter of worthiness from an ecclesiastical leader. The Mormon bishop I met with asked me about my impending divorce and at one point said to me, "Your wife is a good woman. You know, because of this divorce, the sins of your children will be on your head."

I sat for a moment to consider his admonition. Then I responded, "Well, I guess that is okay, because my dad and mom were divorced, and my dad was not really there for me. So, I guess I will just pass those sins along to him." I wasn't being sarcastic or disrespectful. I was merely making a statement about the nature of things, the nature of intergenerational transmission of trauma and woundedness.

It is true that we pass on wounds. We hope to make small improvements and to end some cycles, but we do not escape denting our children in some capacity. I tell this to new parents all the time, to help them avoid the trap of needing to be good, thus dismissing their children's anger and hurt and requiring their children to be enlisted in the project of propping up the idea that they're good parents. In the book *Seeing in Intimacy and Psychotherapy*, the author states, "Of course no one has come from a perfect context—whatever that might be. Therefore, each person will have dents and bruises left over from earlier experiences. It is wise to consider all dents and bruises important and worthy of compassionate understanding."

The opening pages of *The Misery of the Good Child* reveal how these messages are passed from one generation to the next:

> *...all parents have limits. It is routine for us to discipline or punish our children when they exceed our limits. Unconsciously our goal in doing this is to get them to behave in ways we can more easily tolerate...[we] feel we are helping the child...The world...has limits, and the child needs to learn about these...The over the table message is "this is for your own good." The under the table message is "this is my limit; I can't go any farther." That is, the parent is being incapable...The child is likely to be puzzled if not frightened.*

That which is outside of a parent's bandwidth, experience, and sensibility is thought of by the child as wrong or bad. This is a survival instinct. Fitting within a parent's bandwidth ensures that the child is not abandoned, so the child represses the feeling, the thought, or the behavior to survive. The problem here is that the need that underlies the urge will mutate in the closet and become a darker mutation of itself. It will manifest itself in some way and at some time, often in the form of what we will call a mental illness—a pattern of preferred ways or styles of expressing oneself. This mental illness will cause pain to us and to those that love us and if treatment is sought, the primary endeavor of that treatment will be for all to learn to listen to what the disorder is trying to tell us. It is as if the child inside of us is burning the house down, to get some attention for the unmet needs beneath their shame.

The problem we come back to is shame. Shame is the sentinel that stands guard and prevents anyone from discovering the long, lost wound. We try to *hate* away our symptoms. We hate them in ourselves and others. Miller suggests the idea that therapists may cloak their disapproval and derision behind abstract terms like "borderline," "obsessive," "regression," or "destructive," but unless they are willing to explore the three-year-old person inside themselves, they may not see the parallel between these terms and garden variety contempt.

SHAME AND THERAPY

A few years ago, I was invited as a guest on a nationally syndicated radio show with my publisher, Judith Regan. It was her yearly "Thanksgiving Show," and she invited her "favorite" guests from that year to share her gratitude with them and offer them a platform to talk about Thanksgiving and gratitude. That fact that she considered me among her "favorite" guests could have offered me some security, but it didn't. Such an idea found little soil in my insecure *Self*. I planned my comments for the days and weeks leading up to the interview. I talked with peers and read articles on the subject. I was going to show up and show everyone that I wasn't worthless—that I had some value to add.

The day of the interview, my wife and I arrived at the Sirius XM studio in New York. As the other guests joined the pre-broadcast gathering, my insecurity blossomed. I was the only one not from New York and felt small among the group I saw as important people. Despite my anxiety, I did my best to mingle. I tried to meet as many of the guests as I could, and I made sure they knew that I belonged (although I didn't think so myself). I told stories, shared insights, and did my best to make an impression.

When it was time for my interview, Judith asked me a question about Thanksgiving and family. Her question didn't quite fit with what I had prepared, so I did my best to blend the idea I had planned to share with the question she asked. She asked me a follow-up question, and I did more of the same. Later, when listening to the recording of the show, I heard myself and cringed. I didn't answer her question at all, and although she tried to give me a second chance, I was nowhere close to being able to respond to her. I was too busy trying to impress her and everyone else with my wisdom.

As we left the studio, my wife gently asked, "What was that about?" I knew what she meant. I knew it was bad, and I didn't have any inclination to mount a defense. "You were a kind of a wreck in there. You interrupted people, kept talking about yourself, and you were telling stories that had nothing to do with what people were talking about." I felt humiliated. She was precisely right. Her observations resonated with my feelings, and my insides folded over on themselves in shame. I had made a fool of myself. The out-of-towner who didn't belong showed up in a way I despised: self-absorbed, narcissistic, and unable to see and hear others.

Two days later, in my therapist's office in Salt Lake City, I recounted the story. I felt the stinging sense of shame as I told her how I talked about myself and tried to prove to everyone in the room that I had something of value— that I *was* something of value. At one point during my recounting, I said to her, "I hate this about myself. I hate this trait. I hate it in myself and in others. I need to try to make sure I stop it before it starts. It is so ugly and repulsive." I looked at the floor. I didn't want to see her looking at me since I was sure she would reflect back the same distaste I was feeling for myself.

"What were you feeling underneath it all?" she gently asked.

"I was feeling small. I was feeling like I didn't belong," I answered.

"Maybe, instead of hating it, you could write about it. Maybe, instead of running away from it, you could lean into it. I bet if you did, people could relate to it."

I looked up at her, surprised with a spark of hope, as she encouraged me to look into the face of the monster rather than run from it as I had done my entire life. This story, this trait, was not foreign to me. It was my style, my preferred way of dealing with the sense that I wasn't enough. I had spent much of my adult life aware of the defense and spent a lot of energy despising it without much success in extinguishing it. Maybe I could try something different.

I wrote a blog post I titled "The Out-of-Towner: Feeling Small and Being Present," and in it, I told the story of that humiliating Sunday morning in the studio on the Avenue of the Americas in New York City. But instead of stopping at the feelings of shame and disgust for myself, I told about how inadequate I felt. I talked about how this might have originated in the story of my childhood and how it shows up in my adulthood from time to time. I talked about how I would try to recognize it when it came up in the future and hold that young, scared child with compassion instead of judgment for his attempt to solve the problem. It felt good to write about it. And I don't know how many people read it, but it felt better and more effective than despising the aspects of my mental illness.

Since then, the behaviors I exhibited that morning have not disappeared. What has happened is that when I notice myself feeling the need to impress someone, I look for and listen to the little boy inside me. He is well hidden, but I can feel him. I can see what he saw when he was growing up in Southern California to parents who were so overwhelmed by their own wounds that they had little capacity to offer him or his brothers much attention. I can see how he figured out that the only way he could get attention was to impress the adults with what he knew or with a joke. I can hold him and quiet him with my love and attention. Since I wrote that piece, his attempts to impress are quieter. Not silent, and not extinguished, but quieter.

It makes sense that we turn on ourselves, that we learn to hate the parts of ourselves that cause some problems. This is how others responded to us in our childhoods, so this is how we recognized the solution to the problem of pain. Our parents and others who told us they loved us told us that our problematic behaviors, our soul's attempt to signal to the world that we were hurting or that we needed something, were frightening, upsetting, or disturbing. They thought this was the solution, so we thought that too. And if we get lucky, like I did, and find a partner and a therapist who are willing to show something different, we begin to heal.

There is a place on the other side of shame. It is where you get to be loved just as you are. It is a place where you are not at war with yourself. It is a place where your *horrible, rotten Self* is allowed to be. It is a place unlike any other. And I promise, when you find it, you will want to bring everyone you love to that place. You will want to bring everyone in the world to it. You will want to spend the rest of your life loving as you have been loved. You will—because you are touched by the experience of such a place—care for everyone you meet in that same way.

To love yourself without limits is a terrifying prospect. This is what adequate therapy does for you. You may fear that if you allow yourself to be seen and loved in this way, you will become nothing, you will devolve into base pleasures, selfishness, and ruin. But my experience is just the opposite. Loving yourself, even those parts of you that hurt you and others, leads to more love. Loving yourself is where it all starts and leads to more love. It starts by healing you and leads to healing everyone you touch. This is why Maya Angelou encouraged us to choose love, "Because hate has not solved one problem in this world." But we were not shown this. We were shown to hate certain parts of ourselves.

Those who haven't experienced this will need some convincing and it will require patience to show it to them. Those who know this experience won't need it explained. And even though they may not have the words to express it, they feel it deeply.

KEEPING A SAFE DISTANCE FROM THE "DISTURBED"

First, we think of mental health and mental illness as a binary—two piles. You are either mentally ill or not. The binary construct serves to keep us at a comfortable distance from the truly mentally ill.

And while it is true that the manual we use to diagnose people spells out levels of acuity that allows us to diagnose someone, the fact is, as I have mentioned earlier, that mental health and mental illness is a continuum, and we are all on it. Yet most people find the idea of a continuum disturbing—I know I initially did. I remember the first time it occurred to me.

I was working at a clinic treating sex offenders. It was one of my first jobs out of graduate school and I entered it with some confidence. My thinking was, these clients are so sick, so beneath me, surely, I can help them. Certainly, I had something to offer them. I wasn't threatened by them because of our differences and the distance I saw between us. For the first few weeks, I was to shadow another therapist. My first night, I sat in on a group. The first directive from the lead therapist was for each of the men to introduce themselves to me, as I was the therapist that would be taking over the group. Included in their introduction, they were to give an honest and somewhat detailed account of the crime or crimes that landed them in the clinic. The lead therapist challenged a few of them, since he believed they glossed over some of the ugly and harsh details of their offenses. The process for me was a dramatic contrast from the kind of honesty I was used to.

One of the clients was graduating, after years in prison, to a half-way house, and then the intensive outpatient program where I was now working. He talked about a recent episode of going to get a blood test. He was in the waiting room, and a parent left her daughter unattended. Part of his parole included the provision that he was not to be within a certain distance of an unattended minor. If he was found, he would be in violation of his parole and could be sent back to prison. Conversely, his blood tests were required by law, and if he missed the appointment because he left the room, he would also be in violation of his parole. He had to decide quickly to reduce the risk, so he approached the check-in desk and called for a nurse. "I am a registered sex offender," he told them. "I cannot be in this room with an unattended minor, and I cannot miss my test. Is there somewhere else I can wait?" The other men in the group listened and they all talked about their shame and how hard it was to keep going.

By the end of the group, I was unnerved. I told myself I was better than them because I had never done anything close to what I heard them confess to, but I had also never been required to confront my shame with such raw honesty either. I wanted to focus on the fact that their crimes were heinous, but I couldn't stop thinking about how impressed I was with their courage. Even some of the details of their underlying insecurities and my own struggle with self-worth left me feeling a little too close to them—I saw a little too much of myself in them. I felt a lot more comfortable when I saw them as something else—something unlike me in every way.

To further illustrate how uncomfortable it is to see the similarities between yourself and someone guilty of such behaviors, when an outside supervisor was brought in for group supervision, his simple questions about our feelings towards the clients terrified all of us. The fear in the room during these discussions was palpable. We were comfortable talking about sex offenders, their behaviors, diagnoses, and our evidence-based interventions, but talking about our fear, frustration, anger, and compassion (therapists call these things countertransference) was too much for most of us to speak about.

We like to keep a safe distance between us and "the disturbed." Some time ago, I wrote an op-ed after one of the many mass shootings. I wrote about how, after each shooting, we hear the echoing incredulities from talk show hosts and panels, "Why? How could someone do this?" Yet the formula is fairly simple, and this simplicity may be the most terrifying aspect of our analysis and our reflections. I compared the mass shooting to Star Wars. A disenfranchised young man, feeling powerless and isolated, seeks retribution on those (or someone resembling those) who caused him harm. He wants others to feel how he feels, and this motivation, combined with access to weapons of mass destruction, leads to another heart-wrenching tragedy. I wrote,

> *People are going to see these Star Wars movies in record numbers, and these same people watch the news, hands wringing, and wonder how and why a child could enact such devastation in the real world. The reality is that our rhetorical cries of "Why?" are inauthentic—they are actually an attempt to shamefully accuse others of being fundamentally different and provide us a comfortable psychological distance.*

A courageous look into ourselves reveals the seeds of the traits of the clinically mentally ill. John Steinbeck remarked in *East of Eden*, "It would be absurd if we did not understand both angels and devils, since we invented them." This phenomenon plays out in graduate schools all across the country as psychology students study the various diagnoses and shudder to realize they have many of the same attributes. As we explore our inner landscapes, we discover more and more the similarities we share with the disturbed: perhaps it's a fight with a spouse where we abandon all reason and just want to win, or maybe it's the rage that suddenly arises when someone cuts us off on the freeway. I know I have been willing, when feeling hurt or threatened, to forfeit any reason in order to hurt someone who had hurt me—to make them feel what I feel. Although our crimes may pale in comparison to the atrocities we see on the news, the difference may be *quantitative* rather than *qualitative*—similar in kind but distinguished by the magnitude. As uncomfortable as this idea was for me on the first night in treating sex offenders, I could not escape it. Ever since then, when I settle into the comfort of imagining myself better than the client sitting across from me, I recall that terrifying moment sitting across from a sex offender where I saw the worst of myself in him and the best of him beyond my capacity.

The ability to see the similarity between us and *Others*, no matter how disturbed, is a powerful indicator of mental health. I once posted this idea on social media. "The fact that you think you don't need therapy is a powerful indicator that you need therapy."

A friend responded playfully to the post. "Since I know I need therapy, does that mean that I don't need it?"

"No," I replied, "that just means you don't need it as much as the others."

There are two primary courses to take when we encounter someone who seems so different or so much more depraved than us: first, we find what is in common between us. We find it because we have had the courage to look deeply inside of ourselves and realize there are fewer differences than we imagined. This course will require us to feel deep pain and to sort through a myriad of difficult and painful emotions. It is the hero's journey. It is heroic not because it is on a grand or public scale but because it requires great internal courage and capacity. The second course through this is to turn the other person into a monster. This requires very little capacity. We turn our hurt and our fear into anger and hate. This is what George Lucas was showing us when he bifurcated the world into the "force" and the "dark side" and explained it through the words he gave to Yoda: "Fear is the path to the dark side. Fear leads to anger. Anger leads to hate. Hate leads to suffering." And while we may consider the pain and hurt required by the heroic journey inward, it is nothing like the unhappy life lived when we use our anger to cover up our loss.

Furthermore, hate and rage are evidence of unresolved trauma. It is our unprocessed trauma that prevents us from being able to see other people and their humanness; forgiving and moving through it would be too painful, so we get stuck in a mindset of *us* and *them*. Trauma responses turn others into two dimensional beings; we paint others with one color, either good or evil. These days, the weight and scope of so much unhealed trauma has turned everything into a two-sided, borderline world.

LOVE IS MENTAL HEALTH

I have come to determine that the outcome of effective therapy is love for others and love for ourselves. Behind our fear, our shame, and our anger is love. We just need to find it. I remember listening to something on the radio when I was nine or ten, long before I considered therapy as a career. The voice on the radio said something like, "The danger of therapy and therapists is that the nature of it is amoral." What a horrible thing, I thought. Therapists were amoral, devoid of any sense of right and wrong, or of good and evil? I vowed to remember that and do my best to avoid such monsters. Then, I went to therapy. I went to college and something spoke to me. Something about this business of feelings spoke to me, and I switched my major from English Teaching to Family Sciences (and Psychology). And as I sat with sad boys, sad girls, sad mothers and fathers, I began to see that the problem was in their attempts not to feel and to believe there was a right way and that this was creating their shame and ensured their failure in the world.

Again, I refer to Rumi, the wonderful 13th century poet,

> *Out beyond ideas of wrongdoing*
> *and rightdoing there is a field.*
> *I'll meet you there.*

> *When the soul lies down in that grass*
> *the world is too full to talk about.*

This field has been the place where I have found God. This is the place where there is understanding instead of judgment, love instead of fear, grace instead of shame. It is in the rooms of AA or Al-Anon. It is

If I felt better, I would do better.

in my therapist's office; it is in the late-night talks with my wife. It is in my office and in the Utah and Oregon deserts or in a therapeutic lodge in the mountains of Park City, Utah. It is where one person takes the risk to tell the truth and the other person or people listen in order to understand rather than to fix. This is where the ideas of mental health and illness melt away and pain, sadness, and grief are given their voices. This is where we discover the vaccine that heals. It is the place where we come to learn that we are okay, and this makes all the difference in the world. It is everything, and when we find it, we never want to leave.

Maya Angelou is credited with the idea that when we know better, we will do better. The quote goes like this: "I did then what I knew how to do. Now that I know better, I do better." As wonderful as knowing is, all of us can relate to knowing the right thing to do and still struggling to do it. Those who have embarked on the path of self-help, therapy, and self-improvement will attest that knowing is part of a growth equation, but often, it's not enough to fuel or sustain change. In addition to knowing, I think it's *feeling* that's the key. Feeling freedom from shame and fear and a healthier relationship with our pain and sorrow—this is the key to doing better. With this in mind, the saying would go more like this:

If I felt better, I would do better.

And this new feeling leads to a better relationship with oneself which is the foundation upon which rests our relationship with everyone and everything else.

CHAPTER SEVEN

WHAT TO LOOK FOR IN A THERAPIST

"We learn how to be a therapist by practicing therapy. It's good for the therapist. But it's not good for the client."

EXPERIENCING THERAPY

WHAT CAN THE LESSONS FROM THERAPY TEACH US about our relationships with each other? What should one look for in a therapist? When I speak to communities about mental health and addiction, I often point out that I work on the front lines of mental illness and addiction, but the lessons learned there are also applicable for prevention and maintenance. Parents line up by the thousands to get advice and direction from experts when a child is struggling, but few seek out such advice when the child is young before the problems exist. They think their love and the lessons learned from the mistakes of their parents will be enough. Many say to me they wish they had heard the things I was teaching years ago.

My experience is that parents don't find these ideas relevant until there is a problem—until their old ways of thinking leads to a dead end. We approach life, marriage, and parenting our children with naive idealism. We approach our life and our relationships without the understanding of mental health and mental illness, because those around us were never able to teach us what they were. The lessons that help us repair our mental health issues can also inform us on how to prevent some of those same problems from occurring in the first place:

Repair and prevention require the same work and are based on the same concepts.

A colleague of mine, whom I worked with for nearly 20 years, would often take opportunities to pick my brain about issues he was struggling with and during our discussions I would encourage him to go to therapy. This suggestion was not an indictment on his mental health; it was merely a hope that he would invest enough to take care of himself in the way that only therapy can. After each suggestion, he would say, "I am a therapist. What can a therapist tell me that I don't already know? For that matter, what can a therapist tell me that you cannot?"

Like many, my friend had a fundamental misunderstanding of the healing mechanisms of therapy. He thought of it as a place where you gather information, tools, skills, insights and ideas. While those things happen in therapy, that is not what makes therapy unique from reading a good self-help book or listening to a great lecture on relationships or psychology. Skills, tools, ideas, and solutions can be discussed in therapy, but that is not the same experience of *being in therapy*. We can be told we are okay, but we must experience actually being okay by having someone reflect that back to us again and again.

The experience of therapy is sitting with another and risking the re-injury that our earliest context inflicted on us—the response that suggested that something with us was not right. The thing that differentiates therapy from those other experiences is the experience of sitting on the couch and telling your truth at the risk that the therapist will respond in a way similar to those in your past and recreate the feeling something is wrong with you, thus causing you to feel shame.

Therapists who respond to clients with an eagerness to fix or to change the client, hide behind a professional guise but provoke the same feeling of shame. This response is more insidious because it is hidden behind psychologically complex language and delivered from the throne of the therapist-expert. The therapist's eagerness to help may be internalized by the client the same way the mother's fear or frustration was by the young child: something is wrong with me.

When we really love someone, we may not want them to hurt. But, to truly be a safe haven—to hold space for someone who is suffering—we need to resist our urges to make them feel better. We need to allow their feelings— their pain, their suffering, their grief—to just be. We need to sit with them in their pain and be fully present in their experience. This is how we help them to move through it, integrate, and heal.

The one who is lucky enough to have this experience will tell you how powerfully it leads to transformation. If a therapist is capable of empathic resonance, the client will experience something other than what they might receive in the rest of the world: a sense that they are enough—not too much. What my colleague didn't *We can be told we are okay, but we must experience actually being okay by having someone reflect that back to us again and again.* know was that therapy (being the client, not the therapist) is an intense and personal experience. It is not uncommon for therapists to tell me they won't go to therapy because they are not sure it will help, but a little digging and it is really fear that prevents them. They are afraid of not knowing. They are afraid of what they might find. They are afraid to be vulnerable because when they have exposed themselves before it did not go very well.

Most of the therapists I have known during my training and my career become therapists without ever having their own therapy experience or without ever learning what it feels like to receive effective therapy. It is a long and slow experience that goes beyond the exchange of information. In many ways, I often observe that therapy begins after the client is tired of hearing themselves going over the same ground, telling the same stories, and lodging the same complaints. If a client chooses to stick with therapy after becoming sick of hearing themselves talk (fearing the therapist feels the same way), then therapy can begin.

In other words, the healing experience that comes from relating to an empathic *Other* begins. This experience launches the discovery of transformation from part-object to becoming the whole self.

YOU DON'T HAVE TO DO IT ALONE

There's a common toxic message about external validation suggesting we ought not to need it—that it is a weak person who seeks it. The fact is that external validation is necessary. The key is to find a source who values the authentic self rather than some part-object. Valuing part of us (like something we do or some talent we have) is the essence of the narcissistic wound. It is the wound of "not being seen." People may heap praise on us for what we do, but that is not real resonance. It leaves us feeling empty.

The fact is that external validation is necessary. The key is to find a source who values the authentic self rather than some part-object.

Our sense of self comes out of what our early caregivers thought and felt about us—how they held us in their mind. If that is true, we will recognize that repairing attachment wounds is a long, arduous process and requires some new experience of being seen and held with compassion by another. Jacob Moreno, the founder of psychodrama, is credited with this idea that we are wounded in relationships and thus we are healed in relationships. My two oldest children created a simple illustration to underscore the need to find healing in the presence of an empathic *Other*.

THE WORLD THAT TOLD ME THIS...

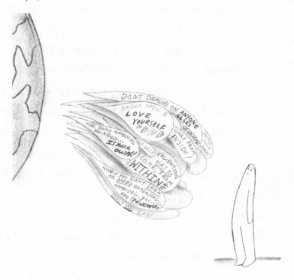

ALSO TOLD ME THIS...

$B U T \ \ IT \ \ WASN'T \ \ UNTIL \ \ THIS...$

$THAT \ \ I \ \ FELT \ \ THIS$

Healing happens in the same way the wounds happened—by participating in a relationship with an *Other*. When the wounds that we carry are created by our experiences, information alone will not suffice in restoring us to a sense of wholeness.

Many times, clients invite me to reveal what I see. "I can take it," they say. "I want the feedback. Tell me if you see something you think I don't see." If I take their requests at face value and offer an insight too early in the process, they will often respond, "You don't understand." When a therapist is too far in front of the client, the client will experience it as the therapist's misunderstanding. An interpretation made prematurely doesn't give enough attention to the context where defenses were created; it doesn't do enough to demonstrate understanding of the client's world. The tricky part is that the client will also feel misunderstood when a therapist truly doesn't understand the client. My daughter, a clinical psychologist in training, pushes it farther by pointing out that when a therapist makes an interpretation that doesn't resonate with the client, the therapist has made an inaccurate interpretation.

The therapist must remain curious and this quality requires the courage of not knowing.

Ironically, the most common confrontation I would offer new clients goes something like this: "I just want to understand. I know you might think if someone is tough on you and calls you on the carpet that it will be helpful, but I have found that seeking to understand you and whatever you find troubling is most effective in supporting long-term growth." The "seeing" that the therapist does must stem from love and compassion. The therapist must remain curious and this quality requires the courage of not knowing. An adequate therapist does see things that the client does not because they see the wound and respond to it with understanding and compassion, and the client may only know to judge the symptom that serves to protect and hide the wound. I remember that some of the early sessions with my own therapist included reflections and interpretations that didn't land. I even remember her making comments about my parents and thinking, "I haven't told you much about my parents. You could not possibly be correct about your interpretation of what they were like." Of course, years later, virtually everything she offered in the way of reflections and interpretations of me or my family are as plain as the proverbial nose on my face.

A therapist must possess the capacity to take in a client's story, metabolize it, and provide a new context in which to understand it. Years ago, I remember struggling to tell my therapist something which must have had a significant amount of shame associated with it. I don't remember the details, but it was probably a confession of a mistake I had made dozens of times before. While I struggled to share this with her, she sensed my resistance and said, "I am not sure you understand, Brad. You see, if you came in here and told me you wanted to have sex with a duck, I would assume you had a good reason and I would try to understand why." I laughed, but I also paused to consider what she said, and the wisdom of it hit me in waves. The example was ridiculous, but I understood the implication. This was not how my mother would have reacted, nor my wife, nor many of countless "well-intentioned" friends. This was something quite unique and precious. This space, this office, was a place "beyond right and wrongdoing" where I could just be me. The invitation to be myself was frightening. I was sure I would eventually exhaust her good will and patience, but to this day, despite my best efforts, she has not ceased to accept me and whatever nonsense I bring with me to our sessions, and this has made all the difference in the world.

There is no idea or story that can substitute for an experience. And experience takes time—years, in most cases—to undo the feeling that we are too much, not enough, or unacceptable in some way. Most people think their feelings of insecurity or inadequacy originated with them, that something in them was inherently broken. John Steinbeck wrote, "Well, every little boy thinks he invented sin. Virtue we think we learn, because we are told about it. But sin is our own designing." They were unable to recognize it when it was happening and so they cannot see that those feelings come from some fractured attachment. When a parent or other authority figure gets frustrated, exhausted, disappointed, or angry with a child, they have lost contact with that child. And what parent or authority figure hasn't discovered this limit in themselves? Unfortunately, for the child, they internalize those feelings as though something is wrong with them. This quote from author Shahidi Arabi powerfully illustrates this process,

> *A child that's being abused by its parents doesn't stop loving its parents, it stops loving itself.*

Thus, we need more than new information; *we must re-experience ourselves* in a different context to let go of the ideas we carry around inside that we internalized from our previous contexts, from the people that surrounded us in our childhood.

ATTACHMENT-BASED RESPONSES

Recently, a client was sharing with me that they get nervous in social situations, and as the anxiety builds, they find themselves rambling about tangential ideas. As they described this pattern to me, I asked them, "Do you ever feel that way in our discussions?"

Without hesitating, he answered, "No, because in here I cannot make a mistake." There it was. As a therapist, it is my greatest hope that I can provide a place where people feel safe. I have the same hope as a husband, father, and friend, but that is a taller order. In these more everyday roles, I trip and fall more often, due to my anxiety and limited differentiation, and have to go back over and over to apologize. Sometimes, I have to let my loved ones know that I may not be capable of providing them with a safe container and that they would be best helped by talking to someone else. Other times, I communicate this more subtly by stating some other need that I have at that time in order to opt out of the discussion.

What we are really talking about here are responses consistent with a securely attached parent-child relationship. Secure attachment provides the child with a sense of security and safety. With secure attachment the child's *Self* feels welcomed. If parents have the capacity and skills to provide secure attachment for a child, the child develops a stronger sense of themselves. But, in an age when anxious attachment is confused by love or euphemistically labeled as "loving too much," the child will be employed in taking on the parental anxiety at the cost of their own authentic self.

For practical purposes, I have composed a list of "dos" and "don'ts" to help us respond in ways that support the child, the spouse, the friend, or the *Other*, rather than unconsciously enlisting them in taking care of us. The statements themselves are not the gold, but these are what it might sound like if we were responding in a way that makes others feel safe, welcomed, and accepted. Providing a safe place must include our awareness and commitment to taking care of our own anxiety, even in the face of alarming information. Taking care of our anxiety does not mean that we ignore or repress it, nor does it mean that we avoid asking ourselves questions. Anxiety and fear can be a signal to explore options and change course, but we don't let those feelings drive the bus, nor do we hand them to the *Other* in the hopes that they will stop doing whatever it is that is *causing* us to worry or be upset.

This list offers practical examples of what safety looks like in response to the *Other*.

Emotionally Safe Responses

- Thank you for telling me.
- Tell me more.
- I appreciate knowing—glad you told me.
- Thanks.
- That sounds hard.
- I am sorry.
- I am here/listening

- You are not alone.
- That makes sense.
- Is there anything I can do?
- You must have a good reason...
  I would like to understand.
- What can I do to help support you?
- I can relate.

Here we see welcoming, curious, and encouraging responses. These responses can start as a practice but over time can develop into internal wisdom born from the experience that the most powerful way to create connection is to make sure others feel the spirit of invitation. The list illustrates the difference between compassionate responses where the other person is contained (provided a safe place to share), and anxious responses, which transfer feelings of fear or inadequacy from the listener *into* the one sharing.

The following responses range from overt discounting to more subtle responses that many might mistakenly consider helpful:

Emotionally Un-safe Responses

- That is silly/irrational/unreasonable/ stupid/ridiculous...
- You're overreacting.
- You're too sensitive.
- You are scaring me.
- You aren't fat; you look perfect.
- You are being selfish.
- You should...
- No, don't feel that way.
- Don't pay them any mind, they are just jealous.
- Ignore them.
- You'll get over it.
- Look on the bright side.
- Why did you do that?
- Have you tried....?
- That is your "depression/ insecurity/anxiety/narcissism..."
- That is your "defense/ rationalization/justification..."
- You've misunderstood or misinterpreted me.
- Let me explain my intention.

Suggesting that one "look on the bright side" or suggesting solutions may seem like they come from a place of love, but just beneath the surface lurks the intention of fixing the "problem" to ease the anxiety the helper feels rather than understanding and offering a context where the *Other* can discover their *own* solutions, which is a key to the development of *Self*.

When I do deep family-of-origin work with clients, many dismiss the statements and actions of parents and others with the adage, "But, I know they had good intentions. I know they loved me." I gently challenge them and suggest that is not the case. When people respond in dismissive ways like those outlined above, it is meant to erase our feelings and protect the one with supposed good intentions from difficult feelings. The *intention* is to protect the person offering help from their feelings of anxiety, inadequacy, or empathic misery. And while it is not a mortal sin to want to protect oneself from such feelings, in no way is this the "best of intentions."

The first list provides the person sharing with compassion and an invitation to share their feelings. The latter list is how feelings, ideas, and struggles are often met, leaving the person sharing with shame and unintentionally causing them to retreat and go into hiding. We employ the second list of bulleted responses because we don't have to own our lack of capacity. We simply shape the other person to fit within our bandwidth. These responses require very little of the listener, which is why they are so appealing. If we can control others, we don't have to work through our own issues. The responses from the first list mean that we have to tolerate uncomfortable feelings and uncertainty. The irony is that when we welcome feelings, others are more able to move through them. When we stifle feelings, they are more likely to go underground or fixate. And in *The Knight in Rusty Armor,* the knight warned of the danger of our unfelt feelings when he concluded, "I nearly died from all the tears I left unshed."

The roles of therapist, parent, spouse, and friend differ in many ways, but the larger brush strokes are similar. In my own work and in my observations of friends and colleagues, the parallel between the way we treat clients and others follow along similar lines. This is because both are rooted in the landscape of our personal anxiety. Both are rooted in our underlying belief that we think it is our job to fix another person—this is really the want for the *Other* to change so we feel better. This need for others to change or be fixed is rooted in the limitation of our ability to tolerate our empathic pain. Most likely it was modeled to us in our family-of-origin in countless and imperceptible examples. If our parents modeled differentiation, then that is the soup we were cooked in and we establish relationships based on that example of intimacy. To the extent our parents lacked differentiation and taught, through example, that family members were responsible for each other's feelings (whether it is upset, sadness, worry, happiness, or pride), then that was the air we breathed, and we look and create relationships based on that level of relational proximity referred to as enmeshment or codependency.

An adequate therapist will not duplicate the behaviors of our earlier contexts—those responses from our parents, teachers, and childhood peers. An adequate therapist will not express (or may not even feel) their disappointment, frustration, or anger at our failures, struggles, and misguided decisions. Adequate therapists hold the client in such a way that the client experiences themselves as enough and okay. Compassion, patience, and curiosity are the hallmarks of adequate holding. Anxiety, anger, frustration, disappointment, fear, agitation, and even an eagerness to fix, are all signs of the therapist's countertransference and need some attention. Because they are human, when an adequate therapist experiences any of these feelings, they can seek supervision or if the problem persists, they refer the client to someone better suited and more capable of helping a particular client. The therapist's feelings can be helpful and diagnostic, but they can also cause the therapist to lose contact with the client, which often results in shame.

Therapy is the unique context that allows us to see things that were previously invisible to us. Like the fish who is the last to discover water, we must experience something other than what we have known to be able to see clearly where we have been. Therapists who bump up against their inevitable limitations can retreat to their practice of self-care or consultation with a supervisor in order to return and be able to provide a better container for the client the next time.

THE MYTH OF THE GURU THERAPIST

Graduate schools and professors arm their students with the latest theories and research in the field of mental health. This can lead to a misunderstanding for young therapists that the key ingredient in therapy are these concepts and tools. My daughter Emma has worked alongside me in running therapeutic intensives for the last several years. Just prior to her first year in graduate school to become a clinical psychologist, we were reviewing a recent case and some of the mistakes I had made. I was letting her know about the importance of the therapist owning his or her issues and feelings and that by doing so, you can improve your ability to provide clients what they need—the safe container. Owning your own feelings unlocks the door for connection.

I told her, "You may not hear much about this in graduate school. At least, they didn't talk about it to me during my training."

"Why?" she wondered. "I think it should be the first thing they talk about."

"Why do you think?" I asked. She had spent enough time with me reviewing cases to see how difficult it was, how much vulnerability was required.

"Because they haven't done their own therapeutic work," she answered.

I told her it was some form of that. Perhaps professors have not been to therapy and done their own work, but at the very least most have not seen it done before. Adequate therapy (that is the highest praise I can attribute to a therapist) is not about the theory or the techniques. Adequate therapists have a strong sense of their own inadequacies or limitations and that usually requires a great deal of work. Only with this sense can they provide clients with the safe space and compassion needed to heal. Only with this sense can they find the client, rather than trying to fix the client.

In contrast to the adequate therapist, let us consider the Guru-Therapist. Socrates taught by asking questions. He placed great value not on imparting wisdom but on teaching people how to think and asking them questions rather than answering their questions. An assumption in our culture is that therapists possess wisdom and this wisdom can be dispensed for an hourly fee. While this assumption doesn't pose a great problem if held by the client—in fact, it is often the assumption that leads clients into therapy—this idea can be very harmful if the therapist believes it. When I am asked how I will approach a specific case or client, the question doesn't make sense to me because *therapy is something you create with your client rather than something you do to your client.* The process is much richer than the dissemination of information, skills, or insight. Therapy is a way of being with a person that changes them at a much more fundamental level.

And if we borrow from the Socratic method of teaching, the person posing the questions is the teacher—the one answering the questions is the student. Some therapists take the position that they are good people and their well-lived, happy, and successful lives are proof. "I have a good life. If you want what I have, do what I do. Follow me and your life will be as happy as mine." In my work with young people, I see this trapping often. The young people with whom I work are clearly suffering and struggling. Therapists in my field often see their role as a guide to show their clients the way to avoid pitfalls, detours, and errors. Like many, they ignore the fact that most of their learned wisdom came from the same mistakes they are trying to help their clients avoid. Gill explains it this way:

> *The therapist or guide we choose must not duplicate the wounds of the past. Thus, if the therapist or guide knows what is right for us and manipulates us to achieve these "treatment goals," it is abuse, plain and simple. It is hard to see how good abuse ever cures bad abuse.*

If therapy is not problem-solving or advice-giving, then what is it? Recently, during a presentation I was giving to colleagues on codependency and co-participation with an addict, a therapist asked how to respond to a client who says, "If I kick my son or daughter out of the house, they could die. At least if they are home, I can keep watch and make sure they are safe."

That therapist's question reveals the problem. Somewhere, from you or from someone else, they are hearing the solution to the problem is to "kick the child out of the house." However, the problem isn't in letting the child live with them or not. That can be evidence of the problem, but the problem itself is the nature of the relationship—first with themselves and then with their child. You cannot solve the problem by kicking the kid out, although that decision may arrive when the *nature* of the relationship changes. Thus, the solution is not what you say or do but is more how you are with the *Other*.

The solution is to work through and heal the codependency (or fractured attachment) and the client can make the decision that feels right to them at that point. The work is to explore the client's ideas about relationships, their notions of cause and effect, of intimacy and connection, and of love and control. Out of the exploration and out of those truths will emerge the "right" decision or *the client's decision.*

Therapists who see themselves as the oracle are the most dangerous of all. Their judgments are insidious because they are cloaked behind a façade of good intentions and dressed in graduate school terminology. Someone asked me during a talk what method I use to find good therapists. I said I look for therapists who don't know everything and spend less time trying to show me what they know and more time being curious about what they don't know. Phrases like "evidence-based" and "the research suggests" are their deities and they take pride in citing experts and studies. They have a list of skills at the ready and refer to the manual. They usually identify themselves with formal classifying designations like "Cognitive Behavioral Therapists" or are certified in Dialectical Behavioral Therapy. I am not suggesting that these models have no value; every therapist relies on research, theories and models. The difference is that the guru hides behind their theory and allows the theory to eclipse the client. They have specific measures that determine when a client is better or even when a client's work in therapy is done and they have "graduated."

The real guru is the one who embraces not-knowing. They find being wrong easy. When a client expresses frustration, hurt or disappointment with something they said in therapy, the real guru welcomes and celebrates such a disclosure. They are comfortable enough with themselves that their not knowing allows them to focus on the client rather than establishing themselves as the expert. A real guru asks more questions and gives fewer answers. The real guru learns while they are teaching because the real discovery is of the *Other* in the session. The real guru finds no comfort as being seen as being a guru and in fact discourages it. When I sometimes still ask my therapist what I "should" do, she's famous for jokingly saying, "You are asking me? Well, I do have some important thoughts about Texas." Adequate therapists recognize when the client idealizes them and sees this for what it is: the client's projection of the wisest and most beautiful parts of themselves.

PROBLEM-SOLVING THERAPY

The goals of problem-solving in therapy arise out of experiencing the client's suffering and the need for the therapist to be helpful. This enterprise is further supported by managed care and insurance companies. The most common questions that bring clients into therapy start with the phrase, "What should I do...?" However, no therapist can adequately answer this question. The question is akin to asking someone, "Should I turn left or right at the intersection?" without knowing where that person is going. In addition, many of life's choices have such profound implications and consequences that it's written in therapists' ethical codes that "clients have the responsibility to make decisions" when it comes to matters of importance.

When clients ask for guidance about decisions, I often remind them, "The answer is not what to do, but what do you want? What is your *truth?* This answer lies in you. Sometimes, these are the hardest questions to answer because we have so little experience with knowing our truth." What we decide does not solve the core issue, but our decisions come out of our understanding of our truth. This way of seeing things relieves pressure from believing that every decision is critical to our well-being and places the emphasis on the lifelong task of finding one's *Self.*

Winnicott's idea of the false *Self* may suggest that the false *Self* brings the real *Self* into therapy. That is to say, that what therapy is in the beginning—a search for answers to what one should do—becomes something different in the end: a search for the real *Self.* We enter therapy to deal with a struggling child or difficulties in marriage, and if we stay with it long enough, we come to realize that the real question is a question about *Self*. As we change our course to finding our center, we realize all relationships are affected by this cornerstone notion of *Self*. As it is with enlightenment, the discovery of *Self* is a destructive process when we unlearn and cast off those ideas and influences that prevent us from knowing.

In the process of hosting family therapy retreats, it is often the case that parents bring in a child struggling with some mental health or addiction issues. The child is usually reluctant to embark on a retreat that lasts several days, but at the insistence of the parent or through some leverage the parent is able to get the child to participate. As the therapy progresses, two dynamics typically emerge. First, the child finds an ally and their voice. They are able, because the therapist asks the parents to listen, to give voice to their concerns. Anger, sadness, hopelessness, self-hate, grief, or fear all are given their time on the stage. The child feels safe and often expresses a reluctance to leave by the end of the experience. They feel safe and heard, and many voice worries that once they're back home, the focus will be, as usual, on them as the identified patient, and their symptoms will be the focus of concern.

The second dynamic that regularly occurs in a successful intervention is that the parent realizes they have a new project—themselves. They realize that their anxiety and fears, their serenity, is their responsibility. They get an understanding that some of the child's problems arose because the child had no safe outlet to express the pain; anger, acting-out, self-medicating, lying, or depression was a last resort. And if they address this new project and have some success with it, then their interactions with their child will be in the service of supporting the child instead of managing the child's behavior so that the parent can feel better.

In couples retreats or couples therapy, the unspoken wish is for the therapist to "fix my partner so I can be happy in this relationship." There is often a dynamic where one is seeking intimacy. They do this by sharing feelings and asking questions, and they are usually the one who initiates therapy or the therapeutic retreat. The other one is the manager responsible for saying and doing the things that will please the pursuer. This partner is the reluctant participant in therapy. They don't have overt complaints about the relationship, for if they did, it would create waves and they would eventually be required to eat their words to keep the peace. But what they both initially think is the solution (or the problem) eventually evolves into something quite different by the end of the experience.

The first person—the one seeking intimacy—learns to listen and comes to understand what they do that creates a lack of safety for their partner. Instead of demanding or asking probing questions, they must listen to disagreeable descriptions of the relationship. Anger, anxiety, and endless conversations that require consensus shift to gentle questioning and listening. They must have an intellectually honest curiosity. Listening must happen without judgment and without retort. One must empty one's mind in this sort of listening to encourage their partner.

As for the second partner, their task becomes to tell their truth—regardless of consequences or reaction. They must abandon the task of managing and taking responsibility for their partner's feelings and reactions. While the project for the first partner is to create a safe container (a safe place to share), the project for the second partner is to tell the truth, and they both enter therapy with the other's project in mind. The pursuer is trying to dig into their partner without considering the risk their partner experiences, and the *Other* is trying to make their partner happy without considering what they need or what will make themselves happy in the long run. Both are trying to control the other.

The above examples represent how what we initially think therapy will be *changes* as we progress. We must have some confidence that the therapist is capable of helping, and an adequate therapist will encourage the client to understand that the problem before them isn't the problem—the problem is the way they were taught and shown how to be in the world and in relationship to others. This will be made clear as the therapist models, reflects back, and reinforces each time the client makes contact with the giant *Self* that lies hidden. The therapist will not offer their solutions but will help the client to discover their solutions. The client will come to learn that the expert is inside of them buried beneath the voices of the supposedly well-meaning and self-proclaimed authority figures of their past.

FIND A THERAPIST WHO CAN FIND YOU

A colleague of mine once shared a story of a client who came to therapy with one request: they wanted to sit in session and text instead of the usual oral dialogue. He presented this case to a group of therapists and asked for their thoughts. Several therapists shared their interpretations and diagnoses, and several offered suggestions for treatment approaches to correct the client's ill-conceived avoidance impulses. After listening to suggestions, the therapist shared his approach, which was simply to allow the texting without judgment and without qualification. For several sessions, the client sat on the couch and texted his thoughts to the therapist and he then responded via text. Eventually, without fanfare, the client spoke. In a profound way, I think this client did well to ensure that the therapist was capable of abandoning his agenda with the goal of finding the client.

Another story was told to me regarding the first meeting between a young adult client and a therapist. The young man said that his wife and family told him he needed therapy. The therapist asked him what he thought and what he wanted, and the young man answered, "I want to be a director. I want to make movies."

The therapist replied, "Okay. Let's work on that."

Therapy is not supposed to satisfy the needs of the therapist. The deal in therapy is the client pays for the therapist's time—end of deal. The client owes nothing else to the therapist. Sure, therapists are allowed to terminate therapy if they find the experience distasteful or abusive, but such termination is in the service of the therapist taking good care of themselves. Inversely, if the therapist is unable to give the client what the client desires, then the client is well-served to terminate the relationship.

Therapy ought not serve the therapist's need to be a good therapist. The need to be "good" gets in the way of being real and present and serves the ego of the therapist. The client can sense this need and will internalize it the same way a child internalizes the parent's need to be good—they will sense the pressure to show up in such a way as to take care of the therapist and consider hiding the parts of the *Self* that present a threat. A good parent or a good spouse will find the need to defend their position at all costs and leave no alternative except that the *Other* must take on the badness: "If I am upset at a good parent or a good spouse, the problem must be me and my feelings."

Any theory or therapist that does not consider the client's impulse to try to please the therapist or make the therapist feel good is inadequate. Compliance in therapy is one of the most common forms of resistance and it is a blind spot for many therapists.

This need to be good will require the client makes progress to provide evidence that the therapist is good at their craft. Ideally, the therapist doesn't need clients to "get better." Of course, no therapist can be unconditionally loving and endlessly patient. When a therapist does experience these limitations, or if a client has the audacity to share with the therapist some hurt or frustration with the therapy, the adequate therapist will issue a sincere apology. A therapist acknowledging a mistake or an offense to a client is one of the sure signs you have an adequate therapist. Many therapists will choose the alternative, the protection of ego, by showing the client how their pathology, not the therapist's misstep, caused the injury. Even further, many therapists suggest that if it hurts, if there is an offense, that is a sign that the therapist is onto something.

A client of mine recently shared that he had a conjoint session with his husband's therapist. At one point during the session, my client shared some disagreeable feelings about the therapist, saying something courageous and benign like, "I don't like this thing you are saying. It makes me feel *this*." Rather than responding from a place of capacity, the therapist went on to explain to my client why his interpretation was off. My client responded by saying, "You're doing it again." The therapist held her ground and explained more authoritatively how the interpretation was off and how it was due to some character flaw in my client. "You just did it again," he told her. The therapist fought back yet again, and my client decided it was not worth his time to help the therapist anymore and waited for the session to be over.

If your therapist is able to respond to you in a different way, in a way the demonstrates capacity instead of insecurity, then you begin to understand others' reactions are not about you. So often in our past people have responded to us and our feelings with angst and frustration. So often, they make the problem about us. But if you have a therapist who is capable, then you begin to consider that who you are and what you feel is okay. And with that sense you can go out in the world and can be yourself with some courage and confidence.

Therapists, like all other humans, have feelings of inadequacy. Left untreated, they run the risk of using therapy to prove their value to the world. This need will cause great harm to their clients. Such therapists need to be "right" or "good," and any information or interaction that suggests otherwise will be rejected and put back on the client. The ability to apologize for missing something or hurting a client is one of the hallmarks of an adequate therapist.

This brings me to an important and often unseen concept. It is easy to go to therapy and talk about other people: friends, partners, children. The courageous and risky endeavor is to talk to the therapist about your experience and relationship with them. It is precarious because you are relying on the therapist's fundamental capacities as a container. An adequate therapist will listen, understand, and apologize. And an inadequate therapist will spin your experience to reflect your inadequacy. This idea can also be carried into marriage and parenting (we will talk more about that in the last chapter under the concept of "learning to lose").

Many in the business of treating mental illness and addiction issues struggle to know how to do it, often because they have little personal experience with it. They don't recognize their inadequacy when it presents itself, but rather they have the experience that they are frustrated or disappointed with clients. When the client is unable to adjust or make acceptable progress or show up in a way the therapist deems acceptable, they describe the client as "borderline," "narcissistic," "sociopathic," or "beyond help." While surely there are people that are limited in their ability to transform or demonstrate progress, severe diagnoses of a client can mask the therapist's feelings of inadequacy.

Therapists are well-armed with terminology that allows them to avoid dealing with their own feelings of inadequacy and their own limitations. They blame the lack of progress on client "resistance," but I often point out that it takes very little skill or even knowledge to point out pathology or diagnoses. *Therapy is treating resistance*—it is what we do. And if we encounter resistance, we would be wise to see if our approach has something to do with it. Recently I heard my friend and colleague Harriet Lerner give a talk on shame—the primary energy fueling resistance. After her prepared talk, the host asked her a few questions from the audience and started with this one: "How do you deal with shame in therapy?"

Dr. Lerner paused for a moment and said plainly, "I think you are just asking me how I do therapy."

Even graduating a client from therapy, deeming them "fixed," can lead to some shame in the client. When a therapist initiates termination of therapy under the guise of graduation, it can also be a signal of the therapist's inadequacy. That is, "I don't know what to do or how to be helpful if there isn't a crisis or a problem to solve." They transfer this feeling of inadequacy onto the client, and while the words seem to suggest the client is "better," the client may walk away feeling confused, unwanted, or ashamed. It is not in the therapist's purview to decide when a client is done with therapy. Many clients have shared with me their confusion, hurt, and shame at being "graduated" by a previous therapist under this guise. I tell them how sorry I am and that the shame they carried away was the therapist's shame.

When a therapist becomes frustrated or disappointed with a client, they have lost contact with them. When we can truly see the *Other*, we won't feel disappointed. Abraham Lincoln said it simply about one of his acquaintances: "I do not like that man. I must get to know him." When people ask me what to look for in a therapist, I simply say, "look for a therapist who looks for you."

This person must be able to consider their own limitations, and this will likely come out of their own work. Look for someone who celebrates a discussion about how you are not getting the type of support and help from them or how hurt or frustrated you may have felt in a relationship with them. You know you are struggling with a therapist who is working through their own narcissistic wounds when they defend their actions and turn it back on you.

There is no talent in calling people on their stuff—first-semester graduate students can do that. When therapists confront clients, they are not providing them with the honor their defenses deserve. Therapy is not a place where we go to **hear** difficult things, but rather a place we go to **share** difficult things because we do so at the risk of experiencing responses that replicate past injuries and abuses.

Identifying somebody's defense takes very little talent or knowledge. Learning how to be with somebody so they don't require the defense (because they don't feel threatened) is what makes therapy unique.

If the therapist is not learning as much from the client as the client is learning from the therapist, then they are doing it wrong. Therapy requires the therapist to grow, transform, and surrender over and over again. It asks the therapist to feel and to work through their wounds and discover their real *Self*. The real *Self* is the basis for any relationship with the *Other*.

Being a therapist is an honor and a gift. Listening to people share their wounds, their fears, and their vulnerabilities as they consider sharing their real *Selves* with me at the risk of receiving the same response they received in previous contexts results in a swelling of love and respect for their courage and a desire to honor the found child inside of them.

A couple of years ago, I was attending a conference on attachment theory that my own therapist also happened to be attending. This experience afforded me the rare opportunity to sit with her during lunch and breaks and have a more casual back and forth conversation. During one afternoon lunch break, after talking about some of the presenters, she asked me, "What was it in your therapy work that made the biggest difference? Was there a moment when it clicked for you?"

I recounted a few critical and memorable experiences, including the duck-sex example, and she listened and nodded. I then turned the question back on her. "What about you? When did it click for you in your own therapy?"

She paused for a moment and then spoke. "I was in analysis twice. Once for eight years and once for ten. I went as often as I could afford. Somewhere around the eighth year of the second analysis, towards the end of one session, I said to my analyst, 'I can't understand how you can tolerate me.'"

"What did she say?" I asked.

"She said, 'That sounds like something we should talk about for a bit.'" Her face was soft with a half-smile as she recounted this story.

As I looked across the table at her, chills ran up my spine and I could feel tears in my eyes. I agreed. "It is almost unthinkable, isn't it? It is unfathomable to imagine someone can tolerate who we are."

She nodded. "Isn't it?"

We both sat there basking in the idea—more than the idea, really—in the *memory* of the experience of being seen by someone. It is hard to teach this idea to others, hard to impart it to new therapists. It is an experience that must be had for one to know it. But once it happens, it makes all the difference in the world. It changes you on a fundamental level. This kind of therapeutic context begins to melt away all the self-doubt, the confusion, the fear, and the shame. In its place, the seed begins to grow. "What if I am okay? What if who I am is okay? What could that mean? How would I treat others?" The answer, of course, is we would treat

Identifying somebody's defense takes very little talent or knowledge. Learning how to be with somebody so they don't require the defense (because they don't feel threatened) is what makes therapy unique.

them with the love and compassion that had also been afforded us. Their darkness would not frighten or disgust us because we will have made peace with and seen a similar darkness in ourselves.

Carl Rogers taught,

> *When a person realizes he has been deeply heard, his eyes moisten. I think in some real sense he is weeping for joy. It is as though he were saying, "Thank God, someone hears me. Someone knows what it is like to be me."*

From time to time, to this day, I reflect with my therapist and express tears and words of gratitude for what she has given me in her ability to find and see me. Inevitably, she'll respond by saying, "You're welcome. I am only doing for you what someone else did for me." I know what she means. I have the same instinct. Although imperfect and limited, I want to provide the same thing for others—for my children, for my wife, for my clients, and, in some small part, even for the readers of this book. However, the process is more alive when you sit across from someone and take the risk of telling your truth, of exposing your *horrible, rotten Self.* I hope you are able to find someone who can do for you what Jami Gill did for me. All you have to do is look for someone who looks for you.

CHAPTER EIGHT

PRACTICAL TOOLS FOR BEING HUMAN

"But if thoughts can corrupt language, then language also can corrupt thought." George Orwell

PRACTICAL SOLUTIONS

MORE THAN ANY OTHER, THE QUESTION I AM ASKED most by clients is for a list of skills to help them in negotiating relationships. I am reluctant to answer because what is so often implied in this request is this question: "What tools or skills can you give me that will change my child or my partner or my circumstances?" This is not a conscious thought most people have when asking this question, but still, it is there. It is there because as I explore their attempts to use this or that tool, they often respond by saying something like, "I don't think that will work," or they return after attempting to implement their new tool and say something like, "I tried it, and it didn't work." When I inquire about their failed attempt to use the new skill, it is clear that the "what works" part of their assessment is a change in another person or a change in circumstances outside of their control. So, like the chapters on behavioral change and communication in my first book, I am including this chapter here with this caveat: the goal in presenting these tools is to provide the reader with something that can change *the individual*, not others around them.

While these tips can be helpful in negotiating relationships and may lead to successful outcomes, the primary purpose of presenting these tools is to influence the reader and the way they think.

Consider this analogy: a hammer is a wonderful tool when, if put to proper use, it helps to build things and to nail boards together, pull nails from boards, and so on. But a hammer can also be a weapon. You can use a hammer to destroy or hurt somebody. And so, for me, the rich work in emotional growth is in transforming the tool user. What's the foundation underneath the skill that allows it to be used to build something wonderful?

If we follow Orwell's logic about how language impacts our thoughts, we understand that sometimes what we do and how we speak can change the way we think and feel. I've witnessed families and couples improve their compassion, develop healthier boundaries, and gain great insight into their relationships by utilizing some simple tools. But tools are not everything. However, if we allow these tools to teach us, they can be of great value to us and can help us develop new ways of being with an *Other*.

In a staff meeting recently, I was pondering those tools as one of our staff asked about my suggestion that simply confronting people's defenses often leads to a refortification of the defense. Telling a client, "You're justifying," or "You're in denial," can provoke the defense. The staff member asked me, "Isn't challenging them helpful for their growth?"

Explaining how confronting the defense can serve to reinforce them or drive the underlying injury further underground only to reappear somewhere else in some other form, I advised, "Be with them so they feel safe enough to let down the wall. I don't confront justifying, but clients do it less and less with me over time." I pointed to a poster where a list of the upcoming "8 Tools" in this chapter hung and explained, "Those don't make you enlightened, but if you were enlightened, you would use these. This is how you would talk and relate to others." It is this way of being with another that makes the difference in the relationship.

While preparing for a parent meeting in Seattle some years ago, I was asked to present on the most common skills and tools that I've seen work for families and make the biggest difference in their lives. I often joke (although it's true) that I originally came up with twelve tools, but since nobody has patience for lists much past eight, I reduced them and combined a couple of them until I got to the top eight. I have created a blog and two podcasts on this subject, and they are some of the most viewed and listened to resources I have produced. Other programs and therapists have shared with me that they use this list in their programs and practices, so I wanted to add it to this book and expand on it. This chapter is based in part on the podcast I did in 2019, with some ideas expanded and stories added. A few of these are found, in part, in my first book, *The Journey of the Heroic Parent*. However, the ideas here are the evolution of those original ideas, and the stories here are expanded to include examples of relationships beyond the parent-child relationship. These are the skills that I've seen make the biggest difference if you allow the skill or the tool to teach you.

8 Tools

1	"I-statements"
2	Reflective Listening
3	Ask or state the intention
4	Avoid imperatives
5	Avoid polarizations
6	Avoid advice
7	Compassion towards self and others
8	Time-out

TOOL 1: "I" STATEMENTS AND OWNERSHIP OF THE *SELF*

The first tool is to use *"I" statements*. These represent ownership and expressing one's truth rather than THE truth. When we tell our truth, we are less likely to arouse a defense in the *Other*, but more importantly, we are acknowledging that we don't know another's truth. These are spoken in the first-person singular: "I feel, I think, I believe, I want, I need." Sometimes we experience shame when speaking in the first person; we feel as if we're acting self-centered. Although subtle, it is common for people to talk about themselves, their feelings, and their experience in the second-person rather than the first person. Instead of sharing, "When I get home at the end of the day and feel exhausted, I am not able to be there for my husband and children," they will say it like, "You know, when you get home after work and don't have much energy to give to your loved ones…" While the distinction is almost imperceptible, the feeling between the two styles can be palpable. The first feels personal, authentic and compelling. The second version will feel more intellectual, academic, and distant. In therapy, I encourage clients to share in the first-person and many don't even recognize it when they don't. But like with all skills, practice can create an awareness and change the way we show up with others.

Most of us don't think that what we feel, what we need, and what we want are enough to justify virtually any boundary that we have. Standing in our own truth and our own opinion can be one of the loneliest places on earth. This is because we grew up in a context where what we felt wasn't enough and instead, we had to be "right," and being "right" is really the opposite experience of being human. Many of us grew up in that context where our feelings don't matter or they're not enough to justify our boundary. This is why you may hear people use a technique referred to as recruiting. This is when people say things like, "Everyone thinks this way," or "My friends agree with me…"

When we say something like, "In my experience," or "This is what has worked for me," we shift how we see ourselves in relationship to others. Using this phrasing, we can avoid advice-giving and merely share what has worked for us. We can say, "I don't know what you should do. I don't know what your journey looks like. I can only tell you what's worked for me, what's worked in my experience, what's helped me in similar situations. For me, what has been helpful is this." Instead of using "you" statements which describe the other person, their rightness or wrongness, and then correcting them, we can simply share our own experience.

Years ago, I had a friend who was newly married. When I asked how married life was going, he responded, "We have a great relationship. We call each other on our crap." Hearing this expression, I always think that's probably going to get old pretty soon. It's not that hard and doesn't take much insight to see somebody's "crap" and call them on it. What does take capacity is the ability to see and understand somebody. It's not attacking, it's not being right. It is being ourselves. And this is the strongest position that we can really take in any kind of relationship.

Instead of using "I" statements, we think it's a stronger position if we just tell people the way it is. This is the way it is about drug use, about certain behaviors, about keeping your room clean, or about getting your tires changed, about setting boundaries with your parents. We think if we just tell the other person the truth, which is really *our* truth, then it is *the* truth. We imagine that this way of talking is unassailable and can't be argued with when we know very well that, on the contrary, it absolutely can.

There is some risk in using this tool when it is aimed at getting the other person to change by tying to instill a sense of duty or responsibility in them. As I mentioned earlier, I often warn parents of the risks of telling children how they feel. It is rare that a parent (or partner, or friend) tells the *Other* how they feel without an underlying feeling that it is the other person's responsibility to change so we feel better. So, I ask clients to look inward and ask themselves why they want to share a feeling. If that exploration teases out some hope that the other person will change, consider not saying it or changing it to a request or a boundary. For instance, you can frame it as a question: "Will you do this?" Or you can lay out a personal boundary: "If you are going to yell or drink, I am going to have to take some space."

The second reason I am reluctant to encourage sharing feelings with a child or someone else is that it is very difficult for children (and some others) to avoid feeling responsible for those feelings even if that is not the intent. With children, we might be particularly intentional and careful with how we use "I" statements. With other adults, we can be intentional and make sure we express our intent (we will talk more about this when we get to the third tool). This is important because the primary idea underlying the "I" statement is *Self*—the defining and discovering of the *Self*. The "I" statement is about owning our *Self* and understanding our own constructs. It is not about imposing those constructs on our partners, our friends, or our vulnerable children. If we use it with this in mind, we will become clearer and pave the way for the possibility of someone connecting to our authentic *Self*.

This first tool is the first step in a three-step process in dealing with your *Other* who might be dealing with mental illness, addiction, or just the dilemma of living. Step one is to notice what you are feeling, to take it out and look at it and work through the feelings. The second step is to decide how to make sense of what you are feeling. What is the feeling telling you to do? Where is the energy coming from? A past trauma? Your childhood? Or just the present circumstance? It can be helpful to work this out with a therapist, sponsor, partner, or another supportive friend. Then, the third step is to return to the *Other* and communicate what you need and what you want to say without all the raw and primitive emotion leaking out. This is learning to feel and learning to respond in ways that are informed by the feeling without the heavy loading of the emotion that can be triggering, shaming, or intimidating. This is a practice which can help you evolve your relationships into intimate ones where both you and your feelings and the *Other* and their feelings both get to be present.

TOOL 2: REFLECTIVE LISTENING AND CREATING SPACE FOR THE OTHER

The second tool on my list is *Reflective Listening*. Sometimes this is called "deep listening" or "active listening." Various models call it different things, but it's deep, profound listening to understand. It's not listening and waiting for a chance at rebuttal. Someone once told me that the opposite of listening is *waiting*. Deep listening requires that we do the work needed so we are not reactive or don't get triggered as easily. To do this we must we clear our mind so we are not having an internal debate or retort in our minds. Earlier in this book, I wrote, "To deeply understand and hear somebody, you often have to lose your mind." You've got to clear the space in your brain and just hear the other person, and that's difficult. If you develop a practice of listening in this way, you will generate more capacity to see others. With practice, the listening muscles grow stronger over time. This is one of the tools on this list you can practice without any insight and it can still make a difference in you and even in the *Other*.

Joseph Campbell taught that every religion is true in one way or another. I had this thought: When people speak, they are always telling the truth, in one way or another—even when they are lying. The trick is to develop ears that can hear what they are trying to tell us.

Listen to others as if they are telling you about their dreams. Listening to a person's lies, exaggerations, and inaccurate stories tells you something about what they cannot express, something they cannot access. To develop this quality, you have to have look deep inside yourself and battle with your own unconscious demons. My young clients, for instance, will try to convince me of something. "A change, of course, is coming," they say. "I am going to stay clean or get good grades this time."

I have said to parents in the past, "When a child tells me they *will not* use drugs in the future. I don't believe them. When they say they *will* use drugs, I don't believe them." What I mean by this is that I am listening to the deeper thing they are telling me. What are they selling me? Why are they telling me this? What are they afraid of me thinking about them? What do they want me to recommend for the next step in treatment? Thus, I am listening to their stories, their dreams, to see things about them they cannot express or are afraid to acknowledge. But most importantly, I am listening to them.

We learn to see others if we are quiet. Since we know that we will not be mounting a rebuttal, we are more likely to use our mental resources to understand. And with all this care and intention, we often do have a profound and positive impact on others. Carl Rogers noted that, "The curious paradox is that when I accept myself just as I am, then I can change." This is also true with others. If we listen, we remove the force pushing against the *Other*, which attempts to compel them to change. Such pressure *tends* to provoke the *Other's* homeostasis—their desire to keep the status quo. They tend to dig in and double down on the feeling, thought, or belief and remain fixated. Again, it is NOT a trick that gets others to change. It is just that when listening, you do not become part of the energy that reinforces stuck-ness.

Several years ago, I was called to an intervention of a former client of mine years after his treatment with us had ended. He wasn't having the same issues that he was having when I treated him, but he had developed a whole new set of symptoms we did not see. Because he and I had a good connection, the family wanted to bring me in as part of the intervention. I wasn't running it, but I was a participant in it. He walked into the room thinking he was just going over to his mother's for lunch, and then he saw a small group of people. He was about to walk out before he saw me. I was the one he hadn't seen in the longest time, so when he saw that I was there, he said, "I'll stay."

We sat down, and the interventionist turned to the father and said, "You've written a letter." Then my former client's dad started to read his letter to the son.

At this, his son shot up and interrupted, "I'm not going to take this shit. I've heard this all before."

"Just wait a second." I asked. "Remember when you were in treatment with me, and remember when you learned, after a few weeks, just to listen to feedback and not to necessarily assume that it was true but just to hear somebody else's perspective? We had that saying, 'If it fits, let it sit. If it doesn't apply, let it fly.' Remember when you could do that? You got really good at it. What if you just did that today?"

You could see his mind adjusting, and he sat down, and said, "Okay, I'll listen to it and just hear your perspective." He sat and listened to father, his mother, a couple of other loved ones in the room, and me. By merely listening, he was able to absorb the messages of love and concern. As he listened, the messages took root in him and began to grow so that by the end of the day he was checking himself into a treatment program with renewed hope that he could get help.

We can learn to listen. We can learn to hear. One of my favorite moments was when a father told me during weeks one and two of our work together that his son was a complete liar, that everything coming out of his mouth was a lie. "He would lie about the color of the sky while we were both staring at it," he said. I saw some of that with his son in our program.

And the son, of course, had a different story, a different perspective on the relationship. He said, "My dad never listens."

I shared that perspective with his father, and the father said, "You know what? Why would I listen to him lie? I'm a great listener, a fantastic listener. I have to be a good listener for my job. I teach people how to listen." I didn't challenge him directly, but I asked that he do some homework, to listen to some podcasts on listening. A few weeks passed. The father listened to the broadcasts, read some of the material we provided, then came back and confessed, "I never realized how poorly I listen to other people. I heard the information, but I didn't deeply listen to understand their perspective."

Shutting your mouth can be the start of the practice. When people just shut their mouth and begin to listen so that they can at least reflect back accurately what they've heard, they find that they don't need to react. Often, I play this game in my head when my wife is talking to me. I try to imagine that she's talking about some other "crazy husband" that she's married to so that I can just hear her. And in a way, it's true. She's describing *her* version of me, not *the* version of me. I can more easily hear her when I am able to separate the two, but I find listening impossible when I think it's about me. If I think it's about me, I want to defend and dispute the facts; I want to share my perspective and defend my intentions. We don't truly listen when we have judgments born out of our vulnerability. We struggle because, essentially, we don't know that we're okay.

There are many reasons that we don't listen. One of them is that our own base is fragile. If our own sense of self is limited, then listening to someone else's thoughts, ideas, and perspectives, especially if it has something to do with us or encroaches on something we aren't sure of, then we will see their expression as a threat and feel triggered by the need to defend our turf.

My therapist once said, "If somebody came up to you and said, 'You don't have a nose,' since you know you have a nose, you would just be surprised and not argue with them. You would look at them strangely and think, 'I wonder what's going on for you? I wonder what that means to you?'" By holding space, we help other people move through feelings.

I was in a lot of family therapy with my sixteen-year-old the spring and summer of this past year. In one of the sessions, my sixteen-year-old was describing a dynamic in the family that was partly about me, and I remember thinking, "That's not true at all." I wanted to defend myself to the family therapist, to cite specific examples that would prove he was making things up or at least exaggerating. And then, because I am a therapist and have facilitated hundreds of these kinds of conversations with parents and children over the years, I realized, "This is what it feels like to the parents I work with when they have to sit with someone else's story and someone else's truth." I looked at the therapist, who was listening and asking us to reflect it back, and remembered therapists aren't assuming that what is being said is THE truth. They're just trying to hear what's going on for the child and then have us hear it. It's almost as if the child is telling us about a dream or a fantasy that they have about us.

And so, it helped me to think about myself as the therapist because when I hear a child talking about a parent, or when I hear a spouse talking about a spouse, or when I hear a parent talking about a child, I run it through the filter I have that says, "I want to hear what your experience is like in this relationship, in this situation. And it's meaningful, and it's important, and it's real." It doesn't matter what the TRUTH is.

I've also had the experience where, after listening to and supporting people listening to each other, over time, their shared truths moved closer and closer together. Oftentimes, we tend to exaggerate and polarize our descriptions of events and situations. If I came home and told you that my boss was slightly disrespectful to me today, that she wasn't listening to me today, and I related this feeling from a subtle experience, many people would be tempted to respond, "Well, your boss might not have been thinking about it, or maybe they just didn't hear you." Or, "Gosh, you might be attributing some intent that's not there." But, if I come home with an exaggerated story about how disrespectful the boss has been and how long this pattern has existed and talk about how she does it to everybody and say what a horrible boss she is, then I will have more confidence that you're going to say, "Wow, I don't know how you deal with that!"

This speaks to the question of whether somebody's truth is enough. Do we need to justify it? Do we need to pass judgment on it? Do we need to approve it? Or if they just say, "This is my experience; this is what it's like for me," can we learn to hear that? Do we have the capacity to do that? If we can do that, we help other people move through feelings. This is actually how we teach other people to feel and how we support them. When people get angry and hurt by what we do, the more that we can contain it, the more we can listen, hold it, be patient with it, see it, and sit with it, the more likely the person is to move through their emotions.

When your child is angry with you for something you did that you thought was right, the most effective thing that you can do is to try to have no attachment to their feelings. Let it be. Even say, "I'm sorry. Maybe it was a mistake. I did the best that I could, but I don't know for sure if it was the best thing."

At a parent meeting recently, my adult son was attending and left halfway through for some plans he had made. Someone asked him before he left if he was ever angry or resentful about me sending him to a program when he was 13. He looked perplexed and told them he never really felt that way. Later, after he left, the group talked about the question further. I said, "It would be strange for my children to be resentful about something that I did because it wouldn't matter to me. Not that I don't care, but anger or resentment wouldn't

178

be something that I would be invested in them not feeling, so they tend to pass through it more easily instead of getting stuck in it."

Miguel Ruiz, in *The Four Agreements*, says this,

Taking things personally is the maximum expression of selfishness because we make the assumption that everything is about me. Nothing other people do is because of you. It's because of themselves.

He uses the world "selfishness," but I would use the word woundedness. Each of us has some narcissistic wounding from childhood. That is, we are not totally and completely seen. How could it not be true since we were raised by human parents? The narcissistic wound leaves a hole in us, an incomplete sense of ourselves and our worth. Because of that wound, we are inclined to feel responsible for how *Others* think and feel. And because of this hole, we are more likely to defend ourselves against attacks, trying to prove to the *Other* that we are, in fact, good.

And that's why it's vital that you be seen and that you find people who can see you and contain you, understand you, hear you, support you—like a therapist, a trusted friend, or a support group. Then, when you show up in your relationship, you can be there for the *Other*, instead of requiring the *Other* to contain you or be there for you.

Because many people, especially in marriage, think that the other person has to be their best friend, confidant, therapist, and support group, it leads to conflict and pain. But this is another unrealistic, romantic idea. In marriage, I had to learn to take care of myself—not that my wife doesn't carry me sometimes, and not that I don't carry her sometimes, but I make sure that she's not the *only* one to carry me. I make sure that I have somebody else in my life (and for me, it happens to be a therapist) that I go to in order to be seen so that when I show up in the marital relationship, I can take my turn at containing and listening. I heal and work on myself over here on the left, so that over here on the right, I can express love, which is a giving thing.

TOOL 3: ASK OR STATE THE INTENTION

The third tool is *Ask the Intention* or *State the Intention*. Of all the tools on this list, this one might be the least talked about by communication experts. Yet if we did it more often, we would avoid so many difficulties in marriage, relationships, and parenting.

Asking and stating the intention is this: if I'm the person talking, I can state my intention or my wishes for what I am looking to accomplish and what I would like from the *Other*. "Hey, Mom, I want to tell you about something, but I just want you to listen." Or I might say to my wife, "Hey sweetheart, I want to share something, some frustration that I'm having right now, and I don't need you to fix it. I don't need any suggestions. I just want you to hear it. Can you do that?"

If I'm on the receiving end of your sharing, I can ask, "What would you like from me? Do you want me to just hear this? Do you want me to respond or react? Do you want me to give my thoughts?" *Be wary and reluctant to offer thoughts in response to someone sharing frustration, hurt, or anger* because you may have a dog in the fight. Your response may be coming from a place of defensiveness, a need to be right or good. Most people overestimate their ability to hear somebody's retort. In my experience, much of the time, people aren't ready to hear, and they don't know that until it's too late.

A good practice or discipline is to take turns. I don't know if it's five seconds, five minutes, five hours, five days, or five weeks, but give the expression or feeling its space. When the feelings are allowed to have their space and that space is going to be determined by each of the people (particularly the sender), you are giving permission for the sender to have their feelings.

My wife and I just had this discussion recently. She was sharing some feelings about our relationship and afterwards she asked, "I want to hear what you're thinking."

I responded, "My goal is to think nothing except to just to hear what you're saying. If I come back with my thoughts and my ideas, then it can easily be dismissive of what you're thinking and feeling. And so, it's not a trick: I'm really trying to just hear you. I'm really trying to have no opinion about what you're saying to me about this issue between us."

If you're the receiver, you ask what they would like before you respond. You might ask on the front end if you know it's going to be an emotional issue. If you're the sender, at any point, you can ask for what you need and check to see if the other person is able and willing to give it. Ideally, you frontload a difficult expression of feelings with, "I just want to be heard. Can you just hear what I'm about to say?" And when the person starts to respond, then you can say, "Remember, I wasn't asking for that. I was just asking for you to listen."

And the amazing thing is that if you can't hear what someone has to say to you, it's okay to tell them, "I don't think I can hear that right now." It's perfectly okay to take care of yourself in this way. If the relationship is important, you can get some help or support so that you can return to hear what they have to say. You can ask for support from a therapist to facilitate the conversation. You don't deserve to be beat up when you are unable to listen because, what you're essentially saying is, "I don't have the psychological energy and resources to do this right now."

Especially if it feels like the person is asking for advice or help in problem-solving, check in with them. If they're being repetitive and expressing essentially the same feelings over and over again, check in with them. Say, "I think I'm hearing you, but this is the third or fourth time you're telling me this, so what do you need from me?" When you state your intention about what you want from the other person, both of you are set up for success, and start to have integrity between what you want and what you're saying. If I know ahead of time what I need from you (that I just want to be heard, or if I want to change your mind about something), stating the intention will reveal the motive for sharing. If I really want to change your mind about something, stating the intention may expose that as long as I'm honest with myself.

When my wife says to me, "Can you just listen?" I know I'm off the hook. I don't have to do anything. I don't have to respond or change, I just have to hear her and understand her. This skill resolves a core dynamic that causes conflict and distance in relationships. One of the most disconcerting things in communication in our relationships is when the content of what we are saying doesn't match the intent of the message we are communicating. Passive communication or hidden agendas tend to provoke hurt, defensiveness, and anger, and stating our intent can be difficult if we are unwilling to own our agenda. However, like the other tools on this list, developing a practice of using this skill can help us to own our feelings and our intentions for sharing them: to say what we mean and mean what we say.

TOOL 4: AVOID IMPERATIVES

Avoiding Imperatives essentially suggests that we virtually eradicate the following words from our vocabulary:

good, bad, right, wrong, evil, have to, need to, should, ought to, must.

If we remove those from our conversations, then when there's any kind of emotional or relational content to it, we find that we start to think about our relationships differently and not say, "You *have to* respect me." Instead, you can say, "I need certain things, or I want to be treated this way." This skill asks us to own our needs and feelings. It's more vulnerable, but it's also more powerful.

Wars are being fought over imperatives: good and bad; right and wrong; have to, need to, and should. Communication based on differentiation, assertiveness, empowerment, vulnerability, and "I" statements—"I feel, I want, I need, I prefer"—is much more effective in conveying not only what we need, but it also demonstrates what it means to be in intimate relationships with others. It begins to outline the concept of relational differentiation—the balance of valuing *Self* and honoring the *Other*—where I am clear about me, about you, about our relationship, and about the separation and connection between us. In addition, when these words are not used to express your thoughts and ideas, it is easier to hear on the receiving end. If someone starts talking to me about good and bad, right and wrong, or what I should do, it's going to be more difficult for me to hear than if they say, "I felt hurt, I felt sad, I felt confused, and I felt frustrated when you said or did x." Imperatives provoke a defense and the need for others to prove or establish their separate sense of *Self*. In such provocations, people often go so far as to fight against reason and common sense because of the need to have a separate sense of *Self*.

Self trumps all other needs, including safety. Maintaining our sovereignty of *Self* will take priority over decisions that may harm us. Teenagers are famous for this type of behavior; they will "cut off their nose to spite their face." Hearing someone share their feelings is not effortless because sometimes one might internalize the insinuation that one did something wrong. So, this doesn't solve the problem of power struggles completely, but it certainly sets one on a more accurate course towards an intimate relationship. Speaking in "I" statements instead of imperatives is a much more accurate way of illustrating what is really going on in a world where interpersonal boundaries exist.

I have loved watching this shift happen through some of the letter writing therapy I do with families and couples. Letter writing therapy slows down communication to a pace where *Self* and intention are more clearly observed. When I tell somebody to avoid using those imperative words in a letter to a child or a partner, I do a quick little edit/find function on Microsoft Word and look for those words. I usually find a handful, so I craft some sentences and give some examples of the way clients might say it differently. Instead of saying, "You have to go to school," you may say something like, "Here's what I value. Here's what I think school can do for you, and here's my boundary around that. If you go to school, this is going to happen. If you don't go, this will happen." Or, to a partner, you say something like, "You don't have to stop being abusive. I am not in charge of that. I can't control it. In fact, I have spent far too long trying to get you to slow down and think about how you are talking to me and the kids. What I can say is that I can't have it in my home or in my life. So, if you want to keep doing things the way you have always done them, I don't think I can stay."

Speaking in this way is much clearer. However, because we don't like the experience of being vulnerable, we make it about the other person, and we make it about right and wrong; there is no vulnerability in making the problem and the solution about the other person. Though this tool may sound simple, it can be very difficult. However, making this shift and eradicating these words from our vocabulary can have a profound impact in how we see ourselves in the world and how we see others and our relationship to them.

TOOL 5: AVOID POLARIZATIONS

Here are a few examples of polarizations:

- "You always…"
- "You never…"
- "You're the worst…"
- "Everyone thinks…"
- "Every time you…"

This tool is no secret; it is very well-known, well-taught, and well-coached. Research shows that families who identify themselves as successful in post-treatment studies say they avoid all or nothing, black and white, either/or, and always/never polarizations. When we talk in those ways with each other, I think we all know that it's more difficult to hear. If I say, "You never listen to me," then my anger is absolutely righteous. However, if I say to you, "This morning when we were talking, I didn't think you were listening to me," it's more vulnerable. But when we say things in a more vulnerable manner, we also hear the voices in our heads that say, "What's the big deal? Why are you making such a fuss about it? You're too sensitive. You're overreacting." We can imagine and discover where those voices came from in our lives and history. They often come from our earliest places, from our parents and family-of-origin. If our partners or children echo those voices, we will likely regress to old feelings and young responses leading to conflict or distance.

As described in earlier chapters, when our feelings were too much for our parents and others, they felt inadequate, and rather than owning their feelings, they made us the problem. In response, we used exaggerated polarizations to justify our hurt and anger and pain. We thought that by amplifying the issues, we justified the right to feel what we were feeling. In that context, the discussion is a battle about who is right and who is wrong—nobody wins. It becomes a power struggle with each person's right to feel how they feel instead of the feeling being enough on its own. Non-polarizing language is a lot easier to hear on the receiving end because it doesn't feel like such an indictment. Using this tool doesn't guarantee that we will be heard, but it can establish our sense of sovereignty—the sense that what we feel is enough. If talking in this way takes root and grows into something larger, we are, simply, *enough*.

TOOL 6: AVOID ADVICE-GIVING

Avoiding advice-giving allows us to share our ideas, thoughts, and experiences without the presumption that we know someone else's truth. For example, in A.A. (Alcoholics Anonymous), or any 12-step group, they have a tradition of *no crosstalk*. This means no one gives advice to anyone in those meetings. If this is violated, a leader is likely to ask members and those sharing to return to regular order. If you find yourself in one of those meetings, you'll hear phrases like "what works for me," or "my experience is *this*, but it may not work for you." "Take what you like and leave the rest" is also commonly heard. The wonderful thing about sharing your wisdom in this way is that if the other person says, "That's the most ridiculous idea I've ever heard," it's easy to back away. But if you give advice as if you know *the* truth about the way that the world works, it's harder to retreat if you bump up against someone's defense or disagreement.

Even in the role of a parent where we think it is our job to know what is best for our children, sharing ideas and feelings rather than advice creates a more effective and differentiated way to relate to our kids. In fact, when my adult children ask for advice, I do my very best not to give it. It's a fool's errand to answer advice questions. Rather, we can explore ideas, feelings, and the goals that arise out of that base. We can explore possible ways of accomplishing those goals and investigate what might be getting in the way of knowing what to do. For example, saying, "What should you do? I don't know. I can't possibly know. I barely know what I want to do in my life a lot of the time. How could I know what you should do? Some of the most important lessons I have learned have come from trying something that didn't work. I can share a similar experience that sounds and looks like yours and describe how I felt and how I responded and what that did, but that's all I know."

Shifting from advising on what people should do to sharing a thought, an idea, or something else that has worked for you establishes clear boundaries—who you are and who is the Other.

Shifting from advising on what people should do to sharing a thought, an idea, or something else that has worked for you establishes clear boundaries—who you are and who is the *Other*.

I love one specific example from David Bowie's life. Shortly after he passed, there was a portion of an interview from the BBC that was circulated. The interviewer was asking him what it meant to be an alcoholic. "Couldn't you just have one drink?" he asked. "At a wedding, can't you just have a toast of champagne?"

Bowie responded, "I can't. I know what's at stake for me. For me, that doesn't work. I don't know what it's like for other people, but for me, I can't do it. I know myself well enough that that won't work for me." Within a very short period, he said the phrase "for me" several times. He was illustrating this way of being in a relationship to the world: knowing yourself first and not extending your truth to assume you know what's best for someone else.

A client I had been seeing in long-term recovery from addiction started dating. He had waited past the often recommended year of sobriety before he started dating, but he was struggling with the typical issues in relationships where we all struggle. His sponsor and others suggested that maybe it was too early to date. He shared that one trusted mentor suggested, "Your *picker* is broken. You need to do some more work on yourself before you know how to choose a partner." He felt a conflict because he wanted to start dating and thought he might never know himself well enough to have a perfect "picker."

I shared my experience with him. "Either way makes sense to me, but for me, I don't know how to fix a picker except by picking and seeing how it works out." In other words, getting married, especially to the wrong person, is a horrible idea; getting married and having children are horrible ideas (tongue-in-cheek). Unfortunately, I can't think of many better ways to learn what it is to be You."

With recovery from co-dependency, they say it's not your business to decide whether or not somebody else in your life is an alcoholic or an addict. You learn to talk about what you're comfortable with and what your boundaries are. You don't have to diagnose your child or your partner as an addict or an alcoholic or being mentally ill to justify your boundaries. You can simply state, "I'm just not comfortable with x. So, I'm going to do y." This is not a passive stance. This way of talking and thinking leads to assertive, clear, courageous, and authentic responses.

When we give advice, we are often hoping that the other person will change so we don't have to deal with our anxiety and our own empathic misery, or we hope they will change so we don't have to set and follow through on a boundary.

In working with teens and young adults in our program, I often playfully remind people, "Children don't need advice. They have parents for that." They need something else: to be heard, to be understood. They need a voice. They need to give a voice to the wounds that their symptoms and defenses are masking, then they need a safe place to heal.

As I've mentioned, I've been seeing my current therapist for more than twenty years now, and I don't know that she's ever really given me advice. I stopped asking a long time ago. Sometimes she may say something like, "You could try this," and I might reply, "That's a great idea. I might try that." Or I might say, "I don't think that'll work."

And my therapist is able to deftly adjust, "Okay. Your probably right. I'm happy to be wrong." After a while, the idea that somebody else could know your truth doesn't make any sense, not in this new kind of sensibility. Lecturing, teaching, preaching, and repetition are all signs that we believe we need to control the other person. We might as well say, "Take my advice—I am not using it."

When we give advice, we are often hoping that the other person will change so we don't have to deal with our anxiety and our own empathic misery, or we hope they will change so we don't have to set and follow through on a boundary.

The Dalai Lama said,

To be aware of a single shortcoming within oneself is more useful than to be aware of a thousand in somebody else.

Application of this idea is embodied in the skill of avoiding advice. Pragmatically, owning your own truth and offering it as an example of what has worked for you but may not work for someone else is more effective than giving advice in encouraging change and maintaining a sense of *Self* and separateness. Advice comes from a place of anxiety, frustration, and a need for control. So, if avoiding advice doesn't square with your philosophy, just think of it pragmatically. If you think your role is to impart your wisdom to others, then the method I have outlined above is simply more effective.

I remember a father once said to me that what he wanted out of therapy was to get to a place where his son would start listening to him again. And I said, "Okay, that's fair. But really, what this work is going to center on is you being able to listen to him." He was quiet. I continued, "This is where the gold is! The gold is not the advice you impart. Be stingy with advice. Be reluctant to offer it. And, ideally, offer it in the form of sharing rather than from a place of 'you should' or 'you shouldn't.'"

Parents often ask me, "How do you avoid imperatives when you have a belief in good and evil or right or wrong? Not sharing those beliefs seems like I am not being true to myself." I asked my therapist about this some years ago. Somebody had asked me a question, and they shared they were getting different information from their rabbi or their priest or their pastor, and my therapist said, "Well, the wonderful thing is, you're not a priest, Brad. You're not a pastor. You're not a rabbi. You get to talk about things through a psychological lens, through a therapist's lens."

Using a psychological lens suggests that you don't know their truth; you know your truth. You don't know anyone else's truth unless they discover it for themselves and share it with you.

You can talk about your thoughts and feelings without imposing them on others, but that is very different from telling other people what they should believe. A few years ago, I was doing a family session, and the parents were talking about their "family's values." They were talking about right and wrong, honesty, integrity, and many things that most of us would identify as worthy values. At one point, their young adult son interrupted, "Those aren't *family* values. Those are *parental* values."

And I thought, he's right. That was a really clear way to say it. They aren't necessarily his values. Some of them are, but some of them are not. And what he was really resisting was the intrusion of someone telling him what he had to believe. You can have your values and offer something like, "This is what's true for me. For me, I

It's only when we can have compassion toward the worst and weakest parts of ourselves that we start to heal the deeper wound.

value honesty. For me, I value authenticity. For me, I value compassion. Those are true for me. I don't know if they're going to be true for you, though. You'll have to figure that out."

Approaching others with that kind of differentiation and clarity is the best way to stoke and encourage the kind of virtues you want to encourage. It steers clear of the power struggle that arises in protection of the *Other's* need to maintain their separate self. In this way, the truth is coming from them, and it's authentic. It's not superimposed. It's not what clinicians call "introjection," which is a psychological defense where somebody swallows something whole without really considering it. Then we end up living someone else's idea of a life with thoughts like, "How did I get here? How did I end up in this job or in this relationship or in this situation? I'm not sure this is me."

Khalil Gibran's beautiful prose *On Good and Evil* explains that when you're doing good, you're good; but when you're not, you're not evil, you're just broken. As many fear might happen, this way of relating doesn't lead to amorality or hedonism. It actually fosters a higher morality—one that's more authentic and deep-seated.

TOOL 7: COMPASSION TOWARDS *SELF* AND OTHERS

Developing a *practice* of compassion towards one's *Self* is one of the more elusive tools because most of us were taught that we need a good butt-kicking when we make mistakes. We need to be chastised. We think that we need a strict schoolmaster and may even hire a therapist to take on such a role. We can try to hate the sin and love the sinner, as they say. But really, hate towards one's *Self* and even one's actions leads to repression, resistance, and denial.

It's only when we can have compassion toward the worst and weakest parts of ourselves that we start to heal the deeper wound. This is when we find the voice of the eight-year-old child inside of us who is actually doing most of the driving.

The Golden Rule says that we should do unto *Others* as we would have *Others* do unto us. While many see this as a commandment, I like to think of it as just the way things are. Every relationship we have with *Others* is a manifestation of the relationship we have with ourselves. This is why, although my first book was about parenting, it really wasn't about parenting. It was about the relationship we have with everyone, beginning with ourselves.

I referenced inner-child work earlier, and many may be familiar with it. This is where one imagines oneself as a small child and then engages in dialogue with lost or hidden parts of the *Self.* The child in us is often scared, hurt, afraid, hopeful, optimistic, and honest. Our ability to hear those parts that need certain things, that has the audacity to dream, and that is willing to dare allows us attend to *Others* when they are suffering and calling out for help. The inner-child is afraid to speak, because when they did so long ago, they may have been met with frustration, exasperation, or disdain.

In a sense, it might be helpful to think of shame as inner-child abuse. We have integrated those voices so completely that we experience them as part of us. These voices lead to shame and we may be reluctant to speak out again. In a sense, it might be helpful to think of shame as inner-child abuse. The kindness we show to those feelings buried deep inside of us will set the stage for the child coming out of hiding. Our capacity to listen to the child within us will predict whether we are able to meet our needs without making a mess of things. That is, if we are able to speak our deepest truths and have them heard, we don't need to act out to get our needs met.

Children make a mess of things when they are ignored. If we are able to listen to our inner-child, we can listen to our own children. The practice of listening to our *Self* predicts whether we will be able to listen to a five-year-old child throwing a tantrum, to an angry and depressed 17-year-old, or an anxious spouse.

We can develop what I call a "Dear One" attitude – a phrase I adapted from Thich Nhat Hanh, the Buddhist monk and teacher. He asks us to approach ourselves and others with the sentiment, "Dear one, I'm here for you." He suggests if we can look at our anger, our anxiety, and our depression like we would a struggling child, we would say to it, "Dear one, I am here for you. What do you need from me?" He explains,

> *You should talk to your depression or your anger just as you would to a child. You embrace it tenderly with the energy of mindfulness and say, "Dear one, I know you are there, and I am going to take care of you," just as you would with your crying baby…The good must take care of the evil as a big brother takes care of his little brother.*

If we can look with compassion at traits like our narcissism, our selfishness, and the things that we do when we are hurt and lash out at others, then we can listen to it, understand it, and get from it the wisdom that it's trying to offer. In other words, we heal.

Instead of cutting the weeds off at the surface, we really get to the root of the matter. We all know what happens when we cut off the top of the weed. Rather, we must dig our hands into the soil, past the worms, dirt lodging in our fingernails, and pull the weed out by its root. Weed chopping is akin to focusing on behavioral change in our children, ourselves, or in others. Sometimes, if we apply enough force to a situation, we can get the behavior to go away. But if we haven't dealt with the root issue, it's going to pop up some other time in some other way. Like Freud observed, "A thing which has not been understood inevitably reappears; like an unlaid ghost, it cannot rest until the mystery has been resolved and the spell broken."

Chasing away our own or others' woundedness with hate, anger, or disgust just doesn't work. It's just shame or guilt even though we justify it as a means to an end. Sadly, this is how we were taught and programmed. It's all we knew. We were taught that when those in authority, those that loved us, were angry or sad or disappointed, then we must have done something wrong. When they were happy, pleased, or proud, then we were doing something right. I have often joked at work that the most effective motivator is shame… too bad it destroys people in the long run. I spent much of my life thinking that the solution to my problems was to hate those parts of myself making the mess:

my symptoms, my defenses, my stupid choices. It took me decades to come to the realization that those things were the voice of my inner-child asking for me to pay attention and asking me for help.

In my experience, becoming angry at, disgusted by, ashamed of, or exasperated with your issues will not heal them. Hating the expressions of our wounds will only cause them to go underground and we will miss the wisdom they have to offer.

When we look at life, at our *Self*, through the lens of mental health, we see wounds and insecurities rather than goodness or badness. This reframe is the same epiphany we have when we see the musical *Wicked* and compare it to *The Wizard of Oz*. We see the other side of the story and realize that the villain is not all bad. Behind the curtain we recognize that the villain is hurt, scared, and human and is more like us than we ever had the courage to consider.

Becoming angry at, disgusted by, ashamed of, or exasperated with your issues will not heal them. Hating the expressions of our wounds will only cause them to go underground and we will miss the wisdom they have to offer.

I mentioned that my partners and I helped to produce a play. The story of *WILDERNESS* was based on six families and their journey of healing through wilderness therapy. In the fall of 2017, I had the privilege of seeing it performed on the opening night at the Kennedy Center in Washington D.C. I took an Uber to the theatre from my hotel and the driver, in broken English, asked me what I was doing in D.C. I told him about the play, and he showed interest in the subject. I described my favorite scenes and explained our work with young people struggling with addiction and mental illness. As is common, he had many assumptions about parents who send their children away for wilderness treatment. I explained that most are nurturing and trying to do their best. Only a tiny fraction of them would be considered "abusive." He asked

When we heal the hurt, we have no need for the anger, resentment, and hate.

about the types of abuse we deal with and I shared some anecdotal examples. As I described these to him, he asked, "Are these parents possessed by devils?"

Surprised at his assumption, I replied, "No. They suffer from mental illness. Many have depression, bipolar, or addictions, and many were victims of abuse themselves."

In his way of thinking, this was the explanation for such things. I suppose it is a suitable metaphor to explain unthinkable horrors, but I prefer to use the language of psychology and mental illness to describe this type of phenomena; I find it more hopeful and helpful.

Therapy taught me to see things as broken and repairable rather than unworthy and worthy. The former is a more compassionate and effective perspective to encourage healing while the latter tends to encourage shame, hiding, and denial. We look at behavior the same way a medical doctor would look at a broken leg. They're not mad at it, they just want to heal it, so they do what they need to do to help it to heal. And that's why I love the mental health lens. It relieves the pressure that comes from other constructs and lenses that can be oppressive and harmful.

It's taken me a long time as a client in therapy to make this shift in my own life. I was capable of making it with others first, but it really wasn't until I started to do it with myself that everything changed and with that my compassion for others greatly deepened.

And that's what I think therapy can do for us. Therapeutic healing is not an imperative. It's not that I took the high road. The work we do in therapy does not lead to hate, but rather to compassion. Nietzsche warned, "Whoever fights monsters should see to it that in the process he does not become a monster." When we heal the hurt, we have no need for the anger, resentment, and hate.

We can look deeply into our past, into our childhood. If we have the courage to walk past the sentinels of guilt and shame and familial obligation, to discover what really happened, to learn where we were wounded, we'll come to understand ourselves and our limitations better. And I think it's from that place that we develop the courage to make difficult decisions, to set difficult boundaries, to interact with our partners, our spouses, our children, and our friends in a more compassionate, whole, courageous, and authentic way.

Jack Kornfield said, "If our compassion does not include ourselves, it is incomplete. Hatred is not the answer to hatred. It doesn't drive out hatred—only love can do that." Similarly, Martin Luther King Jr. taught us, "Darkness can't drive out darkness, only light can do that." In the short term, hate, shame, guilt, anger, and fear can all be very powerful and potent motivators. But when it comes to the long game, these feelings come at the cost of the soul in all of us.

Of course, letting go of shame, the most common expression of self-hate, can be frightening. For many of us, shame has been the thing that has motivated us to be good or be productive. If we let it go, what will happen to the guardrails? Will we devolve into a heartless, lazy, selfish, and unproductive puddle? From my experience as a client and therapist, this is what I know: exchanging shame for compassion doesn't cause one to regress, it causes one to love one's *Self* and *Others* more deeply. It leads to authenticity because actions are not in service of the ego but in the service of giving others the same grace and compassion that someone gave us. My experience is that it begins to feel like every great story or movie where love prevails, even if circumstances don't go the way we initially hoped or planned. I agree with Martin Luther King Jr. when he said, "I decided to stick with love. Hate is too great a burden to bear," especially when it is directed inward.

TOOL 8: TIME OUT

The reason I have put *Time Out* as the last of the eight tools is because, at times, all of us are going to be tested beyond our ability to respond in all of the above ways. When I was working with men who were convicted of domestic violence, we would teach timeouts as a part of the process, and during that time, I learned a few things.

We would have the men come up with an anger scale from one to ten and begin to identify really low levels of anger—feelings like bothered or annoyed—all the way up to a ten, which was something like rage. They could use words like "seeing red" or "out-of-body." They came up with their own labels.

And then we would say to them, "Try to practice taking timeouts when you get to a four or a five at the most. None of them ever wanted to do it. They never wanted to take timeouts when they were at a four or a five—they thought they didn't need to do that yet. But I also discovered that when you're at an eight, a nine, or a ten, you don't care about a timeout anymore. You've been hijacked by the primitive brain, by the "fight-or-flight" part of your brain, and by then, all reason is gone.

The key is to learn to take timeouts earlier. To do that, you must learn to recognize your anger. No matter who you are or how enlightened you are, no matter how many tools you have or how much therapy you've had, there will be times where you may be pushed or triggered to an eight, nine, or ten on the anger scale. It is bound to happen. And so it's important to learn to see that coming ahead of time.

Another issue that prevents people from taking a timeout is that they must own their vulnerability and take some time to cool off, to retreat to a practice. It is easier to see the fault in the *Other* and make that our focus than it is to see the feeling we have inside and our responsibility for it.

If we are unable to hold the *Other* with a "Dear One" attitude, then we can retreat to our practice of self-care, whatever that might be. For some it can be meditation, exercise, or just sitting with yourself. The practice can be on a macro or micro level. Sometimes it is a situation that arises, and sometimes it is something larger. Sometimes we don't go home for the holidays. Sometimes we have to say goodbye to relationships with those we have loved. But in any case, when we lack the ability to hold the *Other* with compassion, we must replenish our reservoirs with a practice of self-care if we are to get back our higher *Self.*

This is the secret: we hold the *Other* in our mind with love and compassion unless we can't. There is no right or wrong, just capacity. There is not good or bad in this, just our humanness.

But this requires us to own our capacity and limitations. It also suggests that if *Others* can't be there for us in the way that we need, they are not bad—they're just human. Many couples devolve to the idea that the other one is a bad husband, wife, or partner. They do this because, again, rather than own their need (which, if too much, can be more than the *Other* can bear, causing shame), they make the *Other* bad. Anger is the bodyguard of our hurt, so in moments where our anger rises, we are least able to let our wall down at the risk of getting hurt some more.

We don't want to take timeouts at a one, two, three, four, or five when we are able because it feels vulnerable and weak. For me, if I need a timeout, I am saying "I can't handle it." I am owning my lack of capacity. And I don't like that. As I start to feel upset and agitated, I don't want to own these feelings or be vulnerable. I want to make it about you and your problem and why you're being a jerk. And by the way, *you* are the one that needs a time-out.

If you have the thought that somebody needs a time out, it's probably truer that you need one.

> *This is the secret: we hold the Other in our mind with love and compassion unless we can't. There is no right or wrong, just capacity. There is not good or bad in this, just our humanness.*

Because really, what we're saying to the other person is, "You know what? You better leave this conversation right now, because if you don't leave it, I'm about to do something regrettable that you're not going to like." So, having the courage to own this is very, very difficult. But I've learned in my own life that timeouts invariably help even though it's also something that we strongly resist. No matter how far I grow, I always find a limit to my capacity.

In working with the men who struggled with domestic violence, we used the concept of "The Cycle of Violence."

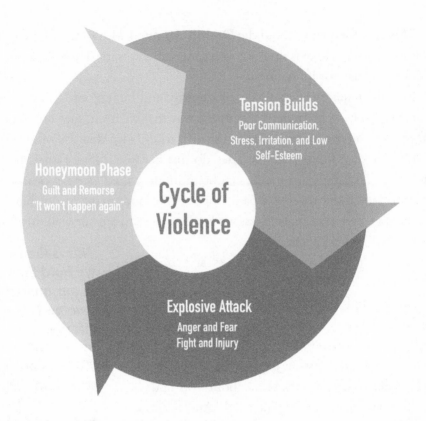

Tension Builds
Poor Communication,
Stress, Irritation, and Low
Self-Esteem

Honeymoon Phase
Guilt and Remorse
"It won't happen again"

Cycle of Violence

Explosive Attack
Anger and Fear
Fight and Injury

This is a very simple model, and it can be used for most repetitive, addictive cycles. The first stage in the cycle of violence is the violent act: the hitting, the abuse (note that it can be punctuated at any point, but for the sake of clarity, I will call the violence itself the first stage). The second stage is the honeymoon phase: giving flowers, apologizing, or promising, "I'll never do this again, let's go to therapy—I'm sorry." The third stage is the tension-building stage where feelings are stuffed. These stages go in a circle: violence, honeymoon, tension-building; violence, honeymoon, tension-building. And it is easy to get stuck in this. These men would stay stuck in it because *they thought the solution was to try not to be angry.* They would try not to feel anger because they conflated it with the act of violence, "Well, last time I was angry, I got violent and I regretted it." But escaping the cycle doesn't work that way. Like all cycles, the only way out *is* the way *off*. We must do something different and unique to break the pattern.

In the studies that I did with these men, we saw that sometimes the victims of the violence would stand in the way of the man when he was trying to leave because it felt too threatening to be left. It was too scary, potentially final, and absolute. It didn't happen in all the cases, but in a statistically significant number of cases, this blocking behavior was present. To get out of such cycles in our lives, even if they're not violent, it would behoove us to become aware of our feelings, own them, and then take a timeout. Owning our feelings means that we take responsibility for our reactions and sit with our anger and listen to it. In a heated situation, none of us is going to have access to the wisdom we have when we are in a place of greater peace. Our biology won't allow it.

Someone wise once told me, "Strike while the iron is cold." If our nervous system is on heightened alert, we lose the capacity for rational thought. Address issues when things are calm. No great issue we have with another will be easily dealt with during moments when we're upset. The adage that says "don't go to bed angry" is, in my experience, ridiculous. It's okay to go to bed angry, because sometimes, doing so will prevent a really unpleasant fight.

A timeout is the last thing on this list of tools because it's the thing that brings us back to the capacity of all the other things. As always, it starts with the relationship we have with ourselves, and the other relationships are merely an extension of that. Tools can change our sensibility if we develop a practice and let them sink into our hearts. This practice is a lifelong project of changing the way we exist in the world. In my first book, *The Journey of the Heroic Parent,* I describe the transformation of changing the question one asks when struggling from "What do I do?" to a series of questions to be answered in this order: "Who am I? (What do I think and feel)? Who is my child, my spouse, or any *Other*? (What do they think and feel)? What is my relationship to their problems?"

I talk about the work this way: imagine taking your two fists out in front of you about eight to ten inches apart. The right fist represents what you're inclined to do, what your natural impulse or response is—what you did yesterday and the day before that. And the left fist ten inches away represents what your higher *Self*, your more enlightened *Self*, your wiser *Self*, and your more capable *Self* would do. The distance between those two places is the work we must do to grow. Think about it like building that bridge between what you're inclined to do and what you can do when you are feeling whole. The larger the space between the two fists, the more work that you have to do. For all of us, this is a lifelong project. The bridge never gets absolutely built, but we can make progress, and that makes all the difference in the world.

No tool is the answer—it will not substitute for the hardest and deepest part of our work. No tool is the manifestation of a healthy *Self* and a connection to an *Other*. But the expression of the above tips is what it would sound like if we were transformed into a new sensibility. We would speak from our center. We would not offer advice or tell people what they should or shouldn't do. We would practice compassion, and when we reached the edge of our capacity for compassion, we would own it and take the time to replenish ourselves until we could. Again, Joseph Campbell said that religion is a defense against a religious experience and the image of God is the ultimate obstruction of God. What I think he is saying is that the form of something that blocks our understanding of the idea falls short of the experience. With that in mind, I invite you to practice these tools while also understanding that they are only an approximation of what it means to be a *Self* and love an *Other*.

CHAPTER NINE

KEYS FOR ENLIGHTENMENT

Enlightenment is more about unlearning and undoing. We must be willing, like the serpent, to shed the skin of our understanding to grow. (adapted from Joseph Campbell)

DEBUNKING MYTHS ABOUT HUMAN BEING

A S I COME TO THE CONCLUSION, I WANT TO RECAP with a list of ideas I have discarded in my search for an authentic life. Some are mentioned in earlier sections of this book, some are from my first book, and some appear here for the first time. These are ideas that I have developed over time and 12 myths from our culture that I think need to be debunked or set straight.

Myths About Human Being

Myth 1	Guilt is your conscience. It tells you when you are doing something wrong.
Myth 2	It is your job to make your spouse happy and to take care of all their needs.
Myth 3	Children should make parents proud, or children are responsible for their parents' feelings and serenity.
Myth 4	Parents, friends, or partners should explain the reasons for their boundaries.
Myth 5	I know what is best for others.
Myth 6	We shouldn't need someone else to validate us. Self-esteem is an inside job.
Myth 7	Intimacy is warm and fuzzy.
Myth 8	Intimacy is a measure of your ability to share your vulnerable, authentic truth.
Myth 9	Tools and boundaries are for changing other people.
Myth 10	It is my duty to give advice to those I love, including children, partners, and close friends.
Myth 11	The entitlement and narcissism of kids today stems from permissive parenting.
Myth 12	I would do anything for my kids or the people I love.

MYTH 1: GUILT IS YOUR CONSCIENCE. IT TELLS YOU WHEN YOU ARE DOING SOMETHING WRONG.

Guilt is NOT a reliable source of right and wrong or morality. Guilt itself is a toxic idea, and it's generally felt when we realize we have or may hurt an *Other*. Yet there are countless "right" and "moral" decisions that can hurt others as well. Stop using guilt as a moral North Star—love is a good replacement. Guilt is expressed most often with the phrase, "I feel bad." Shame is unspeakable, visceral, and often concealed since the experience is so severe and exposing the shame itself is too terrifying.

Very often, we have to learn to tolerate guilt in order to do the right thing. Every reader of this book can think of one thing that we all know is "right" that would trigger feelings of guilt. If we can all think of one so easily, we must find some other way to find our moral way through the world. If we fail to act in this way and do battle with our guilt, we will end up stuck in resentment and anger. Many are happy to point out that shame is distinguished from guilt because shame is feeling bad for who you are while guilt is merely feeling bad for what you do. This may be true, but the distinction isn't important since both prevent wholeness and authenticity.

MYTH 2: IT YOUR JOB TO MAKE YOUR SPOUSE HAPPY AND TO TAKE CARE OF ALL THEIR NEEDS.

Many romantic novels and movies support the misconceived notion that your partner should be able to take care of all your needs and is responsible for making you happy. Instead, *you* are responsible for your own happiness, and if you decide to come together with someone, then that union can be fulfilling for both. This is not a cold abdication of the responsibilities that come with partnership or marriage, but it is a fundamental change in *emphasis*. You help when you can, as you can, and as you are able and capable to. But the inability to give a partner what they want doesn't make you a bad partner or spouse. It makes you human. Owning your humanness can be difficult because of the messages you received in life that good people always help out, especially those that they love, but you can shift the idea towards a healthier differentiation and a more authentic intimacy.

MYTH 3: CHILDREN SHOULD MAKE PARENTS PROUD, OR CHILDREN ARE RESPONSIBLE FOR THEIR PARENTS' FEELINGS AND SERENITY.

This myth is a main point in my first book, but to be more succinct here, I want to remind parents that it is not a child's job to make them proud. They are not responsible for parental despair, serenity, or well-being. A parent is responsible, like anyone, for their own serenity. This debunked myth goes along with the idea I share in this book that parents should avoid sharing feelings with children if the intent is to get the child to change in some way to make the parent feel better. Some parents, partners, or even therapists argue that sharing feelings is a natural consequence for bad behavior, but we learn in life that we must let go of what others think and feel to live our best lives. We can do that most effectively when we find someone (this can be a therapist) who values our whole *Self* instead of some part-object. Part-objects include what we do, our talents, our good moods, our looks, our intelligence, our accomplishments, etc.

Because such messages are so ingrained and unconscious, it takes great effort to interrupt the intergenerational messages from being passed to the next generation. It is important that we take a stand against these patterns and protect our children from the ways of previous generations. It starts with us and we can inform others–babysitters, teachers, and even our parents–of our shift in thinking and behavior towards our children. *It takes great courage to protect our children from being abused by our parents (their grandparents).*

MYTH 4: PARENTS, FRIENDS, OR PARTNERS SHOULD EXPLAIN THE REASONS FOR THEIR BOUNDARIES.

The risk here is that this is most often in the service of trying to convince the other person of the rightness of the boundary. We do this instead of the difficult work of boundary-setting because, if we can convert the other person to our way of seeing things and show them the wisdom of our own boundaries then we don't have to set a boundary. The best explanation for a boundary is to simply state, "This is what I feel good about. I may be crazy, stupid, or old-fashioned, but this is what I am comfortable with." Remember: "no" is a complete sentence.

MYTH 5: I KNOW WHAT IS BEST FOR OTHERS.

Whether it is a parent, child, or a friend, we don't know another person's truth. The expertise of a therapist is not knowing someone's truth but providing a context where they can safely discover it. Lastly, we don't need to know someone's truth to set a boundary—this applies to parenting, friendship, and couples. We set a boundary based on what we need and what we feel good about, not based on us seeking to change the *Other* into something we think they need to be.

MYTH 6: WE SHOULDN'T NEED SOMEONE ELSE TO VALIDATE US. SELF-ESTEEM IS AN INSIDE JOB.

This myth is also covered in this book. And to revive a concept from my first book: the root of the *Self* is found when someone else finds us. We need to be seen. Essentially, our injuries came from a lack of resonance, and healing will occur when that experience is replaced with authentic resonance.

MYTH 7: INTIMACY IS WARM AND FUZZY.

Intimacy is hard. It requires us to sit with difficult and painful feelings. It is terrifying, because we must take the risk to tell the truth with the gamble that our truth will be found as unacceptable, ugly, frightening, repulsive, crazy, stupid, or inconvenient.

MYTH 8: INTIMACY IS A MEASURE OF YOUR ABILITY TO SHARE YOUR VULNERABLE, AUTHENTIC TRUTH.

While that is a part of the equation, the reason I have it on the myth list is because many often focus on this so much that they ignore the other side and maybe more difficult part of the equation. As I have shared throughout this book, the often-ignored aspect of intimacy is the *capacity to hear and see someone without judgment and almost without opinion.* Providing a safe container, listening to someone, and remaining curious and open is a herculean task and takes years for most people to develop. Yet in moments when a loved one is compromised and unable to exude the warmth we so valuably cherish, understanding them is what they need most.

MYTH 9: TOOLS AND BOUNDARIES ARE FOR CHANGING OTHER PEOPLE.

This is embodied by the idea I hear some therapists imply that telling someone how you feel should be enough to do the trick. Tools and boundaries are for self-care. Principally, boundaries aren't for changing others, but for taking care of one's *Self*. The lack of boundaries leads to blame and resentment. Some will respond to boundaries by adjusting, but some will not. If you think of boundaries and tools as a means to an end (specifically, changing another person), then you will likely abandon the endeavor relatively soon and search for tools of a more manipulative nature. If you are looking for those, I recommend guilting, shaming, and intimidating—those are extremely potent at evoking change in others.

MYTH 10: IT IS MY DUTY TO GIVE ADVICE TO THOSE I LOVE, INCLUDING CHILDREN, PARTNERS, AND CLOSE FRIENDS.

Advice relies on the notion that you know someone else's truth. Rather, the only thing you know (and even this has significant limitations) is your truth. Sharing what works for you and your ideas on something is a more accurate demonstration of wisdom. And, from a practical perspective, it is easier on the listening end to hear someone share *their* truth rather than to hear them say they know THE truth.

MYTH 11: THE ENTITLEMENT AND NARCISSISM OF KIDS TODAY STEMS FROM PERMISSIVE PARENTING.

This one is just plain ignorance of human behavior. Narcissism and entitlement are born out of the narcissistic wound of not being seen. Furthermore, the inability to see a child is born out of a parent's narcissistic wound. The antidote begins with the healthy development of the *Self* in a parent. When a parent has a healthy *Self*, they are able to see and connect to the child's needs. In addition, a parent with a healthy *Self* will have needs, limits, and boundaries, and with this in place, the child will have to deal with the presence and the needs of an *Other*. Permissive parenting may be evidence of the lack of *Self* in parenting, but permissiveness is not the origin of the issue that causes the narcissistic wound. This myth, like a lot of popular parenting and self-help adages, is used to shame parents into more "productive methods" of child-rearing.

The conditions that exist in families where children display entitled and narcissistic traits are the result of parents' anxiety and narcissistic wounds. When parents have untreated and unhealed narcissistic wounds, they have problems with boundaries. These parents lack a *Self* and as a result their children are not required to adjust to and live with an *Other*. In these families children are asked to take care of parents; parents hope their children adore, admire, and love them. In such families children are asked to give parents what their parents did not give them: the sense of being welcomed. And when parents ask this of their children, they avoid conflict, they tend to coddle them, and they lavish gifts upon them in the hope for a return of adoration. So, when we shame parents engaged in these behaviors with labels and by pointing out the entitlement of their children, we are punishing the child in the adult who did not get what they needed when they were young.

Narcissism is NOT a result of being *overvalued*. Instead, narcissism is the result of valuing the wrong thing in the child. Valuing talents, looks, good behaviors, achievements, accomplishments, and successes may seem to reinforce aspects in others that we want to encourage, but it also presents a dilemma for the recipient of the admiration. What value do I have when I fail, when I am wrong, or when beauty or talents fade? The result of being objectified like this may be someone who will do anything, including creating a delusional world, where they are more special than anyone else. Or, in the case of the depressed narcissist, they will put themselves at the center of all the problems in their world.

MYTH 12: I WOULD DO ANYTHING FOR MY KIDS OR THE PEOPLE I LOVE.

First off, this is not possible. Secondly, it is not an ideal that we should strive for. In addition to the fallacy or inability of this myth, it sets up a dangerous dynamic. If one can truly be that selfless, and if one is such a saint, it suggests that the people who feel or express anger or hurt with us are somehow wrong. Instead, we do what we can, first by making sure we take on the responsibly of our own happiness and meaning, and then doing what we can for those we love to help them get to where they need to go in life.

There are more of these, but I have to save something for the next book. Also, I haven't discovered all of them yet. I hope this begins to offer the reader some permission to question and even discard some of the ideas and beliefs imposed on us by our earliest contexts—including those in this book. Sometimes, the only way we can find peace is to kill those ideas, the parts of us we have incorporated from well-meaning *Others*.

THREE KEYS TO ENLIGHTENMENT

While a complete definition of enlightenment may be beyond the scope of this work and since I have no personal experience with what the destination looks like, I have some observations about the journey towards it. I have the privilege to sit with parents, couples, and clients who, after years of work, explain the road like this: "At first, I didn't know what you were talking about, but I kept listening and working. Now, I don't even recognize myself, and I find it almost impossible to explain the things I know now to my friends. Many of the conversations about life, family, and love that I used to have with my friends don't make sense to me anymore."

Compromised people can defeat us now because compromised people defeated us when we were young.

As I stated earlier, many of the ideas my therapist shared during the early years of our work together escaped me. At one point, I even considered quitting the work. I considered this because I thought the project of therapy was to provide me with a set of tools or techniques that would change my outside circumstances. I didn't realize that the outside circumstances would only change after I experienced a fundamental shift that provided me with the courage to cross the thresholds that I was previously convinced would be the end of life or happiness as I knew it.

It took years of futility for me to realize that no matter how hard I tried and no matter how many people I recruited, that some relationships would never change. I tried fighting, fitting in, and pleasing, but I still never seemed to find relief from relationships where I felt abused, neglected, and mistreated. In one very specific instance, it took almost ten years to extricate myself from such a harmful dynamic. The great difficulty I experienced getting out of that relationship allows me to be patient with others when the exit appears simple, yet one does everything they can except what they need to do in order to free themselves from such a painful relationship.

Compromised people can defeat us now because compromised people defeated us when we were young. Like the baby elephant who experiences the futility in breaking free from the trainers' ropes—even when fully grown at thirteen feet high and 14,000 pounds, the elephant is still deterred from attempting escape by a mere rope around its ankle—we too learn that there is no escape from the captivity of abusive or neglectful relationships. And in my years of therapy, my therapist patiently listened as I complained about abuse and mistreatment from others before I realized that nobody could save me except myself.

At a therapeutic intensive, one client said, "When I realized some of the beliefs I held as core weren't true for me anymore, I began to realize everything was up for grabs, and it was terrifying." The process of enlightenment is painful, and it's often initiated by a crisis. That is why we jest when we remind struggling parents, "There *is* such a thing as a perfect parent. They just haven't had any children yet."

In *The Letters of Juliet to the Knight in Rusty Armor*, Juliet expresses, through a series of letters to her husband, a similar sentiment after many of the ideas she'd had about life had lost their meaning and their place in her. "I am writing to you through my tears. I have cried so much I don't know who I am anymore...so much has changed! I scarcely know my name. I can't believe a viewpoint can change so much!"

What insight can we glean from those who have experienced such transformations? From my perspective, there are three attributes or characteristics of those who have transformed their lives in fundamentally profound ways. I call these three ideas the *Three Keys for Enlightenment*.

Three Keys to Enlightenment

1 Learn to be okay with being wrong
and get really good at losing.

2 Come to know your darkness and remain
on speaking terms with your mental illness.

3 Learn how to die again and again:
old contexts, beliefs, and relationships.

KEY 1: LEARN TO BE OKAY WITH BEING WRONG AND GET REALLY GOOD AT LOSING.

When I was younger, I caused my mother a great deal of grief. Acting out, drug and alcohol abuse, school failure…the list is long. Any caring parent would have felt the way my mother felt: worried, disappointed, frustrated, and hopeless. The problem comes when a parent feels these feelings and the child senses those feelings and interprets those feelings as "something is wrong with me." My mother did try to get me help. I went to therapy and eventually she sent me to a treatment program, but the behaviors continued, and my underlying anger, sadness, and fear were never fully expressed and heard until many years later. I just thought I was a bad seed. I thought something was fundamentally wrong with me, and I had everyone's fingers pointing at me to prove it.

I have often thought that if I could have escaped childhood with a more secure sense of myself, the sense that I was "okay," I could have spent the subsequent years and energy giving gifts to the world, loving myself, and connecting and sharing more with others.

With this wound, I spent the next 25 years trying to prove my worth, my value, and my goodness to the world. A Ph.D., professional success, money, cars, and a big house were some of my attempts to prove to people that I had some worth, some value to offer. Perhaps more damaging than all of these was how my personal interactions affected others. I needed to be right—right was the measure and evidence of my worth. If I had felt okay about myself, I could have allowed for greater connection in all of my relationships. The energy that it took to try to show the world and others that I had something worthwhile to offer—and, more fundamentally, that I was something worthwhile—was immense. I have often thought that if I could have escaped childhood with a more secure sense of myself, the sense that I was "okay," I could have spent the subsequent years and energy giving gifts to the world, loving myself, and connecting and sharing more with others.

Recently, a friend and colleague named Bill Lane passed away. In the days shortly after his passing, my social media feeds were full of images and tributes to Bill. As I read the stories, a consistent theme emerged. Bill had the capacity to make everyone feel like they were special. When he greeted you and spent time with you, you felt like you were the most important person in the world. If I am honest, my ego was a little hurt that others had the same experience I did, as I almost thought that I was singularly special. But that is how Bill made everyone feel. He would see you and greet you by saying something like, "This guy is here!" and he would look around like he was announcing to everyone that you had arrived and that being in your presence was a privilege that everyone should soak in. I was too insecure and self-absorbed to notice, but he did that for everyone, and everyone was left with the same feeling. I can't imagine a greater legacy to leave behind than giving hundreds, maybe thousands, of people the feeling that they were special and that they belonged. I am not sure I have accomplished anything close to that, and with my friend's passing, I want to cultivate that attribute.

As I have thought of this, I have wondered where this came from in Bill. I know a little of Bill's background. I know he got sober a long time ago, and he often spoke of his addiction and the horrible things that he did to those closest to him. I imagine that he showed up in rooms of A.A. and told his story and some old-timer sitting next to him put his arm around him and told him he belonged. I think I know how that feels—to be told you belong. I know how much it means. I know that it melts away shame. I know it as a grace—something undeserved and more precious than any gift one can receive. I think Bill just wanted to give that feeling back to everyone else.

In *Les Misérables*, when Jean Valjean is freed from prison after 19 years for stealing a loaf of bread, he is taken in by a local bishop in an act of Christian love and grace, and the bishop tells him, "Though our lives are very humble, what we have, we have to share." Though welcomed by the bishop, he steals several pieces of silver in a hasty and thoughtless moment. He is caught the next morning by the authorities, and they bring him back to the bishop for a reckoning. Instead of condemning the thief, the bishop explains to the police that he gave the silver to Jean Valjean, then he adds two more valuable candlesticks to Valjean's bag. With this, he simply asked Valjean to do good to others going forward. This is the turning point in the story, and while one act may not have a transformative effect, there is nothing more powerful than turning people's hearts away from shame and towards love. In this pivotal scene, author Victor Hugo was trying to tell the world what happens when we embrace those things in us that people call "bad"—we heal.

What does grace have to do with losing and being wrong? It is our shame and feelings of unworthiness that create the need to be right. If we are right or successful or prove to the world that we are good, we temporarily escape the unspoken feelings in our center that something is wrong with us. They didn't do it on purpose; our parents and others in our earliest contexts expressed their anxiety towards us, and this made an indelible impression that something was wrong inside of us. Subsequently, we end up needing to try to prove that it is not so, to prove that we are good and okay. Sadly, all along, we were always okay. This is not to say we didn't and don't have missteps. That, I am afraid, is unescapable. But these things do not make us bad. Rather, they make us human.

Trying to be good then can be a serious problem. Trying to be a good friend, a good spouse, or a good parent is a dangerous endeavor. If we try to be good (not knowing we are already always good), we try to enlist others in supporting this notion. We don't allow for others to be angry, sad, hurt, or upset with us. This is an insidious dynamic, particularly in parenting because children are more prone to support parents in this endeavor. The cost of this enterprise for children is the loss of their authentic or real *Self.*

This is the entire premise of *The Drama of the Gifted Child.* But, if on the other hand, a parent is comfortable with themselves, okay with their humanness, the child's feelings are simply allowed to be—they are seen. This is the saving grace. If we can own our mistakes and apologize, then our loved ones don't have to carry it. Almost nightly, my wife tells me that as she puts the kids to bed, she has to apologize to someone. It goes something like this: "Hey, I'm sorry. I lost it again today. That's not about you. Mom's struggling with her own stuff."

When the children were little, they used to say, "That's okay, Mom."

And she would say, "No, it's not."

And they would teasingly say this back and forth: "That's okay."

And, "No it's not."

But now, they usually just say "Thanks." If we can let go of this need to be good, it will not rob others of important feelings and parts of themselves.

Sometimes mothers and fathers struggle to consider how much of their child's problems were created by them. Pointing out origins of our issues by looking to the mother (or father) and our upbringing is not parent-blaming or shaming. It is just describing it. If one experiences shame with this, then that is because their filter is broken—the culture is wonderful at shaming mothers (and sometimes fathers). It doesn't absolve the child of responsibility either. Since the wound is now the child's, the onus for healing sits squarely with the child.

One mother, considering our program for her daughter, related her exploration for the origin of her daughter's issues. "First, I pinned it on our divorce. We had a hellish divorce and I was sure I could trace the issues back to that. But when I shared this with my therapist, she told me I was a 'good mother and needn't take on so much blame.'"

I responded to her with an alternate option. "What if it was your and your husband's fault? Even worse, what if it was mostly your fault? What then? Maybe, the answer is not to remove your culpability, but to let go of the guilt and shame that seems to be stuck to it."

Rather than exonerating parents, because it never truly eradicates their guilt, I will often ask them to participate in the thought experiment, "What if it was your fault? Shall we execute you at dawn by beheading? You see the problem is not whether or not you are the root of the problem, it is your relationship with being human, fallible, and a *Self*. You were taught that to be wrong, to be human, to be limited, or to be a *Self*, was unacceptable. Therefore, you can spend your entire life trying to prove your innocence instead of accepting your *Self*."

With couples, the fight and dissolution of the marriage may occur for this very reason. A partner who needs to be good, will pathologize, attack, and vilify their partner to preserve the notion that they are good. I am farther along with the notion of losing at work, although that took me decades to learn. And I am better with this idea at work specifically because I am more confident at work than I am at home. This confidence affords me the ability to be wrong and apologize with clients whereas I struggle more with my children and even more with my wife. As my daughter said to me while we were driving away from a therapeutic intensive where the clients expressed admiration over my willingness to admit I was wrong, "You know, just so you're clear: you're not that humble at home."

Losing and being comfortable rests on the foundation of a secure sense of *Self*—often referred to as "self-worth" and "self-esteem." And the creation of the secure *Self* most likely occurs when someone important and consistent in our lives holds us with compassion and love. We think and feel about ourselves the way that our parents or other important figures think and feel about us. And if we don't get enough of the good stuff in childhood, we can get it from a support group, a sponsor, a therapist, or a capable friend in adulthood. But this takes years to develop and repair.

Getting good at losing means that we have made peace with ourselves. We can laugh at ourselves and admit fault and failure because our fallibility does not threaten us. If we come to know and admit our faults, we have no need to battle others who try to attack them. If someone points out our ridiculousness or idiocy, we will respond with "You are just scratching the surface of my idiocy. That is the tip of the iceberg. If you got a glimpse of all of it, you would probably run away screaming with laughter or fear or both."

Apologies come easy because we have made peace with who we are. The idea is to shift from the project of being good and of winning because those ideas ensure our failure in the world. Or, as Epictetus explained, "If anyone tells you that a certain person speaks ill of you, do not make excuses about what is said of you but answer, 'He was ignorant of my other faults, else he would not have mentioned these alone.'"

As I have internalized years of therapy and of sitting in the room with an empathic *Other*, I have come to be more comfortable with my humanness— my badness. In fact, I have learned it is not bad at all. The things that I do that hurt others don't make me evil; they merely signal that some part of me is wounded, hurt, or scared. And if I attend to these things, they can be healed.

This is the shift that the lens of mental health offers to us. We learn to be okay with being wrong, and we learn to lose because our worth and our being loved don't hang in the balance anymore. We make peace with those parts of ourselves that we were led to believe were bad or evil because they made those that loved us, those that we needed for our survival, uncomfortable or upset. This brings us to the second key for enlightenment.

KEY 2: COME TO KNOW YOUR DARKNESS AND REMAIN ON SPEAKING TERMS WITH YOUR MENTAL ILLNESS.

While use of the term "mental illness" here may be jarring, I use it to lean into the idea that we are all on the continuum of mental illness and health. Like I mentioned in an earlier chapter, the notion that mental illness and health is a binary may offer comfort by creating distance between "us" and "them." I often hear statistics about gun violence that suggest that the vast majority of gun violence is not perpetrated by mentally ill individuals. The fact of the matter is that violence itself is evidence of mental illness. It may not rise to the level of psychosis or what many imagine as severe, debilitating, mental illness, but it surely is a sign of being unwell.

The idea of befriending one's mental illness emerged for me as I watched parents go through the therapeutic process at our family intensives. Typically, the premise for a family engaging in a family intensive is a struggling child—the identified patient. One family that we worked with helped to crystalize the idea of being on speaking terms with one's mental illness. This was a family of four with a mother, father, 15-year-old son and 17-year-old daughter who came to us because, after several months in treatment, the daughter was still not openly talking with her parents. It wasn't a hot anger, nor were there overt behavioral problems, but the family wanted to improve communication and connection. Like I always do, I spoke to the parents in preparation for the intensive and let them know they would be in the hot seat too. They accepted this premise, yet as they arrived at the lodge where the intensive was to be held, I could feel an intense longing and wanting from the parents. They were there to solve a problem—a cold war with their distant daughter. They wanted tools that would create a different response from their child.

As we settled into the four-day experience, each family member was invited to create a psychodrama depicting what it felt like to grow up in their family-of-origin. I always invite the parents to go first, since their childhood experiences precede their children's, and one can visualize a virtual flow chart as each generation passes on the trauma and resources to the next. In this exercise, the parents' work is independent from the children's, which helps the identified patient see that issues didn't start with them, and everyone is there to work on themselves. Courageous parents embrace this work, but in the back of their minds they are often eagerly anticipating the work that will "fix" the problem—fix the child. Everyone present has the honor to witness and feel what it might have been like to grow up in and get cooked in the particular "soup" of the protagonist. Roles are reversed to create a dialogue, and the protagonist chooses whether their family member responds as they would have back then or as they would like them to now. Either way, the experience of telling the story to a group of witnesses is revealing and healing.

The dialogues depicted unearth the parts that we carry with us through life. Alcoholic or distant fathers, anxious mothers, the scared eight-year-old inner-child, alienated siblings, and compassionate grandmothers all make appearances on the stage. These are the parts of us that show up every day in the quiet moments of our mind and our relationships. The energies that come from a critical mother or a worrisome father rear themselves in our current conversations with our partners, our children, our co-workers, or our friends. The adage that says "if it is hysterical, it is historical" illustrates how unexplored and unconscious forces can often hijack us when we are triggered so that our responses don't match the situation presenting itself. It is not that we are overreacting or being too sensitive, it is that we are reacting to something from our past. These exercises allow for an insightful visit with our parents and siblings from our childhood, so we come to know them better and have a great understanding of the impact they have on our lives. Nothing is immediately fixed or completely healed, but we bring into the light what unconsciously haunts us.

As we explore the landscape of our childhood, our wounds, our ghosts, and our demons, we learn to gently say to them, "I know you are here, and I see you. I know the pain you feel, and I understand why you are reacting to things this way. By honoring these parts of ourselves we are able to realize everything is okay. We are okay. We can sit with it and let this pass through us, and we can let go."

We have few models of someone taking responsibility for their mistakes absent the sting of guilt and shame. Because we have no representation of this, we don't know any other way to consider our mistakes or how we hurt others. The idea of hurting our loved ones or our children is paired with self-loathing and it is this loathing that causes us not to see the issue.

As we explore the landscape of our childhood, our wounds, our ghosts, and our demons, we learn to gently say to them, "I know you are here, and I see you. I know the pain you feel, and I understand why you are reacting to things this way.

My mother recently attended a speaking engagement of mine, and afterwards, she chatted with my brother and me. She offered, "I am beginning to think I should feel guilty for some of the ways I raised you."

"I think it would be nice for you to be aware of some of the mistakes you made while raising us," I replied. "I think that would be good for you and for us, but you don't need to feel guilty. I can't talk you out of it, but the guilt isn't necessary. In fact, guilt will likely get in the way of your discovering how you hurt us as your children."

Making friends and remaining on speaking terms with your mental illness is leaning into one's pain and looking into our wounds to understand the things we do to protect ourselves from similar things happening to us again. Commonly, we regard symptoms or a maladaptive coping behavior with shame and disgust. This characterization prevents the kind of exploration described here. If the shame is intense enough, we deny the trait. We respond this way because that is how others responded to us in the past. We think this is helpful, and we imagine hatred of our unacceptable characteristics will lead to its diminishment or eradication. While it may work in the short term, this is not how deep and long-term growth works.

We must follow the trail where the undesirable trait leads us and listen to the wisdom it has to offer and to the story it has to tell. We honor defenses because they are protecting some wound or some vulnerability. Again, as Alice Miller explains, "We then realize that all our lives we have feared and struggled to ward off something that really cannot happen any longer; it has already happened, at the very beginning of our lives while we were completely dependent." If we have the courage to do our work, to visit our most vulnerable and wounded *Self*, these old stories lose their power. And this important work can last a lifetime.

At the end of the family intensive I previously mentioned, the parents walked away, like so many before them, with a clearer sense of their project. They were able to see how their fears and anxieties created a context where it was not safe for either of their children to tell their truth. And the children, after witnessing the real battle going on inside their parents, were relieved at realizing the entire problem was not about them. When this is realized, and when parents recognize their project, there is hope. There is hope because they comprehend that what they need to work on is within their control, and the identified patient or patients are relieved that they don't have to carry their parents' woundedness anymore and that they are not alone on the journey of healing toward mental wholeness.

Again, as Thich Nhat Hanh implores us, we may talk to our mental illness like we would a little child and say, "Dear one, I know you are there, and I am going to take care of you," just as you would with your crying baby.

Making friends with your mental illness means listening to yourself. It means knowing that your inner-child and your relationship with your inner-child will have direct impact on your relationships with your literal children, your spouses, and all *Others*. The writer George R.R. Martin observed, "Once you've accepted your flaws, no one can use them against you." Parents and partners worry that exposing the weak parts of ourselves offers material for others to abuse or hold us hostage. While revealing them may provide fodder for others to mistreat or blame us, accepting and making peace with our issues, as Martin states, is the antidote. We leave the field of right and wrong, of blame, and we enter the field of *Selves*, of humanity.

Most colloquially, from *The Godfather: Part II*, Michael Corleone said it simply: "My dad taught me numerous things here—he educated me in this room. He trained me—hold your friends close but your enemies closer." This is why we go back again and again to stare at the monsters hiding in our past, and when we find them, we unlock all the mysteries of the universe. Campbell used the metaphor of dragons and articulated that the dragon battle was toward the end of every person's journey, just before they return to the community to share the wisdom from their story. Bob Walter, the President of the Joseph Campbell Foundation, offers this template: "The first thing you have to do is to stop fighting it...what are you fighting...you are fighting yourself." And the self-help author Gay Hendricks explains, "I think loving your dragon is the much more efficient thing to do. It also feels better." And when you stop fighting the dragon, that part of yourself you are also fighting steps aside to reveal the wisdom or the treasure it was hiding and hoarding. Campbell calls this the heroic journey because although each story is unique, the heroic journey is always inward—into the darkness and the forgotten, scariest parts of ourselves. This is what it means to make friends with your mental illness.

KEY 3. LEARN HOW TO DIE AGAIN AND AGAIN; LET GO OF OLD CONTEXTS, BELIEFS, AND RELATIONSHIPS.

The longer I work on myself, the more I realize what I have to disregard. Spiritual teacher Adyashanti explains,

> *Enlightenment is a destructive process. It has nothing to do with becoming better or being happier. Enlightenment is the crumbling away of untruth. It's seeing through the facade of pretense. It's the complete eradication of everything we imagined to be true.*

As I was editing and pruning my first book, the process began to expand from months to years. I kept rewriting, improving, and adding more each time I'd work through it. At one point, a mentor said to me, "You could keep writing that book your entire life because you will continue to learn. But eventually, you will end this project, put it on a shelf, and start your next book." She was right. I could keep writing that one book for the rest of my life because I am constantly learning and growing. While this explanation conjures positive feelings and images, learning and growing also comes with loss.

I have the stories of hundreds of parents and families who share their loss with me. Parents often share how some of the discussions at parties with friends don't make sense anymore. Because of the transformation that occurs when you step into the work due to a loved one struggling with mental health or addiction, the things you used to talk about lose their meaning. There is a saying among those who have been in analysis: "Once you have been in analysis, you can't talk to anyone who hasn't been in analysis." That's also the way it is with transformation. Whether it comes in a moment or over time, when one is changed, the old things lose their meaning. Paul, in his epistle to the Corinthians, said it this way: "When I was a child, I spake as a child, I understood as a child, I thought as a child: but when I became a man, I put away childish things."

I have been broadcasting webinars and podcasts on parenting, relationships, mental health, and addiction for 12 years now. I would estimate that I have broadcast about 1,100 episodes. As a result, I have the opportunity to look back on lectures and subjects that I talked and taught about many years ago. Sometimes, when I dig up an old episode or old notes from one of the broadcasts, I have little or no interest in the topic. Sometimes, I find myself changing emphasis on a topic or going in a completely different direction. This book, while it suits me today, would be different if I were to write it years from now.

Not all people continue to grow. I often playfully say this about my maternal grandparents: "I think they learned all they ever knew long before I was born. I would guess they knew everything by the age of 30." While this may not be accurate, I use it to refer to the idea that many people die long before they are dead. Campbell explains that the motif of dying in storytelling is the story of new life, new growth. And Nietzsche explains, "The snake which cannot cast its skin has to die. As well the minds which are prevented from changing their opinions; they cease to be mind."

Outgrowing old friendships, old ideas, or old conversations feels like loss. Many of us hold onto these old things out of a sense of loyalty. In A.A., there is a slogan for new members that says, "You have to change your playground, playmates, and your playthings." When I freed myself from drugs as a teen, nobody had to tell me not to hang around my old friends—it was immediately evident to me that I could not hang out with the same crew and remain clean.

Sometimes, we hold onto old things because we are not sure what to replace them with. If we let go of an adage that we have long held dear, what guardrails will be in place to keep us from driving off the side of the road? This is why it can be said of those who choose to leave their faith, or the values held by their parents or their culture…that they are such courageous individuals. This is why we are drawn to stories of adventure where the hero steps into the dark cave, sets sails on the expansive seas, or rides their horse into the dense forest.

The ability to adapt, challenge old ideas, and let go of old ways of being rests on our bravery and courage. But beneath those, we must have some sense of our "okay-ness" or that sense that "it" will be okay. When I was diagnosed with multiple sclerosis in late 2015, I drove home from the hospital by myself.

My wife and I had arrived in separate cars, and she was beside me when we got the news. So, on the drive home, I needed to tell someone, and I scanned my mind for people to call. I didn't call my best friend or another family member. My mind came to rest on a friend introduced to me by my son. He was several years younger than me. I met him at a concert—he was the bass player in a band, and I loved their music. I got to know him and learned that several members of his family had M.S. I didn't know what I was looking for when I called him, but I just imagined he would know what to say. He answered, and through tears, I told him bluntly, "Tyler, I just found out I have M.S."

Without hesitation, he responded, "I love you. You are not alone in this and you will never be alone."

I had no idea that I was looking for this, but it was exactly what I needed. It was really all anyone could give to me—their presence and their love. Life changed for me forever that day. I was leaving the non-M.S. life behind and embarking on the M.S. life from here on out. And Tyler gave me what I needed—someone to be with me on this new, unknown road on my journey.

Divorce. Saying goodbye to old friends who once offered you companionship. Changing directions in your career. Letting go of old beliefs and ideas. I recently reflected to a friend that life seems like a long master's course in saying goodbye over and over. He agreed, and told me, "But if you didn't, you wouldn't be growing."

Ash Beckham gave a wonderful TED talk where she talks about this dying in terms of coming out of our closets. Most of us are familiar with closets referring to one's gender identity or sexual orientation. In fact, if we look carefully, however, we will see that all of us have closets. A closet is where we hide who we are because it is not safe to show our true *Selves* to the world. "Coming out" of our closest is telling someone the truth about what we think, feel, believe, or want. Closets are no place to live. A bumper sticker I saw the other day said, "Closets suck." To come out feels like a kind of death. We may lose someone; we may be rejected, judged, or abandoned, and these losses can be profound. They can only be compared to a death. No matter the specifics, everyone has some experience with this. As Beckham explains, "Hard is not relative; hard is hard. Who can tell me that explaining to someone you've just declared bankruptcy is harder than telling someone you just cheated on them? Who can tell me that his coming out story is harder than telling your five-year old you're getting a divorce? There is no 'harder,' there is just 'hard.'"

Therapists, mentors, friends, and family capable of seeing you all can offer you this same kind of comfort as you move through this life. There will be detractors, those telling you to stay put and not abandon your old life for something new. After a parent workshop in New York focused on the Hero's Journey, a father reached out to me with the following dilemma. "You taught us how Campbell said that the path to enlightenment could best be found by following our bliss and that we would have to fight dragons on the way," he said. "I can't even get to my dragon battle because my family won't let me go. They are telling me that I am going on a fool's errand." I smiled as I read his email, then replied, "Those are your dragons. The 'should' and the 'should nots' by those who profess to love us are written upon the scales of the dragon. When we embark on the journey towards change, it is common that those closest to us tell us to stop and change back to the way things were. They do it because they don't want to be left behind. They do it because they don't understand, or because they are too afraid to take the leap themselves. But some will follow. You will lose some, but in the end, you will be with YOUR people."

WHEN YOU'RE DONE WITH THIS WORLD...

When I talk about the concepts in this book, some people tell me, "You must be the most courageous person I know. You must be a great dad or partner or friend." Well, if you ask my family, as someone once did with my oldest daughter at a book signing, you would likely get the reply she gave. "He's alright. Sometimes, he's an idiot, but the good news is that he knows it, so that makes him tolerable." Like Ram Dass said, "If you think you are enlightened, go spend a week with your family."

In the end, or the closer we get to the end, should we have a life that affords us the time and opportunity to make mistakes and learn what we don't know, we would do well to celebrate exactly that. Our unknowing will be a gift to those we love and care about, and it will liberate us and allow for real connection, resulting in an ability to clearly see the *Other*.

This past year, I fell in love with a song by John Mayer called "Walt Grace's Submarine Test, January 1967." It tells the story of a man who decides he is going to build a one-man submarine in his basement, using, among other things, a blade from a fan. Others thought he was crazy, including his wife, and she told their kids as much. Everyone told him it couldn't be done and warned him he would surely die. But he was looking for something new, something different, so he holed up in his basement and set himself on the project. Though the project could end up killing him, he knew that if he didn't try, he would be dead already. Sure enough, he launched the vessel in a particularly rough sea, learning to steer it as he went, and he sailed across the ocean. When he landed in Japan, he called his wife to give her the news.

In this song, the basement and the waves are the journey into the dark cavern of *Self*. The adventure across a rough sea, learning to turn as we go, with nothing but a blade from a fan, is the simple, naked *Self*. But if we risk it all, we will know what Walt came to know, the only way one can come to know something: through experience. The chorus is an invitation to us all to embark on our own heroic adventure: "Cause when you're done with this world, you know the next is up to you."

We walk through life, longing for the company of *our people*—those who have answered the call to find themselves and have developed the capacity to honor *Others*. When we find those people, we never want them to leave us; we would not have reason. I have often said that if my children, friends, or spouse felt that being around me was toxic, if they felt they could not be themselves, I would unconditionally support them in cutting me out of their life. Of course, if this is true, they would have no reason to cut me out. The numbers may not be many, but you will not have to travel this journey alone. Some others and I will be with you on the road. Ram Dass said, "We are all just walking each other home." And I think this is what he meant. This is what it means to be human and to love an *Other*.

NOTES

CHAPTER 1

11 **From Joseph Campbell's,** *The Power of Myth: ...when you reach an advanced age and look back:* The Power of Myth. Joseph Campbell and Bill Moyers, edited by Betty Sue Flowers. New York, NY: Anchor Books. 1991.

15 **Joseph Campbell, a foremost American expert in mythology:** *The Power of Myth.* Joseph Campbell and Bill Moyers, edited by Betty Sue Flowers. New York, NY: Anchor Books. 1991.

20 **A lot of parents will do anything for their kids:** *Wall and Piece.* Banksy. London, England: Century, The Random House Group Limited. 2006.

22 **Campbell stated it this way: We must be willing to let go of the life we planned:** Joseph Campbell. https://www.goodreads.com/quotes/19826-we-must-be-willing-to-let-go-of-the-life

23 **A coward is incapable of:** *The Eden Project: In search of the magical other.* James Hollis. Toronto, ON: Inner City Books. 1998.

23 **Carl Jung explained that in order:** *Letter to Kendig B. Cully,* 25 September 1931; Letters vol. 1 (1973).

23 **Since I know myself:** *The Knight in Rusty Armor.* Robert Fisher. Woodland Hills, CA: Wilshire Book Company. 1990.

CHAPTER 2

25 **In your longing for your giant self lies:** *The Prophet.* Kahlil Gibran. Alfred A. Knopf Inc. 1923.

NOTES

26 **Research in the field of child development:** *Parenting From the Inside-Out: How a deeper self-understanding can help you raise children who thrive. 10th anniversary edition.* Daniel Siegel and Mary Hartzell. New York, NY: Jeremy P. Tarcher/Penguin, a member of Penguin Group. 2003.

26 **I can do nothing for you:** *Be Here Now.* Ram Dass. New York, NY: Crown Publishing Group. 1978.

27 **In her book:** *The Price of Privilege.* Madeline Levine. New York, NY: Harper Collins Publishers. 2006.

31 **Plato, in his search for the guiding principles and laws of a utopian society:** *The Laws of Plato.* New York: Basic Books, 1980.

32 **Innocence is the child, and forgetfulness, a new beginning, a game:** *Thus Spake Zarathustra.* Friedrich Nietzsche. New York, NY. Dover Publications. 1999.

32 **Euripides put it, "The gods visit the...":** http://www.quotationspage.com/quote/24157.html

34 **Thou shalt love thy neighbor:** Matthew 22:39. King James Edition.

41 **From the fear of being found-out:** Sanford Shapiro, personal communication. 2019.

44 **I had the privilege of seeing the musical *Hadestown* on Broadway:** Anais Mitchell. Reeve Carney, Andre De Shields, Amber Gray, Eva Noblezada, Patrick Page, Jewelle Blackman, and Yvette Gonzalez-Nacer. *Hadestown.* 2019. Mara Isaacs, Dale Franzen, Hunter Arnold, and Tom Kirdahy. New York.

CHAPTER 3

47 **Boundaries are the distance at which I can love you and me simultaneously.:** From Prentis Hemphill's Instagram account: see prentishemphill.com.

50 **It has been said that the difference between:** *Addictive Thinking: Understanding self-deception.* Abraham Twersky. Center City, MN: Hazelden. 1997.

50 **What is 2+2:** *Addictive Thinking: Understanding self-deception.* Abraham Twersky. Center City, MN: Hazelden. 1997.

53 **In NPR's Invisibilia:** The Problem with the Solution. NPR: Invisibilia. July 1, 2016.

57 **Salvador Minuchin and Murray Bowen:** Family Therapy: Concepts and methods. Michael Nichols and Richard Schwartz. Upper Saddle River, NJ: Pearson Education. 2010.

60 **Tian Dayton explained that children:** *Emotional Sobriety: From relationship trauma to resilience and balance.* Tian Dayton. Deerfield Beach, FL: Health Communications Inc. 2007.

60 **Researchers conducted experiments on baby mice:** *Nature Neuroscience, 9(8): 1004-6.* Sept 2006. "Maternal presence serves as a switch between learning fear and attraction in infancy." Stephanie Moriceau and Regina M Sullivan.

61 **Part of the business of psychotherapy:** *Forms of Life.* J.D. Gill. Create Space. 2014.

CHAPTER 4

64 **A coward is incapable of:** The Eden Project: In search of the magical other. James Hollis. Toronto, ON: Inner City Books. 1998.

66 **Projection, going home, fusion is easy. Loving another's:** The Eden Project: In search of the magical other. James Hollis. Toronto, ON: Inner City Books. 1998.

69 **Famous psychologist D.W. Winnicott went even further to suggest:** http://web.mit.edu/allanmc/www/winnicott2.pdf

69 **According to Freud, this is the primary purpose of therapy: to free us from unconscious obligations:** General Psychological Theory: Papers of Metapsychology. Sigmund Freud. New York. Simon & Schuster. 1991.

71 **If we really love the Other as Other, we have heroically:** The Eden Project: In search of the magical other. James Hollis. Toronto, ON: Inner City Books. 1998.

71 **Joseph Campbell tells us, "The cave you fear to enter holds the treasure you seek.":** https://www.goodreads.com/quotes/192665-the-cave-you-fear-to-enter-holds-the-treasure-you

71 **Tears from real feelings will release:** The Knight in Rusty Armor. Robert Fisher. Woodland Hills, CA: Wilshire Book Company. 1990.

71 **You're starting to see the differences:** The Knight in Rusty Armor. Robert Fisher. Woodland Hills, CA: Wilshire Book Company. 1990.

72 **The first thing you should know about me is that I am not you. A lot more will make sense after that.:** Author Unknown.

72 **Some of them are bent, and some of them are straight, and some of them are evergreens:** Ram Dass. https://www.ramdass.org/judging-less-harshly/

73 **Here again, the important point:** Parenting From the Inside-Out: How a deeper self-understanding can help you raise children who thrive. 10th anniversary edition. Daniel Siegel and Mary Hartzell. New York, NY: Jeremy P. Tarcher/Penguin, a member of Penguin Group. 2003.

74 **Experience has taught us:** The Drama of the Gifted Child. Alice Miller. New York, NY: Basic Books. 2008.

77 **A few years ago, we helped to create an off-Broadway play:** WILDERNESS. Anne Hamburger and Seth Bockley. En Garde Arts. 2016.

CHAPTER 5

82 **Love itself is a pain, you might say, that is the pain of being alive:** *The Power of Myth.* Joseph Campbell and Bill Moyers, edited by Betty Sue Flowers. New York, NY: Anchor Books. 1991.

83 **Out of a round globe of energy:** *Meeting the Shadow: The hidden power of the dark side of human nature.* Connie Zweig and Jeremiah Abrams. New York, NY: Penguin Putnam. 1991.

84 **This is what happens in projection:** *The Eden Project: In search of the magical other.* James Hollis. Toronto, ON: Inner City Books. 1998.

85 **We then realize that all our lives we have feared:** *The Drama of the Gifted Child.* Alice Miller. New York, NY: Basic Books. 2008.

86 **Whether or not a person is happy:** Will Smith. https://www.facebook.com/aplus/videos/1921514897919437/ 2018.

86 **Alain de Botton explains that success:** *Why You Will Marry the Wrong Person.* Alain de Botton. New York Times online. http://www.nytimes.com/2016/05/29/opinion/sunday/why-you-will-marry-the-wrong-person.html?_r=1 2016

91 **I think one of the problems in marriage is:** *The Eden Project: In search of the magical other.* James Hollis. Toronto, ON: Inner City Books. 1998.

91 **Kahlil Gibran explained it this way: Let there be spaces in your togetherness:** *The Prophet.* Kahlil Gibran. Alfred A. Knopf Inc. 1923.

CHAPTER 6

92 **It took me awhile to figure out the difference between the staff:** Personal Communication. Jami Gill. 2018.

98 **It is important to recognize the defense is doing:** *Seeing in Intimacy and Psychotherapy.* J.D. Gill. Create Space. 2016.

99 **In *Motivational Interviewing,* Miller and Rollnick lay out a model:** *Motivational Interviewing: Preparing people for change.* William Miller and Stephen Rollnick. New York, NY: The Guilford Press. 2002.

99 **What we do to stay safe:** *Letters of Juliet to the Knight in Rusty Armor.* J.D. Gill. Create Space. 2015.

100 **Of the good in you I can speak:** *The Prophet.* Kahlil Gibran. Alfred A. Knopf Inc. 1923.

101 **All parents have limits:** *Misery of the Good Child.* J.D. Gill. Create Space. 2015.

101 **Miller suggests the idea:** *Journal of Therapeutic Schools & Programs.* Vol IX, 1. "Psychology versus Therapy: Implications for the practice and supervision of therapy in residential treatment and wilderness therapy programs." Brad Reedy and Michelle Taggart Reedy. 2017.

106 **Out beyond ideas of wrongdoing:** *The Essential Rumi.* Rumi. Translated by Coleman Banks, with John Moyne, A.J. Arberry, and Reynold Nicholson. London, England: 1995.

CHAPTER 7

110 **My two oldest children created a simple illustration:** Image Credits. Words by Emma Reedy and Jake Reedy. Art by Jake Reedy. 2019.

114 **John Steinbeck wrote, "Well, every little boy thinks he invented sin...":** *East of Eden.* John Steinbeck. New York: Penguin Books. 1992.

114 **A child that's being abused:** Becoming the Narcissist's Nightmare: How to Devalue and Discard the Narcissist While Supplying Yourself. Shahida Arabi. New Yok, NY: Archer Publishing. 2016.

117 **And in The Knight in Rusty Armor:** *The Knight in Rusty Armor.* Robert Fisher. Woodland Hills, CA: Wilshire Book Company. 1990.

119 **The therapist or guide we choose:** *The Mexico Papers, vol one.* J.D. Gill. Create Space. 2016.

120 **It's written in therapists' ethical codes that:** https://www.aamft.org/Legal_Ethics/Code_of_Ethics.aspx

124 **Dr. Lerner paused for a moment and said plainly, "I think you are just asking me how I do therapy.":** Personal communication September 2019, Houston, TX.

124 **Abraham Lincoln said it simply:** As quoted in *Costs of Administering Reparation for Work Injuries in Illinois.* Alfred Fletcher Conard. 1952.

125 Carl Rogers taught, "When a person realizes he has been deeply heard, his eyes...": https://www.azquotes.com/quote/692770

CHAPTER 8

127 But if thoughts can corrupt language, then language also can corrupt thought: *Politics and the English Language and Other Essays.* George Orwell. New York, NY: Penguin Books. 1946.

132 Joseph Campbell taught that every religion is true in one way or another: *The Power of Myth.* Joseph Campbell and Bill Moyers, edited by Betty Sue Flowers. New York, NY: Anchor Books. 1991.

132 Carl Rogers noted that, "The curious paradox is that when I accept myself just as I am, then": http://www.dimensionalpsychotherapy.com/blog/2015/10/12/famous-quote-break-down-part-1-carl-rogers-the-curious-paradox-is-that-when-i-accept-myself-just-as-i-am-then-i-change

138 Research shows that families who identify themselves: *Okay, What Do we do Now? A qualitative study of transition home following youth residential treatment.* Jacob Hess, Eric Bjorklund, Nikki Preece, and Janet Mulitalo. Unpublished Paper from Alpine Academy.

139 I love this example from David Bowie's life: David Bowie, in an Interview with Jeremy Paxman. BBC Newsnight. 1999.

140 The Dalai Lama said "To be aware...": *The Path to Enlightenment.* The Dalai Lama. Ithaca, NY: Snow Lion Publications. 1982.

143 You should talk to your depression: *You are Here: discovering the magic of the present moment.* Thich Nhat Hanh. Boston, MA. Shambhala Publications Inc. 2001.

143 Like Freud observed, "A thing which has not been understood...": https://www.tandfonline.com/doi/abs/10.1080/00754178608254784?journalCode=rjcp20

148 **Campbell said that religion is a defense against:** *The Power of Myth.* Joseph Campbell and Bill Moyers, edited by Betty Sue Flowers. New York, NY: Anchor Books. 1991.

CHAPTER 9

149 **Enlightenment is more about unlearning and…:** Adapted from *The Power of Myth.* Joseph Campbell and Bill Moyers, edited by Betty Sue Flowers. New York, NY: Anchor Books. 1991.

157 **Though our lives are very humble, what we have, we have to share…:** Claude-Michel Schönberg. *Les Misérables: a Musical.* 1998. Exclusively distributed by H. Leonard. London.

159 **Epictetus explained, "If anyone tells you that a certain person speaks ill of you":** https://www.goodreads.com/quotes/227348-if-anyone-tells-you-that-a-certain-person-speaks-ill

161 **As Miller explains, "We then realize":** *The Drama of the Gifted Child.* Alice Miller. New York, NY: Basic Books. 2008.

161 **George R.R. Martin observed, "Once you've accepted your flaws, no one can use them against you.":** https://www.goodreads.com/quotes/870673-once-you-ve-accepted-your-flaws-no-one-can-use-them

161 *The Godfather: Part II,* **Michael Corleone said it simply: "My dad taught me numerous things here":** Francis Coppola and Mario Puzo. *The Godfather Part II.* United States: Paramount Pictures, 1974.

162 **Bob Walter, the President of the Joseph Campbell Foundation…Gay Hendricks:** *Finding Joe* [motion picture]. Patrick Takaya Solomon (producer and director). USA: Balcony releasing. 2011.

162 **Adyashanti explains, Enlightenment is a destructive process…:** https://www.goodreads.com/quotes/7639320-enlightenment-is-a-destructive-process-it-has-nothing-to-do

162 **When I was a child, I spake as a child…:** 1 Corinthians 13:11 King James Edition.

163 **Nietzsche explains, "The snake which cannot cast its skin has to die.":** *Finding Joe* [motion picture]. Patrick Takaya Solomon (producer and director). USA: Balcony releasing. 2011.

164 **Ash Beckham gave a wonderful TED talk:** *Coming out of your closet.* Ash Beckham. Tedx Talks, TedxBoulder. 2013.

164 **Like Ram Dass said, "If you think you are enlightened, go spend a week with...":** https://www.energytherapy.biz/quotes/authors/ram-dass/if-you-think-youre-enlightened/

164 **Song by John Mayer, "Walt Grace's Submarine Test, January 1967":** from the song *Walt Grace's Submarine Test, January 1967*, by John Mayer. Columbia Records. 2012.

165 **Ram Dass said, "We are all just walking":** *Walking Each Other Home: conversations on loving and dying.* Ram Dass. Boulder, CO: Sounds True. 2018.

Made in the USA
Monee, IL
27 August 2020